ROYAL BLOOD

ROYAL BLOOD

KING RICHARD III
AND THE MYSTERY OF
THE PRINCES

BERTRAM FIELDS

SUTTON PUBLISHING

First published in 1998 by ReganBooks, an imprint of HarperCollins
Publishers

This paperback edition first published in the United Kingdom in 2000 by
Sutton Publishing Ltd · Phoenix Mill · Thrupp · Stroud · Gloucestershire ·
GL5 2BU

British Library Cataloguing in Publication Data
A catalogue record for this book is available from the British Library

ISBN 0-7509-2545-0

Designed by Nancy Singer Olaguera

Cover design © by Honi Werner
Cover painting *The Princes Edward and Richard in the Tower, 1483* by
Sir John Everett Millais (1829–96). Royal Holloway and Bedford New
College, Surrey / Bridgeman Art Library, London / New York

Printed in Great Britain by
Biddles, Guildford, Surrey.

So incompetent has the generality of historians been for the province they have undertaken, that it is almost a question, whether, if the dead of past ages could revive, they would be able to reconnoitre the events of their own times, as transmitted to us by ignorance and misrepresentation.

HORACE WALPOLE, 1768

For HMF and MAF.
Thank you for everything.

♛ CONTENTS

I wish to acknowledge the assistance of Roberta Dunner, Ellen Baskin, Christine Baker, John Huggett, Helen Maurer and the gracious men and women who provided guidance at the British Museum, the Society of Antiquaries, the College of Arms, Windsor Castle, Bosworth Field, the Tower of London and the Chelsea Town Hall. I would like to express additional thanks to Professors Ronald Mellor and Simon Varey, and to Dean Scott L. Waugh of the UCLA Department of History.

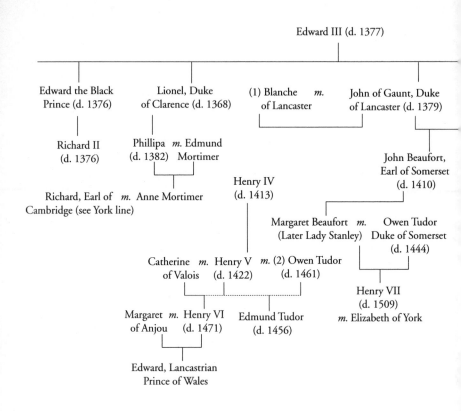

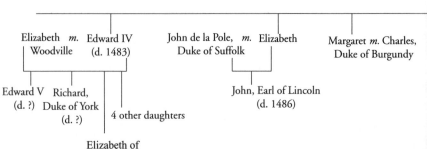

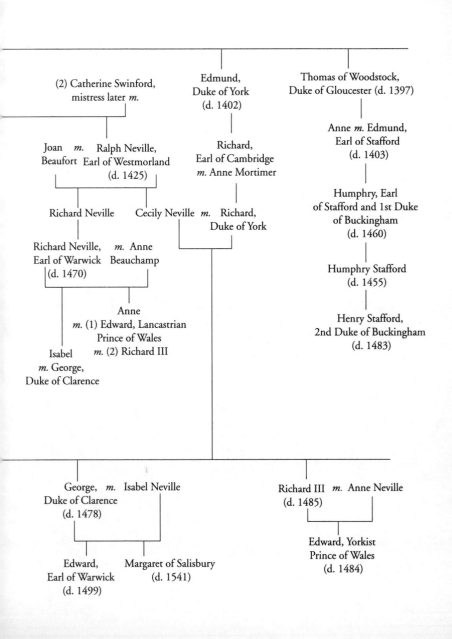

(2) Catherine Swinford,
mistress later *m.*

Edmund,
Duke of York
(d. 1402)

Thomas of Woodstock,
Duke of Gloucester (d. 1397)

Joan   *m.*   Ralph Neville,
Beaufort Earl of Westmorland
(d. 1425)

Richard,
Earl of Cambridge
m. Anne Mortimer

Anne *m.* Edmund,
Earl of Stafford
(d. 1403)

Richard Neville   Cecily Neville   *m.*   Richard,
Duke of York

Humphry, Earl
of Stafford and 1st Duke
of Buckingham
(d. 1460)

Richard Neville,   *m.* Anne
Earl of Warwick   Beauchamp
(d. 1470)

Humphry Stafford
(d. 1455)

Anne
m. (1) Edward, Lancastrian
Prince of Wales
m. (2) Richard III

Henry Stafford,
2nd Duke of Buckingham
(d. 1483)

Isabel
m. George,
Duke of Clarence

George,   *m.*   Isabel Neville
Duke of Clarence
(d. 1478)

Richard III   *m.* Anne Neville
(d. 1485)

Edward,
Earl of Warwick
(d. 1499)

Margaret of Salisbury
(d. 1541)

Edward, Yorkist
Prince of Wales
(d. 1484)

❦ INTRODUCTION

Now is the winter of our discontent / Made glorious summer by this sun of York." With these dramatic lines, Shakespeare introduces history's most infamous villain, Richard III, King of England from 1483 to 1485. With his hunched back and withered arm, Richard scuttles across the stage like a huge spider, spewing out his venomous thoughts. "Since I cannot prove a lover," he confides to the hushed audience, "I am determined to prove a villain. . . . Plots have I laid, inductions dangerous."

And he means it. As the drama unfolds, this grotesque villain kills the youthful Prince of Wales and the aged, saintly Henry VI. Then, he schemes to drown his brother in a vat of wine, to poison his wife, and, worst of all, to murder his two young nephews, the older of whom was the rightful king.

Deserted by subjects so appalled at his bloody conduct that they will not fight beside him, Richard the usurper is defeated by the heroic Henry Tudor at the battle of Bosworth Field. Surrounded, and about to die, he cries out in desperation: "A horse! A horse! My kingdom for a horse!"

Was all this true? For centuries it was accepted "history." After all, Shakespeare's play comes ultimately from the writings of the sainted Thomas More, who was alive at the time. Other historians of the period seemed to share More's view.

Later, however, doubts grew and, with those doubts, came scholarly inquiry. That inquiry created history's greatest unsolved mystery. Were the two young princes murdered by Richard in the

Tower of London, as More and Shakespeare tell us? Or were they killed by Henry Tudor? Or by the unstable and ambitious duke of Buckingham? Were they killed at all? And, if not, where did they go after they were last seen at the Tower windows?

Even today, most writers in the field accept at least some version of the traditional account, and, while varying their degree of censure, continue to hold Richard guilty of the crime. Others, sometimes called "revisionists," offer what they consider to be proofs of Richard's innocence. They insist that he was a brave, sensitive man, a loving husband, a loyal brother and a splendid king who was popular with his subjects and was defeated only by treachery. They charge that after his death, Richard became the victim of a massive campaign of disinformation and slander by Tudor propagandists, who falsely portrayed him as a deformed and homicidal monster.

It will be the aim of this book to explore and evaluate the arguments on each side, to weigh the evidence and, peering through the mist of centuries, to come as close as possible to the elusive truth.

But the fate of the princes in the Tower is not the only mystery bearing on the life and career of Richard III. His times spawned other events and relationships that remain puzzling even today. His contemporaries, the Lancastrian Prince of Wales, the duke of Clarence and that unfortunate king, Henry VI, all died under suspicious circumstances that are still the subject of controversy.

And was his womanizing brother, Edward IV, already secretly married to another woman when he supposedly married the mother of the two princes? Edward died unexpectedly at forty-one, leaving a twelve-year-old boy as his heir. Had he been poisoned by agents of the French king?

How did Richard's future queen come to be hidden away from him disguised as a kitchen maid? What was the true relationship between Richard and his attractive young niece?

Why did Richard pay an enormous sum to the supposed murderer of the two princes, and why did Henry VII grant that same man two general pardons only one month apart? Why did Henry raise no hue and cry when he took over the Tower in 1485 and found the princes missing? Why did his parliamentary indictment of Richard fail to include the explicit charge of regicide? And why did Henry let a man who assertedly confessed to committing the murders at Richard's behest remain free and unpunished for decades? Was the handsome "pretender" who captivated the crowned heads of Europe really the younger of the two princes supposedly murdered years before?

And who was the anonymous "insider" who wrote a secret chronicle of Richard's reign, an account that, if discovered by Henry VII, could have led to the chronicler's imprisonment and possible execution? Why did Sir Thomas More suddenly stop writing his *History of King Richard III*, leaving it unfinished for the rest of his life? Could More's own son-in-law have been one of the missing princes? What is the meaning of the mysterious clues inserted by Hans Holbein in the More family portrait? And, of course, who were the two young skeletons found buried under a Tower staircase in 1674?

While this may seem the stuff of melodrama, it is not. It is about real people and real events. We will explore and analyze each of these issues and many more in the process of trying to ascertain the truth about Richard III and his young nephews who may (or may not) have been murdered in the Tower of London.

✹ SOLVING A MURDER

A number of factors should be considered in attempting to determine guilt or innocence of murder. Motive must, of course, be considered. Did the accused have a sufficient reason to commit that ultimate, most heinous of crimes? What did he stand to gain or accomplish by the victim's death? Wealth? Power? Revenge? Terrorism? Without a strong motive, the inference of guilt is a difficult one to draw. There are killings that appear to be motiveless; but these are typically committed by psychopaths. Even there, a "motive" exists, even though it may be delusional.

Another essential factor is opportunity. Could the accused have been present at the time and place of the crime? If there is evidence that he had an alibi, the inference of guilt is harder to draw. It may even be impossible, unless, of course, the murder was committed by another at the behest of the accused. In weighing the factor of opportunity, establishing the time of death becomes highly significant. If death occurred at one time, the accused may have an alibi. If it occurred at another, he may not.

A third factor is the means. Did the accused have the means to commit the crime? Did he have the physical ability to carry it out? Did he have access to a weapon that could or did cause the death?

Next, we look to the accused's proclivity to commit such a crime. We examine his character and prior conduct to evaluate whether or not he is the type of person that would kill under the circumstances of the particular murder. Some individuals would be likely to kill in certain circumstances, but not in others. The man inclined to violent fits of jealousy may be likely to kill his wife's lover, but the premeditated killing of an aged aunt to inherit her money might be unthinkable. The man who might kill when drunk may pose no danger at all when sober.

Passing the basic elements of motive, opportunity, means and proclivity, we must consider the physical evidence and other relevant facts that create or impair an inference of guilt.

Today we apply scientific methods, such as DNA testing, fingerprints and fiber analysis. In solving a fifteenth-century crime we have no such tools. We can only apply logic and human experience to the known facts. The problem is that the most important facts are not *known*. They have been passed down to us through accounts distorted not only by human error and exaggeration, but often by deliberate misstatement designed to serve a political or religious agenda.

These problems are particularly evident in the case of Richard III. Many of the sources of information are highly suspect, if not completely unreliable. Moreover, we are faced not only with determining who committed the crime, but even whether a crime was committed. The princes disappeared; but it is by no means certain that they were killed by anyone.

THE "WITNESSES"

In a courtroom, we rely primarily on the testimony of witnesses who have personally observed the matters to which they testify. They are subjected to cross-examination designed to test their opportunity to have observed those matters accurately, as well as their memory, their possible bias and their truthfulness in general.

With some exceptions, we do not seek to prove the facts by hearsay, i.e., testimony as to what someone else *said* were the facts. We generally reject such testimony, because the "someone else" who might be quoted is not there in court to face cross-examination.

Solving a historical mystery, such as that of Richard III, is, of course, a quite different and far more difficult process. We must rely entirely on hearsay—second, third and fourth-hand accounts of what others have supposedly observed and reported, written down centuries ago by historians or others and repeated, sometimes accurately, sometimes not, by later chroniclers.

The original sources of such information are beyond the reach of cross-examination to determine their opportunity to have observed the events they described, as well as their bias and truthfulness. Nor can we even cross-examine the historians who spoke to them to determine the truthfulness and accuracy with which they have passed on to us what their original informants said.

Before we can begin to deal with the mysteries inherent in

the life and career of Richard III, we must know something about the chroniclers who are the source of our purported facts. These chroniclers are our witnesses. Deprived of the weapon of cross-examination, we must evaluate their potential bias, the reliability of their sources and the degree of care they used in attempting to separate fact from gossip or deliberate falsehood. Only then can we attempt to assess the truth of what they have written.

From the beginning, writings about Richard and his reign have been plagued with political and personal bias. In 1485, Richard was defeated and replaced on the throne by Henry Tudor, who reigned as Henry VII. The founder of the Tudor dynasty, Henry was a strong ruler with an exceedingly weak claim to the throne. It was politically correct and sound policy for any historian writing during Henry's reign to blacken Richard's reputation in any way possible. Under Henry's son Henry VIII and his Tudor grandchildren, Edward VI, Mary and Elizabeth I, it remained good politics to follow the same line.

Nicholas Pronay and John Cox provide the following description of the Tudors' "insistent and all embracing propaganda":

> Tudor government used the same threefold technique of propaganda for legitimation which is still the standard technique: putting out through all available media a slanted selection of historical facts mixed with a few, but colourful and memorable untruths; persecuting anyone who either questioned them or publicised facts excluded from the official presentation; and seeking to generate an atmosphere where uttering such doubts or seeking after evidence would become socially unacceptable, as an act of disloyalty.

In addition to the advantages of propitiating the Tudors, geographical bias played a part in tearing down Richard's reputation. Most of the Englishmen who wrote or compiled "historical" works at or near the time were from the southern part of England, an area, as we shall see, that was far less supportive of the fallen king than the North, where he was generally revered. Regional resentment was thus added as a source of bias.

Given these general warnings about the major factors that tended to influence fifteenth- and sixteenth-century writers, we can turn to the individual chroniclers of those times. Only by considering them one by one at the outset can we make an informed decision as to how much weight to give their accounts of any particular event or their opinions on any given subject.

John Rous was one of history's most demonstrable hypocrites. During Richard's reign, he wrote his "Rolle," which contained glowing descriptions of the king as "a mighty prince," an "especial good lord" and "a most virtuous prince" who had occupied the throne without "any defiling in the law" and who was revered for his wise and generous rule. According to Rous, these traits won Richard "great thank of God and love of all his subjects, rich and poor, and great laud of the people of other lands about him."

After Henry VII took the throne, however, Rous sang a different tune. He had made two copies of his "Rolle," one in Latin and one in English. He rewrote the Latin copy, deleting his glowing descriptions of Richard and his reign. He also substituted a drawing of Edward III for that of Richard's brother, Edward IV, and deleted entirely the drawing of Richard that originally followed it. Then, when he portrayed Anne Neville, Richard's longtime wife, he placed next to her a drawing of the Lancastrian Prince of Wales, to whom Anne had been briefly "married" as a child, instead of the drawing of Richard, as in the original. He moved Richard to a subordinate position after the slain young prince and substituted, for the high praise he gave Richard in the original "Rolle," the terse caption "*infelix maritus*"(unhappy husband).

Unfortunately for Rous's reputation, he failed to regain possession of the unaltered English version of his "Rolle." His abject hypocrisy can readily be seen by comparing the original English version in the British Museum with the altered Latin version at the College of Arms in London.

Rous later wrote a "History of the Kings of England," which he dedicated to Henry Tudor and in which he absolutely excoriated Richard, referring to him as "like a scorpion." This work was so interlarded with outlandish recitals and provably incorrect details that Rous has little modern support even among staunch traditionalists.

Not all accounts of the time were written by Englishmen. Dominic Mancini, an Italian priest who had lived in France and moved in French literary circles, arrived in London just before the death of Edward IV on April 9, 1483 and left the country just after Richard's coronation on July 6, 1483. Back in France in December 1483, Mancini wrote a report for Angelo Cato, the archbishop of Vienne, who was a member of the French royal council, a physician and also astrologer to Louis XI. It was Cato who dispatched Mancini to England, possibly as a spy, and who later recalled him.

Mancini's report was only discovered in 1934 in the Municipal Library of Lille. The report begins with a reminder to Bishop Cato that he had asked Mancini to put his account in writing for the prince of Taranto. Mancini expresses his hope that the prince will find Mancini's report to his liking. It is conceivable that the reference to "the prince of Taranto" was a cover for someone else for whom Cato was working—possibly even Louis XI. But this is most unlikely. Cato had come to France in the entourage of Federigo of Aragon, who was in fact the prince of Taranto. And Cato appears to have continued his relationship with the prince even after he entered the service of Louis XI.

Mancini did not appear to be writing directly for French eyes. His report included some unflattering comments about the French, such as that they were "bellicose" and used slight pretexts to raid English commercial shipping. Nevertheless, given Cato's relationship with the French king, it is a reasonable inference that Mancini was generally inclined to report what he thought Louis and his aides wanted to hear.

More than anything, the French wanted to avoid aggressive moves by England on the Continent. The Hundred Years War had just ended in 1453. That conflict had begun in 1337; and, by 1429, the English had conquered a vast portion of France, including Paris. In the following years, however, Joan of Arc led a French resurgence, which continued even after Joan was burned at the stake. By 1453, the English had been thrown back, and their holdings on the Continent were limited to the port of Calais on the Channel coast.

But the English threat was not permanently ended; and

Louis wanted no further English incursions. When Mancini wrote his account, Henry Tudor was living in exile in Brittany. Henry was not a trained military leader; and, if he became king of England, especially if this occurred with French support, France would have less to fear.

Richard III was another matter. In 1475, Richard had openly and bitterly opposed Edward IV's acceptance of substantial bribes from the French king. The bribes, given not only to Edward but to other English nobles, were designed to induce Edward to withdraw English troops from France, where he had brought them to support Louis' enemy, the duke of Burgundy.

The French were well aware that Richard had opposed the bribes and had urged his brother, Edward, to pursue the planned invasion. A proven military leader, and a fearless and impetuous warrior, Richard was just the sort of king who might seek to duplicate the feats of Henry V and the Black Prince by invading France and asserting the longstanding claim of English kings to the French throne.

These were reasons enough for the French to mistrust Richard, to attempt to destabilize his reign and to support Henry Tudor. Mancini's report may have been used for this purpose even if that was not what he intended.

Mancini spoke little or no English. His summary of what he heard from others during his three-month stay in England may have been inaccurately translated or intentionally distorted by those who supplied the information. Much of it was only gossip anyway.

Moreover, significant aspects of what Mancini reported may have been told to him months after he left England by Dr. John Argentine, an Italian-speaking physician who had attended Edward V in the Tower. Mancini met Argentine on the Continent later in 1483, when he was writing his account. Argentine was strongly opposed to Richard and later served in the court of Henry VII.

Although there was good reason for Mancini's report to have an anti-Ricardian bias, he does not accuse Richard of murdering his nephews. He writes only that there was a "suspicion" that they had been done away with.

Another non-English source of our "facts" is Phillipe de Commynes, a competent Flemish historian who was sometimes less careful (and probably less interested) in writing about England than in reporting events on the Continent. De Commynes wrote in Tudor times, and, having actually served as an advisor to Louis XI, he was also inclined to a pro-French, and thus pro-Tudor, view of English events. That view was, of course, anti-Ricardian. Interestingly, like Mancini, de Commynes dedicated his memoirs to Angelo Cato, the archbishop of Vienne. Also, de Commynes makes specific reference to conversations with the prince of Taranto, the man to whom Mancini's account purportedly was directed.

One of the most frequently cited English sources is the Croyland (or Crowland) Chronicle. This was a continuing account of current English events maintained at the Benedictine Abbey of Croyland in Lincolnshire. Much of the original manuscript was destroyed or severely damaged by a fire in 1731. As a result, historians have had to rely to a substantial extent on a version published in 1684, the accuracy of which cannot be proven.

There was more than one Croyland chronicler, and the anonymous author of that part of the chronicle covering Richard's reign is often called the "Second Croyland Continuator." He was an educated man who, at least for a time, was close to the center of English government. His work covered the period from 1459 to 1486, but almost as much of it is devoted to the two years between 1483 and 1485 as to the preceding twenty-four years.

The identity of the Second Continuator has created a mystery of its own. Historians have devoted years of study and hundreds of pages to this issue alone. Knowing who the anonymous author was could aid us in assessing his bias and evaluating his account. But his identity has never been satisfactorily established. Because he often presents an insider's view of events and is obviously a man of learning and intelligence, it is worthwhile to consider at some length just who he might have been and what influences and prejudices shaped his views.

Some historians have attributed this part of the chronicle to John Russell, the bishop of Lincoln, who was Chancellor in Richard's reign. Richard dismissed Russell from office in July of

1485. If Russell was the Second Continuator, he may have been an embittered man when his part of the chronicle was written.

A marginal annotation describes the Second Continuator as a doctor of "canon law" and a councillor of Edward IV, who went on a diplomatic mission to Burgundy in 1471. Russell was a member of Edward's council, and he held a doctorate that might have been described as one in "canon law," although that would probably not have been how Russell would have described it. Russell was frequently sent by Edward on important diplomatic missions, but there appears to be no remaining record of who went on the one Burgundian mission singled out in the chronicle.

The Second Continuation states that it was "done and completed at Croyland in 1486 in the space of ten days, the last of which was the last day of April in the same year." Russell made a month-long visit to Croyland in April 1486, and was there during the ten-day period described in the chronicle. But so were a number of others.

While it is possible that Bishop Russell was the Second Continuator, several facts point the other way. First, the style of the Second Continuation does not conform to the style of Russell's known writings. Second, the author has firsthand, inside knowledge of events during the reign of Edward IV, but his information seems significantly less-detailed after Richard took the throne. The account suggests that, under Richard, its author may have lost the inside position he enjoyed under Edward. Yet, Russell's career was just the opposite. He was keeper of the Privy Seal in Edward's reign, but Richard made him chancellor, a much higher position, closer to the center of power. Russell had far greater knowledge of the events of Richard's reign than is revealed by the Second Continuator.

It could be argued that, having attained an exalted position, Russell became reluctant to comment on the events he witnessed. But this does not appear to be the case. The author is open in expressing his opinions, but simply offers less information to support them.

Third, the chronicle harshly attacks acts and policies of Richard's reign that, if not directly attributable to Russell, were certainly measures for which he bore at least partial responsibility.

Fourth, the Second Continuation seems to stress events at a lower level than those handled by Russell. Even the reference to the author's mission to Burgundy seems unlikely to have been written by or about Russell, who had been in charge of a number of much more important missions. Why single out this one lesser assignment, as if it were the only time the king had called on him for such a task? It seems much more likely to have been describing someone who went on only this one mission.

Finally, the Second Continuator, writing during the reign of Henry VII, reveals matters that the new king desperately wanted to suppress, matters that it was treason to reveal. Russell was an intelligent and capable man. He had held high office in Richard's government. By April 1486, it was clear that Henry was going to take no action against him; and Russell could look forward to a pleasant life, if not a thriving career under the new king. Why would he jeopardize that future by recording things that, if discovered, would enrage Henry?

There is a brief third continuation that follows the second. Its author was an unnamed Croyland monk. While describing Bishop Russell's visit to Croyland in April 1486, he states that he is unaware of the identity of the Second Continuator. This seems virtually impossible if the second continuation was written by Russell himself. Russell was a very famous man, whose daily activities during his stay in Croyland would have been widely noted by the monks and whose writing of the chronicle would have been a source of enormous pride to the monastery. The anonymity of the Second Continuator suggests someone far less conspicuous—unless the Third Continuator was simply pretending that the identity of his predecessor was unknown.

An alternate candidate is the lesser known Henry Sharp, who, as pronotory of Chancery in Richard's reign, sat as a sort of ex officio member of the council. Russell apparently paid for twenty-two other guests during his stay at Croyland in April 1486. Sharp may have been one of them. Sharp, like Russell, had a doctorate in what could (inaccurately) have been called "canon law." He also went on some diplomatic missions, although on a lower level than Russell. Sharp did not seem to have Richard's confidence and may have been given little access to inside information during Richard's reign. Possibly this was because of his long association with John Morton, the bishop of Ely, who, as we will see, was Richard's implacable enemy. This would be consistent with the Second Continuator's harsh criticism of Richard and his policies.

Sharp was also older and in retirement. He would seem more likely than Russell to have taken the risk inherent in writing about matters Henry VII wanted suppressed.

Whether it was Russell, Sharp or someone else, the Croyland chronicler generally followed an anti-Ricardian, pro-Tudor line and seems particularly bitter about what he perceived as Richard's favoritism toward Northerners. He portrays Richard as having been rejected by the nobility and describes his policies as "evil," including "things unbefitting which were so numerous they can hardly be counted." Henry VII, on the other hand, is shown as having been accepted by the nation as "an angel sent from heaven through whom God deigned to visit his people and to free them from the evils which had hitherto affected them beyond measure."

Yet, perhaps significantly, the Second Continuator does *not* say that Richard killed his nephews. He reports only that "a rumour arose" that they had "met their fate". He makes no comment on the truth of that "rumour" or as to who might have killed them.

Despite its evident bias, the Croyland Chronicle is a more reliable guide than Rous or the blatant Tudor apologists who wrote in the pay of Henry VII or subject to his will, or those who wrote under his Tudor successors, Henry VIII, Edward VI, Mary and Elizabeth I.

Polydore Vergil, like Mancini an Italian, wrote an "official" Tudor history commissioned by Henry VII in 1505. Vergil completed this work in 1517 during the reign of Henry's son, Henry VIII, who was almost as anxious as his father to blacken Richard's memory. In general, Vergil wrote what the Tudors wanted to read; and what they wanted to read was vituperation about the faults, crimes and unpopularity of Richard III. Vergil has also been accused of destroying a vast number of documents that contradicted the views he was presenting. His history, published in 1534, was the first work in print to accuse Richard of killing his nephews more than fifty years earlier, in 1483.

Robert Fabyan was a London draper and alderman, who compiled various accounts of events that had occurred in the city before and during Richard's reign. A staunch Lancastrian, Fabyan opposed the claims of Richard's family. He compiled his chronicle during the reign of Henry VII, years after the events it described.

"The Great Chronicle of London" was another compilation of "events" made years after Richard's reign. It also appears to have been compiled by Fabyan.

Fabyan's chronicles were not official in nature. They generally present a citizen's view of events. They are demonstrably erroneous in chronology and other matters and are inclined to present gossip as fact. While there is no evidence that Henry VII demanded a pro-Tudor bias in such compilations, it would hardly have been good business for the merchant-politician to have included reports that praised Richard or attacked Henry.

Sir Thomas More is, of course, one of history's most respected figures. Writer, philosopher, lord chancellor and, ultimately, a martyred saint for the principled defiance of Henry VIII that led to his execution, More lends considerable respectability to the traditionalist view.

Some thirty years after Richard's death, More wrote a partial history of Richard's reign that portrays the slain king as a murderous villain. Strangely, this work was neither completed nor published in More's lifetime. The incomplete document was found among More's papers after he was executed by Henry VIII for refusing to support that monarch's plan to divorce Catherine of Aragon and marry Anne Boleyn.

More's "History" was published in 1557 by his nephew, William Rastell. It was based on a manuscript in More's handwriting, which Rastell said had been written in 1513. An earlier and different version had been published in 1543 in John Hardying's "Chronicle," published by Richard Grafton. That version was essentially copied in Edward Hall's "Union of the Families," one of Shakespeare's principal sources, which was also published by Grafton and appeared in 1548. Rastell called these earlier versions of More's work "very muche corrupte in many places, sometyme havyng lese, and sometyme more and altered in wordes and whole sentances: muche varying fro the copie of [More's] own hand, by which thys is printed."

When he wrote his "History," More was thirty-five and was serving a term as undersheriff of London. This was not the work of the mature and courageous statesman who defied Henry VIII and gave his life in support of principle. The "History" is often cited as an authoritative "contemporary account." But More, who was born in 1478, was only five years old when Richard took the throne and only seven when Richard died at Bosworth Field. He was obviously not reporting events he had actually witnessed.

The primary source of More's information was most likely John Morton, the bishop of Ely, in whose home More lived between the ages of eight and fourteen. A lawyer as well as a churchman, the intelligent, devious Morton was Richard's most dedicated and effective enemy. As Bacon put it, Morton had "an inveterate malice against the House of York." Mancini described him as a man "of great resource and cunning," long "trained in party intrigue."

Over and over again, Morton organized conspiracies against Richard, ultimately playing a major role in the plot that put Henry VII on the throne. Henry rewarded Morton handsomely, making him lord chancellor as well as archbishop of Canterbury and ultimately arranging for him to become a cardinal.

It is not likely that the young Thomas More heard anything good about Richard III from his first day in Morton's home until his last. Morton is a likely source of the demonstrably false assertions about Richard that appear in More's "History" and of the long speeches More puts in the mouths of Richard, the queen, Buckingham and others, purporting to quote them verbatim thirty years after the fact. Morton died in 1500, thirteen years before More wrote his "History," but undoubtedly the wily old churchman had ample time to fill More's young ears with anti-Ricardian venom and the Tudor version of the facts.

Probably what Morton told the eight-year-old More was limited to "monster" tales about an evil, murderous king. But by the time his ward was a precocious fourteen-year-old, Morton would almost certainly have filled in all the details of what revisionists call the "Tudor Myth." When he wrote his "History," More had access to other men who had lived through Richard's reign. But by that time, all of them would have been staunch supporters of the Tudor regime and unlikely to contradict the fundamental elements of the story that More had heard from Morton.

Sir George Buck and others have contended that, even though the manuscript of the "History" was found in More's home, it was in fact written by Bishop Morton himself. Certainly, there are parts of the manuscript that seem to have been written by one who was present at the events depicted; and it has been argued that at least parts of the original Latin manuscript are not up to the standards of More's Latin writings. But there is no real evidence of Morton's authorship. As a lawyer and high-ranking cleric for many years, Morton can be assumed to have had Latin skills not significantly less accomplished than those of More. Moreover, the work contains some descriptions of Morton and his conduct not likely to have been written by Morton about himself, as when it describes the Bishop as "lacking no wise ways to win favor" and "craftily" using Buckingham's pride to turn him against Richard.

It has also been contended that More wrote the "History" himself, but did so tongue-in-cheek for his own amusement and not as historical truth. This seems unlikely from the nature of the manuscript.

It is also possible that More neither finished nor published the "History" because, as he worked on it, he began to learn more and more facts that tended to exonerate Richard, to the point that it became dangerous in a Tudor regime to publish or even finish it.

More's "History" appears to have been considerably influenced by Tacitus. Tacitus has been suspected of creating the monstrous Nero of history, just as More's incomplete manuscript was used to portray Richard as a homicidal villain. Like More, Tacitus wrote under subsequent rulers, when denigrating the reputation of their predecessor was probably good politics. Did the young undersheriff of London begin his "History" with the view that it would advance his career? Did he abandon the effort because he

discovered that the stories he had been told could not be reconciled with the facts he ultimately discovered? If his inquiries had
led him to facts of that nature, publishing them would have been
bad politics indeed. But suppressing them and publishing an
account he knew to be false may have been something even the
young, ambitious More was unwilling to do. After all, it was
More himself who said "Let history begin to show either preju-
dice or favoritism, and who will believe history?"

Another theory, discussed below, is that one of the two
princes supposedly murdered by Richard was not murdered at all,
that he adopted a false identity, that he married More's daughter
and was harbored and protected by More, who wrote his
"History" to throw potential enemies off the trail.

More, Vergil and the Croyland chronicler may have given
their contemporaries an early version of the facts, but it was
Shakespeare who gave the world its view of Richard, a view that
has endured for centuries. This he did in his great drama *Richard
III*, which was probably first written in 1591 and was the last play
of Shakespeare's eight-part series on English kings. The cycle
begins in the fourteenth century with the reign and deposition of
Richard II and ends late in the next century with the defeat of
Richard III at Bosworth Field.

Over and over again, scholars have pointed out the anachro-
nisms and inaccuracies in *Richard III*. For example, Shakespeare
relates events that took place over a period of many years as if
they occurred in just a few months, and has Queen Margaret participate in events that took place well after her death. But such
scholarly "exposure" is but a candle in a hurricane. Shakespeare's
Richard forms every schoolchild's view of the villainous, hunchbacked usurper who murdered everyone in sight, including his
poor infant nephews.

Actually, Shakespeare introduces Richard in *Henry VI, Part
III*, giving him the same hideous, yet compelling qualities we see
in *Richard III:*

Why I can smile, and murther whiles I smile,
And cry, content, to that which grieves my heart,

And wet my cheeks with artificial tears,
And frame my face to all occasions.

• • •

I can add colors to me chameleon
Change shapes with Proteus, for advantages
And set the murtherous machiavel to school.

Was Shakespeare a Tudor propagandist? Not really. Certainly
he was practical enough not to portray anything that would dis-
please Queen Elizabeth, who, after all, was Henry Tudor's granddaughter. He knew of the Queen's temper and had seen her close
down a production of *Richard II* because it portrayed the deposition of a reigning king, a subject she did not want publicly viewed
or discussed. A revisionist attitude toward Richard III would not
have been well received at court.

But Shakespeare was much more interested in drama than in
historical fact or even propaganda. A balanced, objective portrait
of Richard, showing his good and bad qualities, would have made
a dull play indeed. A heroic or sympathetic portrait was politically impossible and also inconsistent with Shakespeare's sources,
Edward Hall, who took his account from More, and Raphael
Holinshed, who copied Hall.

It is probable that Shakespeare, writing more than a hundred
years after the events he portrayed, completely accepted the version reported by those "historians." The only effective (and, at the
same time, practical) choice for the great dramatist was to create
a larger-than-life, unforgettable villain. That is just what he did.
He could have made Henry VII that villain. But he undoubtedly
did not believe that was the truth; and, even if he had suspected
it, saying so would hardly have been politic in the reign of
Henry's granddaughter.

In later centuries, particularly after Queen Elizabeth died in
1603, ending the Tudor line, historians and others began to question whether that villainous Richard really existed and whether
he had indeed killed his nephews. Since that time, the writing
about Richard has remained, for the most part, advocacy for one
side or the other.

In 1616, Sir William Cornwallis published an account praising and defending Richard. Cornwallis's account was a "paradox," however—i.e., an intellectual exercise in which one sought to demonstrate that a proposition generally accepted as true was, in fact, false. Exercise or not, it was the first time that the "Tudor myth" had been questioned—at least in writing.

According to the seventeenth-century historian John Speed, his fellow historian John Stow, who adopted More's account in his *Annals,* published in 1592, maintained orally on a number of occasions that the princes had not been murdered at all, but were living incognito beyond the sea.

In 1619, Sir George Buck wrote his five-part *The History of the Life and Reigne of Richard the Third,* vigorously defending Richard. It has been argued that the well-researched work originally created by Buck was carelessly rewritten by his great nephew before its publication in 1646 and was thereby converted into a less precise and less reliable summary.

In 1768, Horace Walpole published his *Historic Doubts on the Life and Reign of Richard the Third,* raising serious questions as to Richard's guilt and undertaking a detailed factual analysis. By this time, the subject had captured the imagination of educated Englishmen, and Walpole's book was an immediate best-seller. Every copy sold within one day of its publication. David Hume and others disagreed with Walpole and said so. But at least now there was thoughtful debate on the subject and not merely fanciful, prejudiced cant.

By this time, anti-Ricardian sentiment among the French appears to have lessened, if not vanished. Walpole's *Historic Doubts* was translated into French by Louis XVI himself while he was imprisoned in the Tuileries. Indeed, the work was apparently so well accepted among French intellectuals that Louis XVIII falsely claimed that he rather than his late brother, had been the translator.

Walpole, who argued in 1768 that no man could have behaved as monstrously as the Richard portrayed by Tudor historians, found that view profoundly altered by the French Revolution. In 1793, he added a postscript to his *Historic Doubts,* conceding that the atrocities of the revolution had led him to accept that men could, in fact, behave toward one another with such violence and viciousness. He made it clear, however, that, while "I *can* believe . . . [that Richard might have behaved so abominably] . . . I do not say I do."

Caroline Halsted, writing in the nineteenth century, concluded that Richard was innocent. Her two-volume work, published in 1844, presents him as a splendid human being and an efficient and beneficent monarch.

James Gairdner, who devoted many years to the subject, presented the opposing view in 1878 in his *History of the Life and Reign of Richard the Third*. Gairdner has often been cited as authoritative; but, while he was thoughtful and diligent, his tendency was to accept "tradition" whenever an issue could not be plainly resolved. This, of course, was true of most of the issues he considered, and the tradition he tended to accept was the Tudor tradition, as set out by More, Vergil and others. Gairdner would probably not have denied this. In the preface to his first edition he said that "[t]he attempt to discard tradition in the examination of original sources of history is, in fact, like the attempt to learn an unknown language without a teacher."

Sir Clements Markham publicly disagreed and debated with Gairdner in the 1890s and wrote his own book on the subject in 1906. Markham presented a flawless, saint-like Richard and concluded that the princes were murdered by Henry VII.

A number of twentieth-century authors have been intrigued with the mystery. Like Shakespeare, Josephine Tey probably had a greater impact on the public's view of Richard than did the historians who were her contemporaries. Tey wrote a popular detective novel called *The Daughter of Time,* in which a hospitalized Scotland Yard inspector, out of intellectual curiosity and to pass the time, considers the historical evidence and "proves" Richard's innocence.

Many other twentieth-century authors have written on the subject, such as Charles Ross, A. J. Pollard, William Snyder, V. D. Lamb, Audrey Williamson, Paul Murray Kendall, Anthony Cheetham and Alison Weir. Recent authors are inclined to portray themselves as objective and open-minded. But most, by their analysis of the evidence and by the facts they stress and those they omit, show that they lean toward one side or the other.

Still, there is a modern tendency to soften the advocacy. Some of those inclined to the revisionist view, assert the probability of Richard's innocence, but concede that he could have been guilty.

Similarly, a number of those who follow the traditionalist view admit the possibility of Richard's innocence, even if they find it improbable. Some reason that if he was guilty, his crime was neither unusual nor particularly heinous, given the situation and the political and moral standards of the fifteenth century, when it was hardly uncommon to kill rival claimants to the throne. Elizabeth Jenkins, for example, sums it up as follows: "The story is not the sensational one of the crime of a habitual murderer, but the awe-inspiring one of a capable, strong minded, dedicated King driven to a dreadful act from which he chose to think there was no escape."

A few, however, have no doubt about Richard's guilt or blame. Alison Weir is one. She tells her readers that she, at last, has solved the mystery: Richard was guilty. What's more, he was a greedy, ruthless tyrant.

However, if Richard was guilty, nothing in Weir's book demonstrates it. Essentially, her "proof" that he murdered his nephews consists of two skeletons discovered in the Tower of London in 1674, some inferences wholly unsupported by the "evidence" she offers and the opinions and assertions of "contemporary" sources such as Rous and More, which Weir is inclined to treat as proven fact. We will analyze that "proof" in detail.

Future writers will struggle with the same problems, looking for new clues to the truth. Perhaps we will never know. Perhaps that's what makes the subject so intriguing.

IV

👑 THE WARS OF THE ROSES

Having examined the sources of our information about the relevant facts, we can turn to the facts themselves, beginning with the background facts that set the scene for the events that led to and constituted the crime—if indeed a crime was committed.

The setting for the drama and mystery surrounding Richard III and his nephews was the Wars of the Roses. This dynastic struggle continued for thirty years, essentially between the house of York, whose symbol was the white rose, and the house of Lancaster, whose symbolic rose was supposedly red. The fact is that the red rose was a Tudor, not Lancastrian, symbol, and the conflict was only named the Wars of the Roses decades after the fighting ended.

For fifty years, from 1327 to 1377, England was ruled by Edward III, a Plantagenet king. This Edward, whose mother was the sole heir of the French king, claimed the throne of France. That claim led to more than a century of warfare.

Edward's oldest son was a warrior hero called the Black Prince, a name probably given him by the French because he wore black armor. Edward and his son soundly defeated the French at Crecy in 1346, and the Black Prince beat them again at Poitiers in 1356. As Edward grew old, there was little fear for the succession, since all expected the Black Prince to have a long and glorious reign.

But fourteenth-century life was uncertain and perilous. In 1377, the Black Prince died following a lingering and, in those times, incurable illness. Edward III, died the next year, leaving three surviving sons. The oldest was Lionel, the duke of Clarence. Next was John of Gaunt, the duke of Lancaster. Then came Edmund, the duke of York, and, finally, Thomas of Woodstock, the duke of Gloucester. Each was a formidable man, up to the task of ruling England, and even France.

Unfortunately, none of these mature, experienced men was entitled to rule. Instead, under prevailing law, the heir to the throne was the eldest son of the Black Prince, Richard Plantagenet (soon to be Richard II). He, rather than any of his capable uncles, was to be king.

But Richard was only ten years old. The nation had reason for concern. The reign of a minor king tempted enemy nations, created power struggles within the kingdom, and brought uncertainty and peril into the lives of every Englishman. Indeed, the dangers of a minority rule had been recognized since biblical times, when it was written in Ecclesiastes 10:16, "Woe to thee, O land, when thy king is a child."

A protector was appointed to govern in the name of the child-king, and somehow the kingdom struggled through. In 1381, at fourteen, the young king showed bravery and coolheadedness in facing down an angry and dangerous mob during Wat Tyler's Rebellion. As Richard II grew into maturity, however, his lack of judgment, arrogance and conflicts with powerful nobles created a fearful instability.

Finally, in 1399, Richard was overthrown and ultimately killed by his cousin, Henry of Bolingbroke, son of the duke of Lancaster. The usurping Bolingbroke became Henry IV, the first Lancastrian king. He was succeeded in 1413 by his son, who reigned as Henry V, the legendary warrior-king and hero of Harfleur and Agincourt ("Once more into the breach, dear friends"). After his French conquests in 1415, this Henry signed the Treaty of Troyes with Charles VI, the French king. Henry was given the hand of Katherine of Valois, Charles' daughter, and, while Charles was allowed to retain his throne for his lifetime, Henry was designated his heir, disinheriting Charles' own son, the dauphin.

Thus, Henry V was destined to become king of both England and France, uniting the two kingdoms, making good his great-grandfather's claim and lending substance to Shakespeare's dramatic rallying cry "The signs of war advance. No King of England, if not King of France!"

Unfortunately, Henry V also fell ill and died unexpectedly in 1422, leaving as his heir to the English and French throne his nine-month-old son, Henry VI. That situation, always a source of trouble and instability, gave rise to many years of conflict in both countries.

As he grew into young manhood, Henry VI was completely unfitted to deal with that conflict or any aspect of governing. He had grown into a weak and unstable man, primarily interested in God and prayer. Meanwhile, the dauphin had repudiated the treaty that had disinherited him. The vast territories in France controlled by the English were enormously expensive to maintain, and Henry had no particular stomach for fighting to maintain them. Gradually, almost everything Henry V had won was lost to the French in battle or ceded to them to avoid a fight.

At twenty-four, Henry VI was married to Margaret, the fifteen year old daughter of the Duke of Anjou. Beautiful, intelligent and ambitious, Margaret became the de facto ruler along with a succession of her male favorites. As Henry VI grew older, he proved less and less fit to rule and was periodically insane, having possibly inherited this condition from his grandfather, the French king. In addition, the loss of the English possessions in France and a pervasive looting of the royal lands and treasures by the queen's favorites had created a furious reaction against Queen Margaret and her current favorite, the duke of Suffolk.

Ultimately, public opinion and the action of Parliament forced Henry VI to banish Suffolk for five years, a sentence far lighter than was desired by the public and the Commons. But Suffolk was not that lucky. His ship to France was ambushed and boarded, and Suffolk was beheaded by six strokes of a rusty sword—not a pleasant way to die. Still the public anger mounted as the Queen turned to another favorite, the arrogant duke of Somerset.

More and more attention turned to Richard, duke of York,

the greatest peer of the realm, who was next in line to the throne if Henry VI died without children. Many felt that York, the father of the future Edward IV and Richard III, had an even better claim to the throne than Henry.

Henry VI was descended from John of Gaunt, the second surviving son of Edward III. Richard of York's grandfather, Edmund, also a duke of York, had been King Edward's third surviving son. This might have given Henry the better claim. But Richard of York's maternal grandmother was Phillipa, daughter of Lione, duke of Clarence, a deceased son of Edward III who was senior to John of Gaun. Lionel's descendants had been next in line to the throne when their Lancastrian cousin, Bolingbroke, ousted Richard II and seized the crown for himself. Thus, if the female line counted, Richard of York had a stronger claim than Henry VI. If it did not, Henry's Lancastrian claim was the stronger.

Under Salic law, a woman could neither succeed to the throne nor pass on the right to succession to her heirs. But the Salic law did not apply in England. Thus, the claim of York seemed stronger than that of Lancaster, even though the Lancastrian Henry VI was the reigning King.

Richard of York was married to a legendary beauty, Cecily Neville, sometimes called the "Rose of Raby" after her father's stronghold, Raby Castle. As a boy, the orphaned York had lived with Cecily's family at Raby, and the two were close long before their marriage. Cecily's mother, Joanna Beaufort, was the daughter of John of Gaunt by his mistress, Catherine Swynford. That Beaufort inheritance (discussed below) gave Cecily some claim to the throne in her own right. Although her claim was not a strong one, it lent even greater force to that of her husband.

After their marriage, the relationship apparently remained a close one. Cecily traveled with her husband on his overseas assignments in the French territories and in Ireland, and bore him many children.

On October 2, 1452, Cecily gave birth to the future Richard III, her eleventh and last surviving child. She and York had three other surviving sons: Edward, then ten; Edmond, nine; and George, who was four.

For some years, York did not encourage those who urged him

to claim the throne. In July 1453, an English army was crushed by the French at the battle of Castillon; and, by the year's end, only Calais remained of the vast French dominions held by the English when Henry VI took the throne. Shortly after the disaster at Castillon, as public anger continued to mount over the loss of the French territories and other grievances, Henry VI suffered a complete mental collapse, apparently a form of schizophrenia.

During the king's illness, Queen Margaret gave birth to a son, whose legitimacy was widely doubted. The queen had been known for years to have dallied with her favorites, notably the dukes of Suffolk and Somerset. Somerset was widely believed to be the father of the newborn prince. The likelihood of the child's illegitimacy appeared even greater when, in a period of temporary lucidity, Henry remarked that his new heir must have been born through intervention of the Holy Ghost.

Even aside from his bouts of insanity, Henry was extremely frail and was not expected to live for long. No one wanted another infant king, and one who was probably illegitimate at that. In the spring of 1454, Parliament elected the duke of York protector of the realm during Henry's illness, and pressure mounted for York to claim the throne. Queen Margaret's resentment at this grew, and, with it, the animosity between the adherents of Lancaster and those of York.

Richard of York ruled the kingdom sensibly as protector. He began putting its affairs in order and committed Somerset to the Tower. Loyally, he swore an oath to support Margaret's son, Edward, Prince of Wales, as heir to the throne.

Just before the end of the year, the king temporarily regained his senses. Despite his lucidity, however, Henry remained in such a weak state that he could be little more than a symbol for his ambitious wife and her adherents. Characteristically, she set out at once to reverse the Yorkist gains. York was turned out of office and his appointed council members dismissed. Somerset was released from the Tower.

In 1455, Queen Margaret called a great council of Lancastrians and their supporters to guard against the "enemies" of the king. York and his supporters realized their danger, and soon the dynastic war began in earnest, with a smashing Yorkist victory at the battle of St. Albans. Somerset, the Queen's favorite, was killed.

However, the war was hardly over. It continued on and off for the next thirty years. In the first part of that period, the Lancastrian forces were led by Queen Margaret herself. The tide of battle shifted from year to year and from place to place. At times, the Lancastrians were victorious; at others, the Yorkists prevailed.

These royal families did not fight with standing armies. Medieval English kings maintained no such institutions. Faced with combat, they called up knights, squires, court officials and relatives, most of whom had been trained since youth in the martial arts. These forces were augmented by other noblemen who controlled vast regions of the land and who gave their allegiance to one side or the other (or switched from side to side), bringing with them their own relatives and retainers, often including large bands of trained soldiers.

During the Wars of the Roses, the population of England was about two and a half million, most of it rural. A third of the land was owned by the church—which, at this time, prior to the Reformation, was the Catholic Church, governed (at least theoretically) from Rome. Much of the remaining land was owned by the Crown, by the dozen or so dukes and earls who were the great magnates of enormous wealth and vast holdings, and by some forty or more other families of the great nobility. Some others, notably knights and burgesses, also had significant property; and there were, by this time, numerous small rural holdings throughout the land.

London, a bustling center of international trade, had a population of about fifty thousand. It had ninety-seven churches. York's population was no more than twelve thousand.

By custom, Parliament was to consent to any taxation of the people and, theoretically, to the making of any law. Parliament, however, was called and dismissed at the discretion of the king. It consisted of a gathering of the leading officials of the church and the greater nobility, the Lords Spiritual and Temporal, sitting as one "house." The second house, the Commons, was comprised at that time of representatives of the landed gentry not included in the great nobility.

No book in English was printed until 1475, and only a small part of the population, mostly the nobility and churchmen, could read.

For the most part, the Wars of the Roses did not involve the general population, except when one warring side or the other swept through an area, commandeering the available cattle and grain. The killing and maiming was confined to the nobility and their retainers.

Phillipe de Commynes commented on this distinction between the fate of the common people and that of the nobility: "Now in my opinion out of all the countries which I have person-ally known, England is the one where public affairs are best con-ducted and regulated with least violence to the people. There are no buildings knocked down or demolished through war and dis-aster and misfortune befalls only those who make war."

The Scots had long had an alliance with the French, by which the French king hoped to balance the alliance between England and Burgundy. Scotland, like France, was sympathetic to Queen Margaret and the Lancastrian cause, as were the northern parts of England and much of Wales. London, the midlands and the southeast favored the Yorkists.

In 1460, after a Yorkist victory at Northampton, the duke of York entered London and asserted his right to the throne. Weeks of debate followed. Finally, in a Solomonic decree, the House of Lords ruled that, since the house of Lancaster had occupied the throne for so many years, Henry VI should remain king so long as he lived, but that the duke of York who, the Lords ruled, had the better claim by inheritance, should be recognized as Henry's heir. Queen Margaret and her Lancastrians would hold sway as long as they could keep poor Henry alive. On his death, the king-dom would be and remain Yorkist. Margaret's son, theoretically Prince of Wales, would never occupy the throne.

An incensed Margaret fled to Scotland, where she assembled a powerful force and invaded England. The ferocious queen and her army reached the duke of York's fortress, Sandal Castle, before the duke's allies could join him. His oldest son, Edward (later Edward IV), was away raising an army in Wales.

Taunted by Margaret's men, the duke unwisely left his castle to give battle, rather than awaiting reinforcements. This was the battle of Wakefield, fought on December 30, 1460. It was a disaster for the Yorkists. Perhaps, Duke Richard ventured forth to attack what appeared to be a small Lancastrian force outside the castle, only to be overwhelmed by a much larger body of troops that had been concealed in a nearby forest.

Whether or not this was the reason for his unwise decision, the duke was captured by the Lancastrians. His second son, Edmund, only seventeen, was also captured and was slaughtered while a prisoner, after vainly pleading for his life. The duke was placed on an anthill throne, where he was ridiculed and humiliated. Then, on Margaret's order, he was killed, and his head, wearing a paper crown, was impaled on a lance and placed, alongside the head of his young son, over the gates of York.

The emotional impact on the duke's surviving sons must have been staggering and indelible. Richard was only eight when his father and brother were killed in a single day. He and his eleven-year-old brother George were quickly spirited across the channel to Utrecht in the territory of Phillip the Good, the duke of Burgundy.

Their older brother, Edward, was then nineteen. Enraged at the humiliation and death of his father and brother, Edward returned from Wales and took command of the Yorkist forces. During February 1461, in a swift and brilliant campaign, he defeated the Lancastrians at Mortimer's Cross and entered London. He was cheered by the citizens; and, with the approval of the council, he claimed the throne as Edward IV. In March, he utterly destroyed the Lancastrian army at the decisive battle of Towton. Margaret was forced to flee to Scotland, taking with her the Prince of Wales and poor Henry VI.

Returning to London, Edward IV was formally crowned, and his two younger brothers, Richard and George, were returned from Utrecht. Edward made George duke of Clarence, and, in November 1461, he made Richard duke of Gloucester.

The tall and handsome Edward, widely acclaimed now as a skilled military leader, quickly became popular with the people. By contrast to the pious but weak Henry VI, Edward IV looked and acted like a true English king.

At this time, the most powerful peer in the realm was Richard Neville, the immensely powerful earl of Warwick. Warwick had enormous wealth in his own right. Moreover, his wife was the heiress of the great Beauchamp fortune. Through her, he acquired the Warwick title and even greater holdings. Warwick's family, the Nevilles, were closely linked to the House of York.

The estates of such peers as Warwick were sources of great power, not just because they involved vast and profitable land holdings, but also because the greater the estate, the greater the number of men who could be called upon to render military service in the name of the lord of the manor. Warwick's numerous men were a reliable and effective force in combating the Lancastrians and placing Edward IV on the throne.

In the early years of Edward's reign, former queen Margaret attempted to continue the war against the Yorkists with the aid of the Scots, but without much success. Time after time, her forces were defeated by Yorkist armies led by the redoubtable Warwick or his brother John Neville, Lord Montagu. The Scottish king was losing his enthusiasm for Margaret's military adventures, which were costly in men and money. Finally, he negotiated a fifteen-year truce with Warwick and Montagu promising to end the Lancastrian-Scottish forays into the North of England. Margaret returned to France with the Prince of Wales, leaving a bewildered Henry VI in Edinburgh.

Edward IV showed his gratitude for the splendid service of the Nevilles. Warwick's brother Montagu was made the earl of Northumberland and his youngest brother, George, a churchman who was already chancellor, was made archbishop of York.

Warwick himself became known as the "kingmaker" for his part in winning the throne for Edward IV. The great earl possessed such strength, wealth and alliances that, as More put it, "he made Kinges and put down Kinges almost at his pleasure, and not impossible to have attained it himselfe, if he had not rekened it a greater thing to make a King then to be a King." A report to Louis XI of France referred—probably tongue-in-cheek—to there being two kings in England, "M. de Warwick and another whose name escapes me."

Nevertheless, Edward was enjoying his role as monarch.

While engaged in the process of governing the realm, he involved himself in many amorous adventures, a proclivity that seemed only normal for the handsome and vigorous young Plantagenet.

On May 1, 1464, however, the king secretly married a commoner, Elizabeth Woodville (or Wydville) an act that had a profound effect on many fifteenth-century lives. Presumably he did so because, unlike most other women of his acquaintance, the flaxen-haired widow with the sensuously lidded, ice blue eyes would not succumb to his charms until they were married.

Edward's secret marriage to Elizabeth may have cost him the loyalty of the proud and powerful Warwick. The earl, who favored a French alliance, had been negotiating with Louis XI for a marriage between Edward and Louis's niece, Bona of Savoy. He was embarrassed and enraged when the news finally came out in late September 1464 that Edward had married a commoner five months earlier and had not even bothered to let Warwick in on the secret.

Elizabeth Woodville was the widow of a slain Lancastrian with whom she had two sons. She was five years older than King Edward and came from a family of little distinction. Her father, Sir Richard Woodville, had been assigned to accompany Jacquetta, the beautiful young widow of the duke of Bedford, on a voyage to England from Rouen, where the duke had died. One thing led to another, and Woodville, known for his good looks and engaging manner, married the widow. They produced twelve children.

Once their daughter, the highly ambitious Elizabeth Woodville, became queen, she quickly set out to make up for her relatively low birth. As concerned for her family's advancement as she had been for her marital status, she brought a horde of Woodville relatives to court and into positions of power. Her two grown sons, five brothers and six unmarried sisters, along with their spouses and friends, formed an ambitious and acquisitive group. One of the group, the queen's brother, Anthony, Lord Rivers, was an intelligent and scholarly man, famous for his skill in tournaments. Rivers played a leading role in the drama that was later to unfold.

Elizabeth saw that her sisters were married to wealthy and

high ranking nobles. In 1465, even the eleven-year-old duke of Buckingham, in whose veins flowed the royal Plantagenet blood, was forced to marry the queen's sister, Katherine, also a child at the time. This coerced marriage may have led to serious trouble for the Yorkist cause years later, when Buckingham, still smarting from this "insult," attained maturity and power.

Elizabeth's nineteen-year-old brother, John, wed the enormously rich dowager duchess of Norfolk. Since the duchess was almost eighty, the nobility was scandalized. The match was dubbed the "diabolical marriage." It also had an impact on later events.

It was not only her relatives whom the queen brought to the court. Dominic Mancini says that she "attracted to her party many strangers and introduced them to court, so that they alone should manage the public and private business of the crown, give or sell offices, and finally rule the very King himself."

King Edward seemed completely tolerant of the growing Woodville power, perhaps because it took his wife's attention away from his numerous infidelities.

In 1465, Edward made his younger brother Richard a Knight of the Garter. The young man, only thirteen, was now one of twenty-four Knights of the Garter and one of only six English dukes.

In that year, following the custom among noble families, Richard was sent to live in Warwick's home at Middleham Castle. As a youth, Richard's father had lived in the household of Warwick's grandfather, Ralph Neville. As we have seen, he had married his host's daughter, Cecily. Now Cecily's son, Richard, was to enter Warwick's household. There, he would become a companion of Warwick's daughter, Anne, whom he would later marry.

At Middleham, Richard would learn the social graces and martial arts, along with other young "henxmen" such as Francis Lovell, who would remain his lifelong friend. Richard spent the next three and a half years virtually as a member of Warwick's family. Ironically, he would first demonstrate his martial skills against Warwick. But that was later.

Also in 1465, Henry VI, who had been left behind in

Edinburgh, was captured by English royal forces. After another Yorkist victory, the poor deposed king had been found wandering in a confused state, followed by a handful of nervous attendants. He was immediately sent off to the Tower of London, where he was generally well treated and permitted such visitors as wished to see him. As things stood, the Lancastrian cause seemed lost.

But the Wars of the Roses were not over. Four years later, in 1469, Edward was betrayed by his longtime ally, Warwick, and by his own brother, George, duke of Clarence. The immensely powerful Warwick had several grounds for his dissatisfaction. First, there was the earl's resentment of the ambitious and greedy Woodvilles. Then, there was Edward's permitting him to negotiate the king's proposed marriage to Bona of Savoy, while Edward was already secretly married to Elizabeth Woodville. Another ground was Edward's flat rejection of Warwick's advice on foreign policy.

Louis XI, the cleverest of schemers, had long cultivated Warwick. He flattered the powerful earl and tried his best to lessen Warwick's embarrassment over Edward's Woodville marriage. What Louis wanted was Warwick's aid in bringing about an Anglo-French alliance against the duke of Burgundy.

Louis desperately sought to make Burgundy a part of France. The duke of Burgundy, naturally, wanted his dukedom to remain independent. England, it seemed, was the key to which man would succeed.

Warwick tried to influence Edward to adopt the Burgundian policy urged by Louis—an alliance of England and France to crush the stubborn dukedom. But Burgundy was England's traditional ally and Burgundian trade was vital to English commercial interests, a situation of which Edward was keenly aware.

France, on the other hand, was the traditional enemy. An alliance with Burgundy against France would be widely applauded by the merchants, the public and most of the nobility. An alliance with France against Burgundy would almost surely be unpopular. Not only did Edward ignore Warwick's counsel by signing a treaty with Charles the Bold, the new duke of Burgundy, he emphasized his pro-Burgundian policy by giving Duke Charles his sister Margaret's hand in marriage. Once again Warwick was humiliated.

Warwick's brother, Archbishop George Neville, was lord chancellor. The archbishop indicated his displeasure at Edward's Burgundian policy by declining to attend the opening of Parliament. Edward, who was beginning to realize that the archbishop placed the interests of Warwick above those of his king, summarily dismissed Neville as chancellor, giving Warwick still another reason for anger.

The duke of Clarence had his own reasons for resenting Edward. Probably from the beginning of Edward's reign, Clarence envied his older brother's kingship. And, always conscious of class and position, Clarence, like Warwick, hated the low-born Woodvilles, whose pretension, he felt, was becoming intolerable. Edward seemed blind to their overreaching and would do nothing to stop it.

Also, Warwick had cultivated Clarence, just as Louis of France had cultivated Warwick. Clarence had joined in urging Edward to adopt the earl's Burgundian policy. To Clarence, Edward's rejection of his advice on that important matter lessened Clarence in Warwick's eyes, just as, to Warwick, it lessened the proud earl in the eyes of Louis XI.

As time passed, Edward's relationship with both Warwick and Clarence went from bad to worse. Warwick had for some time proposed a marriage between Clarence and his older daughter, Isabel. Clarence was enthusiastic about the prospect. But Edward had flatly forbidden the match, feeling that such an alliance between Clarence and Warwick would be too powerful and too dangerous.

Evidently, Warwick thought that, as Edward's cousin and his mightiest subject, one who played a significant role in placing him on the throne, he had been rejected and humiliated once too often by the king he felt he had made. Ignoring Edward's order, Warwick brought Clarence to Calais, where the earl was governor. There, in July 1469, he proceeded with the forbidden marriage, having already obtained the pope's dispensation, which was required since the bride and the groom were cousins.

Returning to England, Warwick and Clarence openly took up arms against the king. Catching Edward unprepared, they defeated his vastly outnumbered supporters at Edgecote and captured Edward himself. Also among the captured were the queen's father and her brother John, who, in the "diabolical marriage," had wed the aged dowager duchess of Norfolk. Unfortunately for young John, the dowager duchess happened to be Warwick's aunt. A vengeful Warwick, considering that his aunt had been grievously imposed upon, that the May-December marriage was a bizarre disgrace and that the queen's father was an ambitious upstart, had the two Woodvilles quickly beheaded.

Evidently, however, the rebels lacked the will or the courage to kill the king. Presumably they intended to bring about his abdication and to place Clarence on the throne. But as word of Edward's captivity spread, the people were stunned and outraged to learn that their handsome and popular king was a prisoner. When Warwick went north seeking to put down a Scottish invasion, he was unable to raise the necessary troops so long as he held the king captive. Even Warwick's brother John Neville, now the earl of Northumberland, refused to join in Warwick's scheme.

The rebels came under pressure from all quarters to release their royal prisoner. Even the duke of Burgundy threatened to come to the aid of Edward, who was now his brother-in-law. Ultimately, his captors allowed Edward to show himself to the people at York and then to travel to the castle of Pontefract.

When Richard and Lord Hastings arrived near Pontefract with a strong force of armed men, Edward coolly advised Warwick and Clarence that his brother and friends had come to escort him to London. Lacking the strength or resolve to offer further resistance, Edward's captors stood aside and allowed him to leave. He entered London to the jubilant cheering of his subjects, once again a free man and their king.

In the months before the rebellion of 1469, Richard had still been a part of Warwick's household, and he had always been fond of his charming older brother, Clarence. It is likely that, before the rebellion began, he had been asked to join Clarence and Warwick in what was undoubtedly portrayed not as an attack on Edward, but as an attempt to rid the kingdom of Woodville power and influence. If so, Richard, evidently realizing that the scheme was necessarily against Edward's interests, refused and stood by his brother, the king.

After Edward's release from captivity, Richard was granted valuable estates and accorded many honors, presumably for his loyalty to Edward and possibly also for the part he had played in securing the king's freedom. Among other things, Richard was appointed constable of England for life. Always a position of great power, the constableship was made even more powerful by Edward, who was determined to see order restored to the kingdom. In addition to many other powers, the constable was now empowered to determine and punish treasonable acts without the need for further judicial proceedings.

The Woodvilles were, of course, enraged at the execution of the queen's father and brother. They urged Edward to take decisive action against Warwick and Clarence. He decided, however, on a policy of amnesty and forgiveness, issuing a general pardon to all who had participated in the rebellion. Warwick was hardly in Edward's favor. He lost some valuable estates and offices; but, despite the extreme gravity of their crime, Warwick received no punishment of any real significance, and Clarence received none at all.

Nevertheless, the earl must have realized that his position would never be the same with Edward on the throne and a vengeful Woodville queen at his side. Clarence was also concerned that his brother's view of him had been adversely affected. That concern was aggravated by the growing respect and regard Edward showed for Richard.

Gradually, Edward had come to recognize the marked differences between his two younger brothers. Clarence was charming and eloquent, but, even before betraying Edward, he had shown that he was mercurial in temperament and generally unreliable. By contrast, as Richard grew into young manhood, Edward began assigning him serious tasks, which he performed loyally and well. Exercising his first military command, Richard successfully put down a Welsh rebellion, recapturing two royal castles. Edward made Richard his principal representative in Wales and bestowed on him offices previously held there by Warwick. Instead of feeling gratitude for Edward's leniency, Clarence felt growing resentment and humiliation over what he considered the unfair favoritism shown his younger brother.

Given these circumstances, the peace was short-lived. In March 1470, Warwick and Clarence once again fomented and led a rebellion with the aim of deposing Edward and putting Clarence on the throne. Edward declared Warwick and Clarence traitors and, personally leading an army, defeated the rebel forces at Eppingham. Once again, John Neville refused to join in his brother's treason, as did other key nobles.

Seeing their cause lost, Warwick and Clarence fled to the coast and escaped to France. There they were welcomed by Louis XI, who still sought an Anglo-French alliance against the Burgundians and who now realized that his best chance of attaining that goal was to replace Edward with some other monarch.

Louis succeeded in affecting a reconciliation between Warwick and the exiled ex-queen, Margaret, who had despised the earl as the Lancastrians' most implacable enemy. After Margaret's probably feigned reluctance was overcome, an agreement was reached. A new invasion would be mounted by Warwick and Margaret with Louis' aid. Henry VI would be restored to the throne. Margaret's son, the Prince of Wales, would marry Warwick's younger daughter, Anne, the marriage contract being conditioned upon Henry's successful restoration.

Everyone but Clarence got something from the deal. Margaret would finally get the support she needed to restore poor Henry to the throne and, more importantly, to have him succeeded by her son. Warwick, who apparently had given up hope of placing the unreliable Clarence on the throne, could put his new son-in-law there on Henry's death and so regain the power and influence he had once enjoyed under Edward. Louis, of course, would get his Anglo-French alliance against the Burgundians.

Clarence was rendered virtually irrelevant. He had committed his most serious act of treason thus far and had nothing significant to show for it. His only solace was Warwick's promise that if the young Prince of Wales died without an heir, Clarence would succeed to the throne.

In September 1470, Warwick and Clarence landed in England with an invasion force in ships supplied by Louis. The Lancastrians rallied to their cause, and their force increased.

Edward placed his reliance on an army being raised by Warwick's brother, John Neville, long a dependable friend and ally.

Earlier in the year, however, Edward had tried to regain the support of the powerful Percy family by restoring to them the earldom of Northumberland, which he had previously bestowed on John Neville. Neville was now to be satisfied with just being Lord Montagu. As Edward waited for Neville's forces to join him, he suddenly got the terrible news that his longtime friend, probably resentful at losing his earldom and faced once more with a conflict between brotherhood and loyalty to Edward, had gone over to Warwick's side. Worse still, he was rapidly descending on Edward's smaller force with a large and powerful army.

Realizing that the situation was hopeless, Edward raced for the coast with Richard and a few loyal followers. They were able to find small craft and set sail for Burgundy. Evading hostile ships of the Hanseatic League through the last minute intervention of the governor of Holland, they successfully reached the Low Countries. They stayed for a time at the Hague, while Edward's brother-in-law, the duke of Burgundy, fearful of antagonizing the new powers in England, refused to receive them.

When the invasion of 1470 succeeded in driving Edward from the throne, Richard elected to accompany him into exile. Did he have a choice? Perhaps not. Despite his years in Warwick's home, Richard would have faced a dangerous situation had he remained in England after Henry VI's "restoration." Even if he still retained Warwick's goodwill, he would have posed a serious threat to Margaret and her son and would necessarily have found himself in extreme peril.

Still, it is more likely that loyalty, rather than fear of death, impelled Richard to follow his brother into exile. Loyalty to Edward—indeed loyalty in general—was critically important to Richard. He adopted as his motto *Loyeaultlé me lie*—"loyalty binds me"—and at least professed to live by those words.

On October 6, 1470, Warwick and Clarence entered London in triumph and proceeded to the Tower, where they "released" Henry VI in order to place him once more on the throne. The saintly, feeble-minded old king had been held in the Tower since 1465 and would probably have been happier remaining there with his books and prayers than once again facing the pressures and disturbances of being, even nominally, the reigning king.

At the behest of Warwick, Parliament adopted his unpopular policy of peace with France, unaware that the earl had promised Louis XI even more—an alliance with France to attack Burgundy, England's ally and trading partner.

It was becoming clear to the duke of Burgundy that, with Warwick ruling England in the name of Henry VI and allying the English with Louis of France, there was little chance for an independent Burgundy to survive. Recognizing that danger and urged by his wife, Margaret, Duke Charles finally relented and welcomed his brothers-in-law to the Burgundian court.

During Henry VI's restoration, Elizabeth Woodville remained in England in sanctuary. Sanctuary was a designated area of a cathedral or church in which a person accused of a crime or otherwise threatened could, by tradition, remain in safety indefinitely. As Mancini described it, "In England these places of refuge are of ancient observance, so that up to these times, either from religious awe or from fear of the people, none had dared to violate them. For whatever reason a man may be accused or disliked, it is not lawful even for Kings to drag him thence against his will."

On November 2, 1470, while still in sanctuary, Elizabeth gave birth to Prince Edward, ultimately Edward V, the older of the two "princes in the Tower." The news was spread throughout the kingdom and had considerable impact. Edward IV had a male heir!

By this time, Henry VI was almost consistently insane. Margaret, who had promised to return to England with the Prince of Wales, delayed her arrival. For once, the usually bold queen was cautious. It was the one time she should not have been. The Yorkists established clandestine contacts with Clarence, who realized with bitterness that Louis, Margaret and his own father-in-law, Warwick, had cast away his claim to the throne to serve their own interests. He was urged to make peace with his brothers and return to the Yorkist fold.

At the same time, support for Lancastrian rule was slipping. Probably sensing that, Louis XI declared war on Burgundy, undoubtedly expecting that, if the English would not join him in attacking the Burgundians, they would at least stay neutral so long as Warwick retained control.

In February of 1471, the English government, controlled by Margaret and Warwick, joined France in its declaration of war. Now, the danger the Duke of Burgundy had been slow to perceive had come to pass. Duke Charles was left with no real choice. His fate plainly depended on the restoration of Edward to the throne.

In March, with aid from Burgundy and the Hanseatic League, Edward crossed the channel with a small but loyal band including, of course, Richard. Landing at Ravenspur, they proceeded inland, avoiding early resistance by announcing that Edward sought not the throne, but only the re-establishment of his rights and holdings as Duke of York.

The band marched South. On their way, they revealed their true goals and attracted considerable numbers to their cause. Reaching Coventry, they threatened Warwick, who remained within the city walls awaiting reinforcements from his brother and Clarence. Edward's forces moved on toward what seemed a confrontation with a sizeable force under the leadership of Clarence himself.

When the two armies seemed about to clash, Edward and Richard rode out ahead of their troops. Having been persuaded, by the secret Yorkist contacts, Clarence rode out to meet them. Dismounting, he knelt before his brother the king. With kisses and embraces the three brothers were reconciled. Clarence, always eloquent, returned to his troops and convinced them that their true enemy was Warwick, their true king, Edward.

With their combined armies, Edward turned toward London. He was able to outmaneuver the Lancastrians and entered the capital on April 11, 1471. He did so triumphantly to the cheers of the people lining the streets and with Richard proudly riding at his side. King once again, Edward was reunited with his wife and saw his new young son for the first time.

Next, Edward led his army out of London and, in a brilliant campaign, defeated the Lancastrians at Barnet and Tewkesbury, settling the Wars of the Roses in favor of the Yorkists for the next eleven years. In these critical battles the eighteen-year-old Richard established himself as a brave and skilled commander and a ferocious combatant.

At Barnet, on Easter Sunday, 1471, Richard found himself in a dense fog on the flank of the Lancastrian forces. He pressed his attack so fiercely that Warwick was forced to commit his reserves. With superior numbers, they turned and attacked Richard in wave after wave, for hour after hour. Edward offered to send his own reserve to aid his brother, but Richard refused. He would not weaken the Yorkist center, sorely pressed from the other flank, to save himself. He would hold—without reinforcements. Swinging his battle-ax in the thick of the fight, he slew foe after foe. Two of his squires were killed at his side, and he himself was slightly wounded. At last the Lancastrian front broke, and Richard led his men in a triumphant charge with the enemy fleeing before them.

Warwick and his brother were both killed in the battle, but not before the breathtakingly perfidious Clarence had suggested that he might, once again, switch sides and reconcile with his father-in-law. The proud earl refused, reportedly answering that "Warwick, true to his word, is a better man than the false and perjured Clarence."

On the very day of Barnet, Queen Margaret finally returned to England with the Prince of Wales. She had been advised that Edward's position was not a strong one and that she could win an easy victory. The advice was wrong. The Queen and her son were too late.

At Tewkesbury, Richard's men were attacked on their flank by a large force led by the Lancastrian duke of Somerset, the son of the man who had been Queen Margaret's favorite and who had been slain at St. Albans. Somerset had successfully screened his flanking movement behind heavy hedgerows. Surprised, the Yorkists began to fall back. But Richard encouraged them and gradually reformed their line. Then, leading them in a fierce counterattack, he forced the Lancastrians to retreat to a place from which Edward's spearmen, hidden in a nearby wood, were able to launch a sudden and unexpected attack, putting the enemy totally to flight.

Queen Margaret was captured at Tewkesbury, and the Prince of Wales was killed, either fleeing the battlefield or immediately after the fighting ceased. Somerset and other rebel leaders took sanctuary in Tewkesbury abbey. But an infuriated Edward, evidently claiming that the abbey was not a valid place of sanctuary, had them dragged out and executed in the market square.

A few days later, Henry VI died (or, more likely, was killed) in the Tower of London. A cynic might say—perhaps correctly—that poor, gentle Henry had been kept alive before Tewkesbury, only because he had a male heir who, until Barnet, was living safely in France. Given the existence of the Prince of Wales, killing the harmless old king would be pointless. If so, the death of the Prince of Wales at Tewkesbury would have sealed Henry's fate. Despite his own disinterest in holding secular power and his manifest inability to govern, Henry would have remained a potent symbol to mask the dangerous schemes of ambitious nobles and a focal point of potential rebellion. Probably Edward realized that he could not take that risk.

Ultimately, Queen Margaret was ransomed by Louis XI and allowed to return to France, where she remained for the rest of her days. The Wars of the Roses were over—or so it seemed.

V

♛ EDWARD IV

After Tewkesbury, Edward IV became England's unchallenged king, ruling until his death in 1483.

More and more, Edward relied on Richard. His loyal younger brother had become his foremost military commander and the man on whom he could most depend. Earlier, when Edward had placed Richard in charge of protecting the king's interests in Wales, giving him powers there like those of the king himself, Richard had performed admirably. After Tewkesbury, Edward made his younger brother "Lord of the North," with broad authority to govern and deal with the troublesome Scottish problem.

For generations, kings of England had relied on great northern families, such as the Percys and Nevilles, each with its contingent of armed retainers, to fend off Scottish incursions. For years, the rivalry and fighting between these two powerful families had rendered the English strategy less effective. Now, with the Nevilles in decline and the Percy family led by the twenty-year-old earl of Northumberland, Edward decided that his younger brother would exercise control over this troublesome part of the realm.

The king's wish was carried out through agreements between Richard and the principal northern peers, particularly Henry Percy, the young earl of Northumberland. Percy may have signed the agreements, but he cannot have been pleased with the new arrangement. This subordination of the Percys' standing and power may have had an unfortunate long-term effect on Yorkist interests.

In the North, Richard acquired not only power and authority, but also considerable wealth. After Warwick's death, he was awarded substantial parts of the earl's estates, including Middleham Castle, where he had lived with Warwick's family in his youth.

Possessed of Warwick's castle, Richard's thoughts turned to Warwick's daughter Anne, his childhood friend. Along with her sister, Isabel, Anne was heiress to the great Beauchamp fortune on her mother's side. But sixteen-year-old Anne was now father-less and alone. Her mother, the countess of Warwick, was in sanctuary in Beaulieu abbey. In the autumn of 1471, Richard asked the king's permission to marry Anne, and, over Clarence's vehement objections, permission was granted.

Anne had been at least nominally married to the slain Prince of Wales. In a marvelously crafted scene, Shakespeare shows her despising Richard after the prince's death, but being swiftly won over by Richard's bold and sexually charged wooing. The facts, of course, were completely different. We have no idea what, if any-thing, Anne felt for the Prince of Wales. It may well be that her marriage to the Prince was never consummated. Be that as it may, if she was bereaved at his death, it is highly unlikely that she blamed her childhood friend Richard, and it is virtually certain that she did not despise him.

The Neville estates of Anne's father were to be forfeited by reason of his treason. While her mother was in the sanctuary of Beaulieu abbey, the Countess's vast Beauchamp estates were being commandeered by her rapacious son-in-law, Clarence. Richard was not only an old friend to Anne, but a royal duke and, next to the king himself, the leading citizen of the realm. He was probably the only person who could protect Anne's interests against the powerful and unscrupulous Clarence. It is probable that Anne welcomed his suit from its inception.

The events leading to their marriage provide further evidence of Clarence's unstable character. Married to Anne's older sister, Isabel, and determined not to share the family fortune with Richard, Clarence kidnapped Anne and hid her in London to prevent the marriage. After a desperate search, Richard was able to locate and rescue Anne, who had been disguised as a kitchen maid.

This disguise leads to additional questions. Did Clarence or his men force Anne to put on the kitchen maid's clothing when Richard came searching for her? Had Anne escaped from Clarence and hidden herself away in this disguise? We cannot tell.

Given the power and proclivities of Clarence, Anne was probably fortunate not to have been spirited overseas by Clarence's men, never to be seen again. Certainly Clarence had the motive and the means to arrange Anne's "disappearance." Possibly his fear of retaliation by Richard or even punishment by Edward deterred him from such draconian measures.

Alison Weir, never reluctant to apply a pejorative term in describing Richard or his conduct, refers to his dramatic rescue of Anne as a demonstration of Richard's "craftiness." More charitable and probably more accurate words might be "intelligence" and "determination."

In any event, Clarence was outraged at the possibility of the marriage and determined not to share the vast Beauchamp estates with Richard. Edward intervened and attempted to settle the dispute between his brothers. Clarence, adamant, insisted that if the marriage was to proceed, he must have, or at least control, the vast bulk of the property. As Sir John Paston put it in a letter dated February 17, 1472, "The King entreats my lord of Clarence for my lord of Gloucester; and, as it is said, he [Clarence] answers that he [Richard] may well have my lady his [Clarence's] sister in law, but they [Richard and Anne] shall part no livelihood," i.e., they may not take away any of the income producing Beauchamp property controlled by Clarence. Richard agreed, retaining only Middleham and those other Neville properties that Edward had already given him. In early 1472, Richard and Anne married without waiting for final adjudication of the property dispute.

In 1473, Anne gave birth to a son, Edward. Soon thereafter, Richard persuaded the king to permit Anne's mother to leave sanctuary in safety and to join their household. Later, Richard even tried unsuccessfully to obtain a pardon for Anne's uncle, George Neville, the archbishop of York.

In 1472, the duke of Oxford, ablest of the Lancastrian military leaders, had attempted an invasion of England with the backing of Louis XI of France. There were indications that Clarence planned still another treasonous escapade. When Oxford gave Louis a list of English nobles who could be relied upon to support an invasion, only one duke was on the list—the perfidious Clarence. But Oxford's invasion failed. He surrendered and was imprisoned in Calais. Edward took no action against Clarence, even though he was probably aware of his brother's potential treason.

Twenty-three years later, in December 1495, depositions submitted at a hearing claimed that, back in 1472, Richard's servants had bullied Oxford's mother into signing over her estates to Richard. The 1495 hearing took place under Henry VII, and the depositions may not have been reliable. Nevertheless, it has been argued that in order to amass a landed estate for himself, a greedy Richard appropriated the properties of a helpless widow by disgraceful and coercive tactics.

But the "evidence" of Richard's coercion is subject to serious doubt. In 1472, the countess of Oxford legally assigned her lands to Richard. According to Richard's statement to the Court of Chancery, made at the time of the transfers, Richard agreed, in return, to pay all the countess's debts, to provide her with an annuity yielding an annual income of 500 marks, to provide benefices for her son then studying in Cambridge, who desired to enter the priesthood, and to grant other unspecified "benefaites costes and charges" for the countess, her children and grandchildren.

Thirteen years later, in 1485, after successfully leading Henry Tudor's army at Bosworth Field, the earl of Oxford retook his mother's lands. Ten years later still, Oxford became concerned about his title to those lands, fearing that charitable institutions and other nobles (possibly including Henry VII himself) might assert adverse claims. The earl petitioned the Court of Chancery to establish his ownership, claiming that Richard had obtained the lands from his mother by coercion. He provided the chancellor with six depositions. These documents generally supported his position. To a great extent they were based on hearsay. But there was direct testimony that certain of the deponents had seen the countess of Oxford weeping while at Richard's home in Stepney, and one deponent stated that the countess had told him that unless she signed over her lands to Richard, she feared she would be sent to Middleham Castle in the North, where the cold weather would shorten her life.

Interestingly, one of Oxford's deponents was Sir James Tyrell, who had been a principal aide to Richard, and who was later accused of having killed the two princes in the Tower. At this time, with Richard dead ten years, Tyrell had become a valued and honored part of the government of Henry VII. Sir James was undoubtedly chosen by Oxford because of his former relationship with Richard, but his deposition is rather vague as to the supposed coercion on Richard's part. He does say that he saw the countess weeping at the Stratford convent, where she had been living, when she was told her property was to be confiscated, and that he saw her weeping again in Stepney, "but for what cause he cannot certainly say." He adds, however, that there was "talk in the household" that she was weeping because she was being entreated by Richard to convey to him "certeyn of her landes."

Evidently there was no opposition to the earl's petition, and it was granted by the chancellor—Richard's old enemy, Bishop Morton.

Some historians have considered it probable that the earl's petition had merit, and it has been argued that 500 marks per year was not a sufficient price for the countess's valuable lands, so that the countess would not likely have made the sale of her own free will. We cannot, of course, know the true facts, but before we accept the charge of coercion, we should consider the evidence and the situation more carefully.

Firstly, all of the countess's wealth had previously been turned over to Richard by order of Edward IV. This was not an unusual occurrence. Quite frequently, the wives and mothers of traitors were confined and their lands and wealth impounded lest they should make it available to the king's enemies. In this instance, it appears that the countess was to be deprived of all of her real and personal property at least during her lifetime. It is probable that she could have devised her property by will. But her three sons had all been attainted or were about to be, and so could not inherit; and they were her natural heirs. Besides, how would she support herself for the rest of her life? Even if King Edward decided to grant her some allowance, it would undoubtedly be a small one, and she would hardly be able to maintain a comfortable lifestyle.

Thus, the countess's lands were no good to her during her lifetime and no good to her sons on her death. The 500 marks per year that Richard was offering for a legal transfer of title may well have been only the income from her own lands. But, if he had wanted to, Richard could have kept the lands and the income, at least so long as the countess lived. By accepting Richard's offer, she would have sufficient income to live comfortably for the balance of her life, rather than hoping that the king might relent and grant her a few crusts, despite her son's treason. Five hundred marks, while considerably less than the income required for a dukedom, would still support a comfortable lifestyle.

Considered in that light, the deal was not that bad from the countess's point of view and one that she might well have made of her own free will.

Yes, Richard may have obtained a significant bargain, especially since, at sixty-two, the countess was probably not expected to live many more years. But the issue here is coercion, and the countess's situation renders that charge somewhat more doubtful than has been contended.

As to the depositions, they were made twenty-three years after the fact, when memories as to specific conversations would not likely have been accurate, even had the witness not been trying to aid Oxford's cause. And it is highly probable that they were trying to aid that cause. The depositions were made under Henry VII, when Richard was dead, and it was good politics to revile him and blacken his reputation. They were also made in aid of Oxford, by then an extremely powerful magnate.

Moreover, the depositions were not subject to cross-examination. Any experienced lawyer knows that even an honest witness, when handed a written statement prepared in advance by a litigant whose cause he favors, will often sign it without being too careful about the details of its contents. When the witness is cross-examined, the true facts often turn out to be quite different from those in the written statement.

And, assuming the countess was seen weeping at the Stratford Convent, wasn't this understandable given the fact that all of her wealth was being confiscated by King Edward's order? The other episode of weeping supposedly occurred in Richard's house in Stepney, where the countess resided after being moved from the convent to which she had previously been exiled. Was there something cruel in bringing the countess from a nunnery to the comfortable London home of the king's brother? It would seem not.

But what about her fear of the cold weather at Middleham? Here again, assuming that the countess actually expressed that concern twenty-three years earlier, the possibility of living in the former home of the wealthy earl of Warwick, the place where Richard had spent his own youth, was hardly the equivalent of being put on the rack. Wasn't it preferable to a return to the convent?

Isn't it possible that the countess had already realized that the deal Richard was offering made good sense, given her situation? If she complained at all, it may well have been that she had no real choice. If she rejected Richard's offer she would be dependent on the king's charity and might be relegated to the great northern castle with its blustering winters. If she accepted, she could afford to live as she liked in the region of her choice. Would that have been coercion? Maybe, but not in the usual sense of the term.

Arguably, the claim of Richard's greed is also supported by the treatment accorded the estates of Warwick's widow, the mother-in-law of both Richard and Clarence. The property dispute between the two royal brothers arose again in 1474 and was once again settled by Edward. Richard retained those Neville properties he had occupied since 1471. But this time an act of Parliament divided the Beauchamp properties of Warwick's widow between her daughters as if she were no longer alive.

Actually, the records of chancery confirm an act of Parliament giving Clarence, Richard and their wives the right to "possess and enjoy" the property of the countess of Warwick "as though she were naturally dead." Taken literally, this would seem to convey only a right of possession, rather than outright ownership. But the grant has not been construed that way.

Was the countess subjected to this treatment because Edward wished to treat even *her* lands as forfeit for her husband's treason? Or was it because Clarence and Richard pressed for that result? The matter is not clear. More of the Beauchamp lands went to Clarence's wife, Isabel, which meant that they were controlled by Clarence. To a somewhat lesser extent they went to Anne.

The widowed countess spent the next decade in retirement in the North. Whether or not this was voluntary or imposed on her by Clarence, Richard or Edward is also a matter of dispute. Since Richard had obtained the King's permission in the first place for his mother-in-law to leave sanctuary and to live with him and Anne, it seems unlikely that it was he who pressed for her departure and retirement. Possibly Edward ordered this to placate Clarence, who may have considered her continued residence in Richard's household a threat to his position.

It has been argued that Warwick was never formally attainted for his treason, so that Edward's settlement, in granting Richard parts of the Neville holdings, deprived Warwick's minor nephew, George, of his rightful inheritance. This would seem something of a technicality. Edward could have formalized the matter at any time. Moreover, the divestiture he ordered was designed to punish only the *disloyal* Nevilles and *their* descendants, including George and his heirs. If George died without heirs, Richard's rights terminated on his own death, and the properties reverted to other lines of the Neville family that had not been disloyal. Had he wished, Edward could have declared the land itself permanently forfeited through a formal bill of attainder, which would have created an even more harsh result for the Nevilles.

In 1475, Charles, the duke of Burgundy, asked Edward for help in making war on Louis XI of France. Despite the loss of most English territory on the Continent, English kings still asserted their right to the throne of France. Burgundy, which controlled what is now Belgium and the Netherlands, had become England's natural ally against the French. Trade with the Low Countries was extremely important to English merchants, and Duke Charles was married to Edward's sister. In addition, Edward remembered with bitterness Louis' support first for Margaret and the Lancastrians, then for Warwick and Clarence, and finally for the Duke of Oxford's attempted invasion. Considering all of those factors, Edward agreed to come to Burgundy's aid.

With Richard, now his most trusted military leader, Edward landed at Calais in June 1475, accompanied by a large invasion force including more than one thousand men supplied by Richard, himself. This contingent, wearing Richard's white boar badge, was the largest private force in the expedition.

On arrival, Edward sent a message to Louis formally demanding the French throne. But Louis had a keen knowledge of his opponents. He offered Edward a handsome pension for life in return for the withdrawal of his forces. Lesser payments were offered to other English nobles. Louis promised, in addition, that the dauphin, Louis's five-year-old son and the heir to the French throne, would marry Edward's oldest daughter, the ten-year-old Elizabeth of York, who, like her father, would receive an annual payment from the French.

Edward agreed to the bargain. Louis put on a fantastically lavish party for the entire English army, after which the formal agreement was signed personally by the two monarchs on the bridge at Piquigny.

Disagreeing for the first time with his brother's policy, Richard argued vehemently against abandoning the war, and refused to accept any payment. Reportedly he was furious and conspicuously absented himself from the peace talks and signing ceremonies. Louis marked the young duke as a man to be watched. He dined with Richard and gave him gifts; but it was apparent to Louis that Edward's intense younger brother could pose a problem in the years to come.

Philippe de Commynes has described the events at Piquigny, having been personally present as Louis' advisor. De Commynes was given the dubious honor of dressing in a costume identical to that of Louis, so that any assassination attempt might mistakenly be directed at the advisor, rather than his sovereign.

Despite Richard's strong feelings, Edward's motivation at Piquigny may have been more than simple greed. By 1475, the English archers and dismounted fighting men who had won so brilliantly at Crecy, Poitiers and Agincourt were no longer invincible. The French had developed a trained army that used guns, artillery and other weapons with growing effectiveness, as they would prove in succeeding decades. Edward had brought his own artillery, along with 11,000 archers and 1,500 men at arms. He could probably have defeated the French, but it was by no means certain.

Besides, the duke of Burgundy, on whom Edward had counted for substantial military support, had turned his attention elsewhere, besieging a distant city rather than preparing his army for the campaign Edward had envisioned. Edward's English army would have had to carry the major burden alone. Without effective Burgundian support, the English would have found it impossible to pacify all or even most of France.

Instead, Edward could return to England having shown his courage by starting the expedition and having made the French pay "tribute," thus creating a fund that would lessen the need for harsh taxation and give his reign added fiscal stability.

And Edward could tell himself that he was not abandoning the concept of a France ruled by his descendants. If an English king could not immediately occupy the French throne, at least an English princess someday would; and, even better, she would be succeeded by a male heir of Edward's line.

From the French point of view, Louis had not done so badly either. The English had withdrawn without the necessity of a fight. Since the promised payments to Edward and other English nobles were to be made periodically in the future, they could serve as a means of controlling English foreign policy. The cynical Louis correctly assessed Edward as a man who would not be inclined to sacrifice his handsome pension in order to mount another invasion of France.

As to the dower payments to Princess Elizabeth, Louis made it clear, after the English withdrew, that by French custom they could not begin until the marriage was consummated. That would be some years in the future, since the dauphin was still a child. In short, with the English gone, Louis was in a position to keep his promises or not, depending on what served his interests at the time.

Louis looked at the result with considerable satisfaction. As he later joked, "I have chased the English out of France more easily than my father ever did; for my father drove them out by force of arms, whereas I have driven them out with venison pies and good wine."

There may have been long-term consequences of the Treaty of Piquigny that were not perceived by either side. Colin Richmond makes the interesting argument that fifteenth-century England was a warrior society that actually needed foreign wars to bring the nobles together in support of their king, in order to avoid the eruption of local jealousies and rivalries into serious combat and to make the people accept rigorous and steady taxation. This is not a theory applicable only to England in the fifteenth century. In early twentieth-century America, Theodore Roosevelt held similar views about the desirability of an occasional war.

In support of his view, Richmond contrasted the relatively peaceful decade after Henry V's victory at Agincourt with the turmoil and conflict in the period following Edward IV's withdrawal at Piquigny. Perhaps then, Piquigny laid the foundation for the revolution that was to come in 1483 and the events that led to Bosworth Field in 1485.

The betrothal of Princess Elizabeth to the dauphin, a match greeted enthusiastically by the queen, may have started Edward thinking about the marriages of his other children. Presumably Prince Edward, who was to be the king of England, would be saved for a brilliant match, creating a powerful alliance, such as a marriage to the Infanta of Spain.

On January 15, 1478, however, his younger brother, four-year-old Prince Richard, was married to Anne Mowbray, the six-year-old duchess of Norfolk. Poor Anne died in November, 1481, when only nine. As discussed below, her remains are a part of the evidence debated in a twentieth-century controversy over the true identity of the skeletons found in the Tower in 1674.

Pursuant to the marriage contract between Prince Richard and Anne Mowbray, the young prince received the title duke of Norfolk and the right to his wife's estates. Edward IV, however, pronounced that if the prince died without heirs, the Norfolk inheritance would go back to family members who otherwise would have had it. Later this marital settlement came to have significance in the mystery of Prince Richard's disappearance.

After the victory at Tewkesbury, Edward IV had generously forgiven Clarence for his treasonous alliance with Warwick and had ignored Clarence's apparent readiness to support the duke of Oxford's unsuccessful invasion. But the relationship between the two soured again. The arrogant Clarence behaved as if he were totally above the law, as he had in kidnapping Anne to prevent her marriage to Richard.

As time passed, Clarence seemed more and more obsessed with the old promises made by the Lancastrians that if Queen Margaret's son, the Prince of Wales, died without heirs (as he now had), he, Clarence, would be king. Apparently he did not openly assert a claim to his brother's throne; but, almost certainly, he became involved in further conspiracies with Louis XI of France and the Lancastrian exiles on the Continent.

In December 1476, Clarence's wife, Isabel, died after a lingering illness. This opened the door to a new source of power—a favorable marriage. Clarence was more than willing to pursue that goal. A few days later, an opportunity arose. On January 5, 1477, Charles the Bold, duke of Burgundy, was killed in battle, leaving his daughter Mary the greatest heiress in Europe and Clarence's sister, Margaret, a widow.

Louis of France immediately asserted that since Duke Charles had no male heirs, Burgundy reverted to France. Mary and Margaret desperately needed help. But Edward IV, reluctant to forfeit his French pension (as Louis had predicted), temporized and did nothing. The only solution for Burgundy seemed a powerful husband for Mary.

Clarence, perhaps at Margaret's suggestion, determined that he should be the one. Not only was Mary enormously rich, she was the great-granddaughter of John of Gaunt, the duke of Lancaster. Accordingly, she had something of a claim to the English throne. Perhaps Clarence sought only to acquire power and prestige on the Continent, or perhaps he saw the marriage as a means of attaining his long-term goal—the throne itself.

Louis XI was now threatening an attack on Burgundy, one

that would be difficult to repel. With her duchy in a precarious position, Mary had no intention of marrying the unstable and ineffective Clarence. Before she expressed this view, however, Edward forbade the match. Once again, Clarence was incensed. Then Edward made things worse by proposing, at the urging of his wife, that her brother, Lord Rivers, should become Mary's husband. Mary rejected Rivers as well. His pedigree was hardly sufficient.

Since Edward must have realized this would occur, his proposal was probably an easy way to appease his wife without taking any real risk. To Clarence, however, the insult was inexcusable. His own brother had denied him the match of his choice and had proposed that match for Rivers, a lowborn upstart. Meanwhile, with Edward's support, Mary was betrothed to Maximilian of Austria, son of the Holy Roman Emperor.

Clarence worked himself into a state of fulminating rage. He would rarely appear at court; when he did, he would pointedly refuse to eat, indicating that he feared that the king and queen intended to poison him.

Next, accompanied by a body of armed men, Clarence broke into the home of his late wife's servant, Ankaret Twinho. He dragged her off to one of his castles, robbed her of her jewels and money, and charged her with poisoning his wife. There was no evidence whatsoever to support the charge. Nevertheless, after coercing a terrified local jury into finding the poor woman guilty, Clarence immediately hung her. In the eyes of most, including the king, he had acted contrary to law, as if he were some kind of Oriental potentate.

When Edward expressed his anger at his brother's arrogant behavior, Clarence openly denounced the king before his own council. To others, he accused the king of using poison and sorcery. Apparently he also spread the story that Edward was the illegitimate son of a French archer, so that he, Clarence, was the rightful king. As will be discussed later, Clarence may have spread another, even more dangerous story about Edward, one that may have cost Clarence his life.

Whatever the true cause, in May 1477 Edward finally ordered Clarence's arrest and confinement in the Tower.

Evidently this course had been strenuously urged on Edward by the queen and her family.

But the king was still in no hurry to act against the younger brother he had forgiven so many times. Conceivably, Edward told his wife that Clarence, shut up in the Tower, no longer posed any danger, while the queen argued that, so long as the perfidious Clarence lived, their son could never be secure in his inheritance of the crown.

It was eight months before the king's action finally came. On January 19, 1478, Parliament was summoned to pass a bill of attainder against Clarence.

A trial ensued at which the king read out the charges against his brother. They included treason as well as making the claim that the king was illegitimate and that Clarence himself was entitled to the crown. As the Croyland Chronicle reported, "No one argued against the Duke except the King; no one answered the King except the Duke." The result was foreordained. Clarence was convicted of high treason and sentenced to death.

Having obtained the conviction, however, Edward seemed hesitant to see the sentence carried out. He delayed and temporized until, at last, the Speaker of the Commons appeared before the House of Lords and urged that the execution take place. Apparently under pressure both from Parliament and the Woodvilles, Edward finally gave the order, and Clarence was executed in the Tower on February 18, 1478.

The Croyland chronicler sums up Edward's feelings on the matter, noting that he "privately repented very often what had been done."

The mode of Clarence's execution was not officially recorded. This, of course, gave Shakespeare license to invent the colorful scene in which murderers hired by the scheming Richard suggest that, after he is stabbed, poor Clarence will be drowned in a cask of Malmsey wine, the now famous "Malmsey butt."

Shakespeare's means of execution may be fanciful, but he was only passing on what historians alive at or near the time had said. Thus, Mancini had Clarence "plunged into a jar of sweet wine." De Commynes had him "put to death in a pipe of Malmsey." The Great Chronicle reported that he was "drownyd in a barell of

Malmesy." Virgil too placed the drowning in "a butt of Malmsey." Alison Weir reports that, around 1530, Clarence's daughter had her portrait painted wearing a miniature wine cask on a bracelet.

One story is that Cecily, duchess of York, the mother of Edward, Clarence and Richard, requested of Edward that Clarence be allowed to choose his own means of death and that, whatever he chose, it be done in private. Molinet gives some support to this, reporting that drowning in wine was the condemned duke's own choice.

Perhaps the dramatic mode of execution portrayed by Shakespeare was the one really used. Contrary to Shakespeare's play, however, there is no indication that Richard had any hand in his brother's execution. Most modern authorities believe that Clarence's death came at the vehement urging of the Woodvilles. They were his staunch enemies, and the queen's brother, Lord Rivers, was considerably enriched by Clarence's death, receiving control of his vast estates.

Moreover, the Woodvilles evidently believed Clarence was spreading the story that Edward was illegitimate and that he was about to claim publicly that Edward and Elizabeth Woodville were never legally married. This would mean that their children were illegitimate, even if Edward was not. The latter claim was to play a great part in the drama to come.

If Edward himself had been a bastard, Clarence would have been the rightful king. Even if it was only Edward's children who were illegitimate, Clarence, rather than they, would have been entitled to the throne on Edward's death. There was no evidence to support the claim of Edward's illegitimacy other than the fact that he did not resemble his father, the duke of York. But the validity of Edward's marriage to Elizabeth was another matter and ultimately the source of much greater concern. The Woodvilles could not take the chance of Clarence's living if either story gained popular currency. Too many discontented peers were always ready to rally around a serious contender for the throne in order to further their own ambitions.

There is good reason to believe that Clarence's spreading these tales of illegitimacy was a significant part of the reason for his arrest and trial. The indictment, read by the king himself, included the charge that his brother "had falsely and traitorously intended and purposed firmly the extreme destruction and disinheriting of the King and his issue," and that he had "spread the falsest and most unnatural coloured pretence that man might imagine, that the King our most sovereign lord was a bastard, and not begotten to reign upon us."

The charge that Clarence had attacked the validity of the king's marriage, and thus the legitimacy of his children, was not explicitly made. Probably it was considered too dangerous an assertion even to be officially mentioned.

Richard was well aware of Clarence's failings, but, despite them, he felt love for his handsome and charming older brother, the companion of his childhood. Even writers generally hostile to Richard describe him as being extremely upset with Edward over the order to execute Clarence. They report that Richard withdrew from court at that time and retired to his northern estates in sorrow or anger. More states that Richard openly opposed his brother's execution, but suggests that Richard's opposition and his grief may have been feigned.

Mancini, however—no Ricardian sympathizer—wrote that Richard "was so overcome with grief for his brother, that he could not dissimulate so well, but that he was overheard to say that he would one day avenge his brother's death. Thenceforth, he came very rarely to court."

Richard appears to have returned to London only twice more during the life of Edward IV. One occasion was the 1480 visit of his sister Margaret, widow of the late duke of Burgundy. The second was in late 1482, to report to Edward on the situation in Scotland.

Following Clarence's death, Edward had Parliament pass a bill of attainder excluding Clarence's heirs from the succession. Thus, if Edward and his children should die, Richard would be next in line to the throne.

In the final years of his reign, Edward became more and more dependent on Richard, particularly in handling problems in the North of England and especially in dealing with the Scots. Richard was now a proven military leader, and Edward had grown too fat and infirm to take the saddle and lead his troops into battle. That became Richard's task.

From 1480 to May 1482, Richard led frequent border raids into Scotland. These forays restored English morale in the area and enhanced his reputation and popularity in the North and among the common soldiers. In 1482, he laid siege to Berwick Castle. Queen Margaret had ceded this great border fortress to the Scots in 1461, permitting them to attack time and again down the eastern coast and into the North of England.

Leaving the siege of Berwick in the hands of Lord Stanley, Richard moved northward with a large force, driving the Scottish army before him and burning towns in an attempt to force a major battle. In July 1482 he entered Edinburgh, and the Scots sued for peace.

But Richard had more faith in holding military strongpoints than in signing treaties. He returned to the siege of Berwick, which fell on August 24, 1482.

It has been argued that Edward would have been better off without the entire Scottish campaign, since it diverted men and money that could have been used to frustrate the designs of Louis XI. But to the citizenry—and particularly in the North—the campaign had been a manifest success; and, at Christmas 1482, Richard returned to London, where he received the thanks of a grateful king and people.

Richard had firmly established his reputation as a skilled warrior and military leader. Not only had he been brave and brilliant in the fighting at Barnet and Tewkesbury, he had captured Edinburgh and retaken Berwick from the Scots. Mancini put it that "[i]n warfare such was his renown that any difficult or dangerous task necessary for the safety of the realm was entrusted to his direction and generalship."

Richard had also loyally fulfilled his duties to Edward in the North of England. From 1471 on, he had exercised the power of governance of all England north of the River Trent, although, by agreement, he upheld Henry Percy's traditional rights in Northumberland and the East Riding of Yorkshire.

Richard had become truly "Lord of the North." He exercised his power in a way that won him the admiration and loyalty of the king's northern subjects. He founded and endowed colleges and chapels and calmed the quarrels and feuds among northern nobles, including the Nevilles and the Percys. He dispersed even-handed justice even to commoners who had claims against the landed gentry and even when the law required him to rule against his own adherents.

Mancini reported that Richard "set out to acquire the loyalty of his people through favours and justice. The good reputation of his private life and public activities powerfully attracted the esteem of strangers. By these acts, Richard acquired the favor of the people, and avoided the jealousy of the Queen, from whom he lived far separate."

On December 24, 1482, just as Edward and his court were lavishly celebrating the Christmas holidays, Louis XI signed a treaty with Maximilian and Mary of Burgundy. The treaty provided that his son and heir, the dauphin, was betrothed to the daughter of Maximilian and Mary.

Edward and his queen were furious. By the treaty signed at Piquigny in 1475, Louis had committed the dauphin to Edward's own daughter, Elizabeth of York. They had waited years for the dauphin to be of sufficient age for the marriage. In the interim, Princess Elizabeth had even been called "Madame la Dauphine."

Finally, her anxious parents had inquired of Louis when they might send his intended daughter-in-law to France. Louis had promised that he would send for her as soon as he could resolve his troublesome Burgundian problem. Now he had. Evidently despairing of receiving military aid from Edward, Maximilian and Mary had been forced to accept an unfavorable peace treaty with France. The betrothal of the dauphin to the their daughter had sealed the bargain.

This grievous insult to Edward's daughter called for a declaration of war. But with the Burgundians out of the game, war with an ever stronger France was a more daunting prospect. To a great extent, this unfortunate situation was the result of Edward's own reluctance to come to the aid of the Burgundians and risk forfeiting his handsome French annuity. Even Edward's sister, Margaret, the dowager duchess of Burgundy, had traveled to England in 1480 to urge him to commit the English to the unequivocal support of the duchy in its struggle with the French.

But Edward had declined. Louis's pension was simply too good to give up.

In 1475, at Piquigny, Louis had correctly assessed his man. The money had bought Edward's complaisance when it was needed. Now, when it suited his policy, Louis reneged on his promises. Edward's daughter was left out in the cold, and, ironically, Edward himself had seen his last gold crown from the French king.

This was by no means the Edward of Barnet and Tewkesbury. Although he was only forty, the king had grown fat and indolent. His health had deteriorated. The Croyland chronicler reports that, by 1482, Edward IV was "thought to have indulged too intemperately his own passions and desire for luxury," Mancini said that "in food and drink [Edward] was most immoderate," that "he used to take an emetic for the delight of gorging his stomach once more" and that "he had grown fat in the loins."

Large as it may have been, Edward's stomach did not seem to interfere with his extramarital sex life. He reveled in licentiousness and enjoyed sharing his pursuit of sexual adventure with his friends. Mancini said that although Edward had "many promoters and companions of his vices," the "more important" were Rivers, Dorset and Grey, the queen's own brother and her two grown sons. Another was the king's closest friend, Lord Hastings, who, according to Mancini, was "the accomplice and partner of the King's privy pleasures."

Hastings was in his early fifties at this time. As a youth, he had been placed in the household of Edward's father, the duke of York. The two young men became lifelong friends. Hastings fought for Edward at the battle of Towton and was handsomely rewarded with both lands and offices, including an appointment as lord chamberlain, which allowed him to control access to the king and gave him enormous political power. Like Edward, Hastings had accepted a substantial bribe from Louis XI.

Hastings had great personal influence with the king and maintained a formidable body of armed men. Nevertheless, like so many other powerful men of the time, he resented and feared the Woodville power. He had a bitter rivalry with the queen's son Dorset, primarily over women. He also had a serious dispute with her brother, Lord Rivers, over the governorship of Calais. In that controversy, Hastings was barely saved from the queen's wrath by his close friendship with the king.

Perhaps King Edward intended to mount an invasion of France, with others (such as Richard and Hastings) leading the English forces. He never got the chance. In March 1483, Edward went fishing with friends on a cold, damp day. He contracted some kind of rapidly devastating illness—possibly pneumonia. In a very short time, he was obviously dying.

Vergil wrote that "ther was a great rumor that he [Edward] was poysonyd." A 1997 article by Michael Bongiorno theorizes that this "rumor" was correct; that Louis XI, near death himself, fearing an English invasion and realizing the peril that would face a France ruled by his minor son, ordered Edward's assassination in order to put England in that same vulnerable position, when Edward was succeeded by the twelve-year-old Prince of Wales.

Whatever the cause of his suffering, the dying Edward implored those close to him to mend their differences. Hastings and Dorset pretended to be reconciled and pledged to love each other. So did Hastings and the queen. It is doubtful that any of them meant the pledge. Certainly none kept it.

Finally, on April 9, 1483, Edward died. He was forty-one years old. More reported that he was fifty-three, which suggests that Sir Thomas's research before abandoning his "History" may have been less than thorough.

VI

♔ THE PROTECTOR

At the time of Edward IV's death, his older son, Edward, the Prince of Wales, was twelve. His younger son, Richard, the duke of York, would be ten in August. Young Edward was now to be King Edward V. He was residing at Ludlow Castle, near the Welsh border, in the care of the queen's brother, Lord Rivers.

Rivers was not the only Woodville around the prince. His household, his schedule and his views were all shaped by the queen's family. Sir Richard Grey, Elizabeth's son by her first marriage, was the prince's comptroller, assisted by Elizabeth's cousin, Richard Haute. Another of the queen's brothers, Lionel, bishop of Salisbury, was the prince's chaplain. Two more brothers, Sir Edward Woodville and Sir Richard Woodville, were the young man's councillors. Even the prince's Master of the Horse was Lord Lyle, the queen's brother-in-law by her first marriage.

As More put it, "everyone as he was nearest of kin unto the Queen, so was planted next about the Prince." The prince's chamberlain was Sir Thomas Vaughn. He was not a family member, but was a strong Woodville adherent.

The entire nobility and much of the common people were well aware of the dangers of a minority rule. The example of Henry VI was still fresh, and those who were educated knew of the troubles that had followed the accession of the young Richard II just over a hundred years earlier. Still, no voice was raised in opposition to the right of twelve-year-old Edward to rule.

By his will, Edward IV named Richard as protector, leaving to him the care of his son's person and the government of the kingdom until the young king came of age. The will is no longer in existence, but there is substantial evidence of its contents. Mancini refers to the opinion that Richard should govern "because Edward in his will had so directed." Even Rous refers to Richard as the "brother of the deceased King and by his ordinance protector of England." Virtually every other commentator writing at or near the time concurs that Edward's will designated Richard protector of the realm and gave him governance of the royal heir.

Shakespeare (in *Richard III*, act I, scene iii) has Elizabeth Woodville, while Edward IV is still alive, decry the fact that her son Edward "is young; and in his minority is put into the trust of Richard Gloucester." Lord Rivers asks, "Is it concluded he shall be Protector?" The queen replies, "It is determined, not concluded yet. But so it must be if the King miscarry."

This has been misconstrued as an indication that Edward had not yet designated Richard as protector. But, given the line, "But so it must be if the King miscarry," it is evident that Shakespeare used the response "It is determined, not concluded yet" to mean that Edward had already designated Richard as protector, but that the matter would not be "concluded" unless and until Edward should "miscarry," i.e., die. If Richard's appointment had not already been made, the king's death would not require that appointment, and the line "so it must be if the King miscarry" would make no sense.

Edward IV's prior will, made in 1475, had left the care of the Prince of Wales to Elizabeth Woodville and had given her the power to dispose of the king's property. Edward made the new will on his deathbed. It threatened a radical and negative change in the power and fortune of the Woodville family, and the Woodvilles knew it. It eliminated the family's longstanding control over the new young King. It gave Richard that control and could be construed to give him the power to order and forbid "like another king." Perhaps most importantly, it gave the former queen no power at all.

To Edward, it must have seemed perfectly normal that while he lived, his eldest son should be entrusted to the care of the brilliant, scholarly Lord Rivers and that the boy's thoughts and views should be shaped and dominated by the Woodvilles. Undoubtedly, he believed that the Woodvilles wished the boy well and had every incentive to protect him and preserve his claim.

But Edward must have foreseen that, on his death, the situation would be very different. Perhaps he realized that without his own tempering influence, Hastings and other powerful nobles would never accept a government dominated by the despised Woodvilles. Perhaps he feared that such men, unhappy enough with the prospect of a minority rule, might even depose the new young king in order to throw off the yoke of unrestrained Woodville power.

Perhaps he decided that only by turning power over to the strong and reliable Richard could he avoid civil war, while protecting the position of his son. Richard had always given Edward unconditional loyalty. Now, with the backing of men like Hastings, Richard could control the disparate elements clambering for power, while keeping young Edward on the throne.

But the Woodvilles were not likely to accept such a reversal of their fortunes without a struggle. They certainly realized that without control over the new king they would be extremely vulnerable to acts of revenge by those, like Hastings and Buckingham, who had been injured, angered or humiliated by their arrogant conduct during Edward's reign.

It was probably not just coincidence that shortly before Edward's death Rivers had written his attorney in London seeking a copy of the patent appointing him young Edward's governor, as well as another patent giving him the power to raise armed men in the marches of Wales. Rivers also directed that his own position of deputy constable of the Tower, an office to be given and taken only by the king's order, was to be "transferred" to his nephew Dorset. This transfer, without the king's assent, was unlawful. But that did not deter the Woodvilles. Dorset was in London, where he could take quick and decisive action. Making him deputy constable would give him access to the treasure and arms stored in the Tower at a time when they might be sorely needed to protect Woodville interests and when Rivers himself was in far-off Wales with the boy king.

Richard was at Middleham Castle in the North of England

when he received the news of his brother's death. That news appears to have been intentionally delayed by the Woodvilles. It did not reach Richard until mid-April. Even then, it was not the Woodvilles who informed Richard, but a messenger dispatched by Lord Hastings. Shortly thereafter, Hastings sent a second message. It told Richard that the Woodvilles aimed to seize control of the kingdom and to ignore Richard's position as protector. He was advised to come at once, in strength and with the king.

Richard's response was to direct a letter to the queen and council. To the queen, he expressed his sorrow at her loss. To the council, he wrote of his loyalty to his brother's heir and of his desire that law and justice be observed. He reminded them that he held his position as protector pursuant to his brother's will and warned that any acts contrary to the law or to Edward's will would not go unpunished.

Meanwhile, as Hastings had warned, the Woodvilles determined to ignore the late king's wishes. Not only were they in charge of the young king's person they also held numerous positions of power in the government of the realm, which they immediately began to consolidate.

The family intended to exclude Richard from any kind of control and to retain, by force if necessary, the power they had previously enjoyed through the queen's influence. Having been unlawfully made deputy constable of the Tower by Rivers, Dorset took prompt and effective action. According to Mancini, he seized all of the Tower's arms and the vast treasure stored there, dividing the treasure among himself, the ex-queen and her brother, Sir Edward Woodville.

At the Woodvilles' urging, Sir Edward was given command of twenty ships, comprising virtually all of the English fleet, on the pretext that this was necessary to protect English shipping against French piracy.

The Woodvilles simply ignored the protectorship created by the late king's will. Royal orders were issued not in the name of Richard, as protector, but in the names of Rivers or Dorset, as uncle or brother of the young king.

Weir argues that, despite the will of Edward IV, Richard had no valid status as protector until appointed by the council and approved by Parliament. This is a questionable proposition, and no one appears to have taken that position at the time. It seems to have been generally perceived that the protector's appointment was controlled by the late king's will and became effective on his death. But what power went with the protectorship and how long it lasted were different matters. On those issues, there was serious disagreement.

Hastings and other members of the council were of the view that the protector was to govern the realm until the new king was old enough to rule in his own right. The Woodvilles and their supporters contended that Richard's position as protector made him simply one member of the council, albeit the chief member, and that, in any event, the protectorship ended as soon as the young king was crowned.

Based on that proposition, the queen's family sought to hold the coronation at the earliest possible time and convinced the council to set it for May 4. According to Mancini, when it was suggested that such choices should await the arrival of the protector, Dorset replied "We are so important, that even without the King's uncle we can make and enforce these decisions."

The Woodvilles' position was not without precedent, but the matter was by no means clear. In 1377, when ten-year-old Richard II inherited the throne from Edward III, England was ruled by a regency council rather than a single protector, although the young king's uncle, John of Gaunt, exercised enormous influence in governing the kingdom.

Under the will of Henry V, his youngest brother, Humphrey, duke of Gloucester, had been designated the principal guardian and protector of the infant Henry VI. But substantial powers were also given to Humphrey's older brother, John, duke of Bedford, and to Thomas, duke of Exeter. The forceful Bedford proved a significant check on Humphrey's ability to govern.

To a great extent because of Bedford's influence, Humphrey's claim to rule as sole regent during the minority of Henry VI was rejected by the council and Parliament, and he was relegated to serve solely as the chief member of the council. Then, in 1429, when the seven-year-old Henry was crowned, Humphrey's protectorship was deemed at an end.

On the other hand, during the madness of Henry VI, when the duke of York had been protector, he had exercised full powers of governance, rather than merely serving as the chief member of the council. It is likely that this most recent precedent, set by their own father, established the meaning of "protector" as understood by Edward when he made his will and by Richard when he heard its terms. Moreover, Edward's will, which did not divide the power to govern or provide checks and balances, gave Richard governance of both the kingdom and the person of the heir. The wills of Henry V and Edward III did not.

Weir supports the Woodville's argument on the length of a protectorship. She argues that the *only* purpose of a protector was to govern until the minor king was crowned. Presumably this is her view even if the heir was a young child, crowned within weeks of inheriting the throne. The argument is difficult to accept. Providing a mature leader until the king is not merely crowned but old enough to govern would seem a far more cogent reason for establishing a protectorship.

As a matter of sound public policy, the age at which a young monarch is considered old enough to rule would seem a far better measure of when a protectorship should end than the date on which the minor king is crowned, which may have nothing to do with his ability to rule. It is difficult to believe that when Edward made his will designating Richard "protector," he intended that status to end in less than thirty days, if that is when the coronation happened to be scheduled.

The populace apparently supported the view advocated by Hastings. Mancini reported that Richard's earlier letter to the council was made public—perhaps by Hastings—and that this "had a great effect on the minds of the people, who, as they had previously favored the duke in their hearts from a belief in his probity, now began to support him openly and aloud, so that it was commonly said by all that the duke deserved the government."

But fifteenth-century governments did not follow public opinion polls. Although it had some independent members like Hastings, the council was dominated by the Woodvilles and their clerical allies—Thomas Rotherham, who was chancellor as well as archbishop of York, and John Morton, the bishop of Ely. The majority of the council, at the urging of the Woodvilles, voted that the kingdom would be governed not by the protector but by a council of "many persons" of whom Richard would simply be "accounted the chief."

It is by no means clear that the council's decrees had legal force. A king's council was a group of advisors, primarily nobles and churchmen, gathered by the king to provide guidance. On his death, its legal status would appear to have ended. Even the Croyland Chronicle refers to the council in this period as "the counsellors of the dead King." A new king was to appoint his own council.

Nevertheless, the council of a deceased king sometimes continued to function until his successor's coronation. Did its decrees have legal effect? If it was an advisory body, whom did it advise in that interim period? And, if the new king was a minor, who appointed the new council? Seemingly, that would be a function of the protector, acting in the name of the minor king.

In any event, seizing and holding control of a fifteenth-century government was more likely to be a matter of power, rather than one turning on precedent and law, and the Woodvilles did not hesitate over legal niceties. The key piece in the game being played in April of 1483 was control of the young king. Naturally, the queen intended to see that her son remained totally under her family's control. She proposed to send a large force to meet him and escort him into London, where he would be surrounded by his Woodville relatives.

But some members of the council were growing increasingly wary. According to the Croyland Chronicle, they had concluded that "the uncles and brothers on the mother's side should be absolutely forbidden to have control of the person of the young man until he came of age". Hastings was one of the members of the council who had become seriously concerned at the Woodville grab for power and was ready to do what he could to uphold Richard's position as protector.

Whether he acted out of loyalty to his late friend, Edward, or out of distaste for the Woodvilles and fear for his own position in a regime dominated by the ex-queen's family, Hastings now openly took sides. At a council meeting attended by the former queen herself on April 11, the powerful knight argued vigorously that sending a large force to escort the young king into London would create a most unfavorable impression.

In addition to being the lord chamberlain, Hastings was the governor of Calais. He threatened that if the escorting force was not limited in number, he would withdraw at once to Calais. Presumably, this meant that he would occupy one of the heavily fortified castles guarding the port city, where he could indefinitely withstand a siege by the Woodvilles or anyone else rash enough to attack such a stronghold.

The former queen, perhaps not yet ready for an open break with the formidable Hastings, suggested, as a compromise, that the force accompanying the king be no more than two thousand men. Hastings agreed, apparently believing that Richard would be accompanied by at least that many.

Now Dorset wrote to Rivers urging haste. He directed that the king reach London three days before the May 4 coronation. Perhaps Dorset sensed a lack of commitment, and even a growing reluctance, in the scholarly Rivers.

Dorset may have been correct in that assessment. Despite his urgent message, it was April 24 before Rivers and the young king set out for London, accompanied by the two thousand men agreed upon by the queen and council.

Meanwhile, on April 20, Richard had begun his own journey to London, accompanied by only three hundred men, all arrayed in the black of deep mourning. Richard proceeded to York where, on the 21st, he had his nephew acclaimed king. According to the Croyland Chronicle, he required all of the York nobility to take an oath to support young Edward's rule. Richard himself was the first to take the oath.

It has been contended that, by this time, the Woodvilles were conspiring to have Richard killed. This may well have been the case; and certainly, Richard must have considered the possibility.

To the ex-queen's family, Richard was a dangerous adversary, having proven himself a formidable military leader not only in the battles against the Lancastrians, but in his campaigns against the Welsh and the Scots as well. If, as seems the case, Richard was embittered at the Woodvilles for their part in Clarence's execution, they certainly were aware of his feelings. As the protector designated by the late king, he would possess considerable legal and moral authority. Backed by Hastings and other anti-Woodville nobles, he would have a substantial armed force at his disposal. And, while England was not yet a functioning democracy, Richard was popular with the people. In a pinch, that could count.

The Woodvilles might prevail upon the council to curtail Richard's legal rights, but, while he lived, he posed a severe threat to the family's interests. To determined and aggressive fifteenth-century pragmatists like Elizabeth Woodville and her son Dorset, these factors would have been more than sufficient reason to have Richard killed. He was certainly aware of these factors and would have been likely to believe any report that the Woodvilles planned to kill him.

Richard was certainly aware of the fate of Humphrey of Gloucester, the last Englishman to serve as protector during the reign of an infant king. When Humphrey was named protector, his nephew, Henry VI, was only nine months old. Most historians believe that once Henry VI and his "advisors" took over the reins of power, Humphrey was slain. Protectors could be vulnerable to such a fate when power was relinquished to the young king and those who controlled him. In Richard's case, the Woodvilles were already moving heaven and earth to advance that time.

In meeting this challenge, Richard gained support from what seems an unexpected source. Henry Stafford, the duke of Buckingham, hurried from Wales with three hundred men to join Richard in facing the serious peril before him. Buckingham was a descendant of Thomas of Woodstock, the fourth surviving son of Edward III. He was now a peer of the realm next in rank to Richard himself and to the new king's nine-year-old brother, Richard, duke of York. Buckingham was also head of what was now the wealthiest and most powerful of the great English families. He had not been active in political matters up to that point. But he was a bold, unpredictable young man, filled with pride of family and position.

When he was only nine, Buckingham was placed in the queen's care. At eleven, he was forced to marry her Woodville sister. Although he spent a good part of his youth in the queen's household and was her brother-in-law, Buckingham felt disdain for the entire Woodville clan. He considered them ambitious upstarts and burned with resentment at having been forced to marry one of them in a match he considered far beneath him.

Buckingham and Richard had other things in common besides resenting the Woodvilles. Both had the royal Plantagenet blood in their veins, and they appeared to hold similar views on at least some aspects of foreign policy. As a youth, Buckingham had been a part of the English invasion of France in 1475, but he had returned to England before the treaty of Piquigny was signed. De Commynes noted that other English leaders joined Richard in opposing the treaty. Possibly Buckingham was one of these and, like Richard, was disgusted at Edward IV's acceptance of payments and the cancellation of his French campaign.

Whether for these or other reasons, Buckingham determined now to ally himself with Richard. Alison Weir writes that Richard initiated the alliance. It seems more likely, however, that the initiative was Buckingham's and that he first wrote to Richard offering his aid. Elizabeth Jenkins reports that Buckingham not only took the initiative but also offered to bring a thousand men. She adds that Richard replied indicating his pleasure at having the duke's aid, but asking that his escort be limited to three hundred.

Richard and Buckingham dispatched messengers to the young king asking his route to London and offering to accompany him into the city. The messengers encountered the king's party on the road. When Rivers learned that Richard was to meet Buckingham at Northampton on April 29, he agreed that the young king would join them there.

Richard and his men arrived at Northampton on the 29th, as agreed. They were now only sixty-four miles from London. But Rivers and the king were nowhere to be seen. Young Edward and his Woodville uncle had been in Northampton that very morning. Instead of staying there for the rendezvous, however, they had traveled on to Stony Stratford, fourteen miles closer to the capital. Evidently, Rivers's plan was to speed the new king on to join his mother and the rest of the Woodvilles in London, without even meeting Richard. Most likely this was pursuant to orders sent up from the capital by Dorset or the ex-queen.

Shakespeare, who should have known better, reverses the

order of things and places Northampton closer to London than Stony Stratford was. The error is interesting to scholars, but it has no impact on the effectiveness of the play.

In any event, Rivers, accompanied by only a small part of his force, rode back from Stony Stratford to Northampton after Richard arrived on the 29th. Apparently his plan was to stall Richard while young Edward was hurried on to London. On his arrival, Rivers explained to Richard that the king had proceeded to Stony Stratford without waiting because he feared there might be insufficient accommodations in Northampton for both Richard's men and his own. Richard acted as if he accepted this. It is certain that he did not.

Richard invited Rivers to spend the night in Northampton and to dine with him at Richard's inn. He proposed that in the morning they would ride together to Stony Stratford to join the king on his journey to the capital. During the meal, Buckingham arrived with his men, and the duke joined Richard and Rivers. Buckingham was cordial, and the conversation was pleasant and animated. When Rivers finally excused himself to retire for the night, the two dukes stayed on, planning their strategy for the next day.

After a long discussion, they decided to arrest Rivers at first light. Between them, they had only six hundred men, while Rivers had a force of two thousand. But Rivers had left most of them in Stony Stratford, apparently not wishing to give Richard the impression that he had any forceful intent. Rivers was widely noted for his jousting skill, and he had held some military commands. But the two dukes formed a plan that they expected would nullify whatever military skills he had.

Before dawn, they posted guards surrounding Rivers's inn. Other guards were placed along the road to Stony Stratford to prevent any rider from warning the king once the dukes' plan went into effect. At dawn, a surprised Rivers was arrested without resistance.

Richard and Buckingham rode swiftly on to Stony Stratford. There, they encountered a large number of troops starting to move on to London. Young Edward was already in the saddle, about to depart for the capital. The king's Woodville half-brother, Richard Grey, was with him, as was his chamberlain, Sir Thomas

Vaughn. Plainly, the king's party had not planned to wait for Richard or to have him accompany the king into London.

Despite this now obvious deception, Richard kneeled to the youth and treated him with every courtesy. He advised Edward that he would accompany him into the city and that Rivers and Grey would be sent elsewhere for the time being.

Mancini reports that the two dukes expressed their grief at the death of the boy's father, which they blamed on his "ministers" (meaning Dorset, Rivers and other Woodvilles), who they said were "the servants and companions of his vices, and had ruined his health." They insisted that such "ministers" be "removed from the King's side," not only lest they "play the same old game with the son" but also because "a child would be incapable of governing so great a realm by means of puny men." Richard added that, as the boy's own father had directed in his will, he, Richard, could best "discharge the duties of government" as "a loyal subject and diligent protector."

According to Mancini, the young king responded that his ministers were only those his father had given him and that, as to governance, he had complete confidence in the peers of the realm and his mother, the queen. Hearing mention of Elizabeth, whose family he detested, Buckingham intervened, declaring testily that "it was not the business of women, but of men to govern Kingdoms."

Now Richard turned boldly to Rivers's troops, calmly but firmly ordering them to return to their homes. They could easily have arrested Richard and Buckingham and executed them on the spot, had anyone in authority ordered them to do so. But no one did. Aware of Richard's high station and his reputation as a soldier, and having no leader of their own, the soldiers broke ranks and began moving along the road in the direction of their own villages.

Young Edward was undoubtedly upset at his separation from Rivers and Grey, which he certainly realized was involuntary on their part. Nevertheless, having no real choice, he agreed to accompany Richard on the rest of the journey. His attitude toward Richard can only be a matter of speculation, but it is likely to have been one of sullen resentment rather than familial affection.

Before leaving for London, the party returned to Northampton. Richard had elected to wait there until he learned the effect in the capital of his having taken control of the king. Grey and Vaughn, like Rivers, were treated courteously but were confined to their quarters in local inns. That evening Richard had a dish from his own table sent to Rivers, telling him to be of good cheer, that all would be well. Rivers asked that the dish be taken to his nephew, Grey, whom he said was less used to adversity and in greater need of comfort.

Meanwhile, the startling news of Richard's action had reached the Woodvilles in London. They took swift measures to protect themselves. Sir Edward Woodville set sail with the twenty ships entrusted to him, evidently taking his share of the royal treasure with him.

Dorset and the former Queen tried unsuccessfully to rally support from such noblemen as were in London at the time. Failing this, they went into sanctuary at Westminster, accompanied by Elizabeth's younger son, Richard, and her five daughters. Evidently, reconciled to spending considerable time in sanctuary, Elizabeth took with her a store of furniture, furnishings and treasure so vast that a portion of the walls had to be knocked down to get it all in.

Hearing that the ex-queen had taken sanctuary, Archbishop Rotherham, who was lord chancellor and a Woodville adherent, rushed excitedly to Westminster, where he placed in her hands the Great Seal of England. The next morning, summoned to attend a meeting of the council, Rotherham realized that he had acted rashly and that there could be no lawful basis for the former queen to possess the Great Seal. He arranged at once for it to be returned to him. Hearing of Rotherham's action while still at Northampton, Richard ordered him removed as lord chancellor and directed that the Great Seal be delivered over to Thomas Bouchier, the archbishop of Canterbury.

Now Hastings sent word to Richard that the Woodvilles were in disarray and that the time had come to bring the king to London. Rivers, Grey and Vaughn were dispatched to separate castles controlled by Richard. Rivers was sent to Sheriff Hutton, Grey to Middleham and Vaughn to Pontefract. The three were held under guard, but were not imprisoned. If they felt optimistic about their fate, they were seriously misled.

VII

👑 TAKING THE THRONE

On May 4, 1483, Richard, Buckingham and young Edward finally rode into London. The new king wore blue velvet. The two dukes rode with him wearing mourning black. They were greeted by cheering crowds and the ringing of church bells, as well as by the mayor, the sheriffs and aldermen, all clothed in scarlet and accompanied by five hundred horsemen all in violet. Richard showed great deference to Edward. Repeatedly, he bowed low in his saddle, crying out to the crowd "Behold your prince and sovereign."

Four wagons loaded with barrels of weapons were displayed to the people. They bore the Woodville coat of arms. Criers told the crowd that the Woodvilles had secreted weapons near London for use in attacking Richard as he approached the capital. Much of the crowd was outraged. But Mancini says that others considered the display a sham, saying that the weapons had been placed there long before Edward IV's death, for use in the war against the Scots. Mancini provides no explanation as to why weapons to be used in a Scottish war would be stowed so very far south.

More also says there were doubters among the populace. He does not attribute these doubts to the story of a Scottish threat, but to "wise men" who perceived that someone intending to ambush Richard and Buckingham "wolde rather have hadde theyr harnets (armor) on theyr backes than tave bounde them uppe in barrelles."

According to Elizabeth Jenkins, Rivers had purchased a large quantity of Spanish armor with which he intended to outfit a force to accompany the King. Since Rivers expected his force to be far larger than the two thousand men he had been allowed, there were cartloads of excess armor. Were these the carts put on display? It seems unlikely that, with the young king and Rivers in Wales, the armor for their accompanying force would have been stored this far from their point of departure. There is little remaining evidence from which we can discern the truth.

According to the Croyland Chronicle, Richard, acting as protector, compelled the Lords Spiritual and Temporal, as well as the mayor and the aldermen of London, to take an oath of fealty to Edward V. Once again, Richard took the oath himself.

These solemn oaths, taken first at York and then in London, acclaiming young Edward as king, were considered very serious matters. Although the act of coronation had symbolic importance, it was only a ceremonial confirmation of the heir's right to rule. The rightful heir became the monarch when acclaimed king and accepted by the people.

Accordingly, the oaths demanded by Richard in both York and London had both constitutional and religious significance, as well as considerable impact on the people. If Richard planned to usurp the throne at this early stage, it is not likely that he would have been so quick to insist on public oaths proclaiming Prince Edward's rule or that he would have so prominently taken those oaths himself.

On arriving in London, Richard moved in with his mother at Baynard's Castle, her splendid home on the banks of the Thames, just west of St. Paul's Cathedral. However, when Richard's wife, Anne, reached London on June 5, he left Baynard's Castle and moved with Anne to a leased home, Crosby Hall, then on Bishopsgate Street. He continued on good terms with his mother, holding important meetings in her home even after he no longer resided there. Crosby Hall, having been moved, can be seen today in Chelsea, on Cheyne Walk near the Thames embankment.

At first, young Edward resided at the bishop's palace in St. Paul's Churchyard. However, at the suggestion of Buckingham and with the unanimous approval of the council, he was moved in mid-May to the royal lodgings in the Tower of London. In 1483, residence in the Tower did not have the ominous connotation it acquired under the Tudor monarchs. The royal apartments there were spacious and handsomely appointed. Indeed, they were the place at which newly acclaimed kings had traditionally resided while awaiting their coronation.

It has been claimed that the Tower was not considered a prison at all until Tudor times. It may be that it was not *primarily* considered a prison. But certainly prisoners had been held there. The first was Ranulf Flambard, the bishop of Darham, who was imprisoned in the Tower in 1100. Later, such illustrious prisoners as King John of France and the duke of Orleans were held there.

In the thirteenth century, Edward I imprisoned Jews in the Tower—presumably those who had not obeyed his order expelling them from the land. Before that, Norman kings, who had brought the Jews to England for the monarchs' own financial benefit, used the Tower as a place to house and protect them during periods when their safety was jeopardized by the superstitious and brutal London mobs. During the coronation of Henry III, for example, when anti-Semitic violence was rampant, the entire Jewish community of London was kept within the Tower walls. It is unlikely, however, that the Jews' "protective" housing in the Tower was much more comfortable than imprisonment.

It is clear, nonetheless, that young Edward, who was placed in the royal apartments, was in no sense imprisoned—at least at this point in time.

Soon after arriving in London, Richard appointed and assembled his first council. It included allies, such as Buckingham and Hastings, as well as men who had supported the Woodvilles, such as Morton and Rotherham. Rotherham, although appointed to the new council, was replaced as chancellor by John Russell, the bishop of Lincoln.

Whether or not it was legally required, the council confirmed Richard's right to be protector pursuant to Edward's will. It also gave him "tutele and oversight" of the young king. More characterized the council's action differently. To him "the lamb was betaken to the wolfe to kepe."

Now Richard began issuing orders and proclamations as protector, signing them with his motto *Loyeaulté me lié*. Having acquired the power, Richard had to face the problems. Among the first problems was the matter of the twenty ships with which Sir Edward Woodville had set sail, giving his family control of the English fleet.

Here again, the Woodville plans were thwarted. Richard sent the swashbuckling Sir Edward Brampton on a dangerous mission to recover the fleet. Brampton, a converted Portuguese Jew who had been a trusted associate of Edward IV, had fought at Barnet and Tewkesbury and had successfully commanded English warships in critical naval engagements. He was the first Jew ever to be knighted. A clever and highly skilled seaman, Brampton managed to persuade the crews of all but two ships to return home to England. Sir Edward Woodville escaped to Brittany with the remaining two ships and apparently with his share of the royal treasure.

Meanwhile, Richard summoned Parliament to convene on June 25. Although the protectorship of Humphrey of Gloucester had formally expired with the coronation of seven-year-old Henry VI, there were strong feelings that ending Richard's protectorship would lead to a fierce and destructive political fight, with each side seeking to curry favor with the young king.

The May 4 coronation had been postponed, with the date to be announced later. In mid-May, the council proposed that, despite the coronation, Richard's protectorship be continued until Edward was old enough to rule. The matter was left to be submitted to Parliament when it assembled on June 25. Presumably, Richard's governance was to continue until Parliament ruled on the matter, even if the coronation took place before it met.

On June 5, Richard issued detailed orders for the coronation to be held on June 22, and for the attendance of forty squires who were to receive knighthoods at the coronation ceremony.

There are those who contend that, in May or even earlier, Richard had determined to seize the throne. There is no hard evidence of this; but, of course, a person's subjective intention is always difficult to prove. At a distance of five centuries, the difficulty becomes vastly greater.

There is evidence to the contrary, such as Richard's insisting on public oaths recognizing Edward V as the rightful king and taking those oaths himself. There is his preparation for Edward's coronation and his agreement to submit to Parliament the question of how long his protectorship should last.

Revisionists find another indication in the speech drafted by Bishop Russell for the opening of Parliament on June 25. In the speech, which was never given, Russell planned to urge that Richard's authority be continued as both protector and tutor of Edward V. However, we do not know when Russell drafted the speech; and, although he was lord chancellor, he may not have known the protector's true intentions.

It is certainly possible that, at some point in April or May 1483, Richard did form a secret intention to usurp the throne. Unquestionably, after April 1483, he had a significant motive to do so. He knew he had aroused the enmity of the Woodvilles by the arrest of Rivers and Grey and that their feelings would necessarily be shared by the young king, who had grown up dominated by Woodville influence. That resentment would not be easily removed from the king's mind, even by the passage of years. And, in any event, very few years would pass before the young ruler became a serious threat.

Even assuming that Richard could succeed in persuading Parliament to extend the protectorship until Edward V was of sufficient age to govern, what age was that? The young king and his family would surely assert his right to govern alone at fourteen—just two years away—or, at the latest, when he was sixteen. There were good arguments that fourteen or fifteen was sufficient; and very few would deny a sixteen-year-old monarch the right to rule for himself.

The concept of delaying a young man's adulthood for political or dynastic purposes until he reached twenty-one was essentially a creature of later centuries. It was not the governing principle in matters relating to medieval kings or their families. Henry VI was declared "of age" to govern when he was fifteen. He had attempted to assert his authority from the time he was thirteen.

When he was only fifteen, Edward III had engineered the over-throw of his mother's consort, Roger Mortimer, who had gov-erned as if king. From that point on, Edward governed directly, although with the advice of his nobles. Richard II faced down Wat Tyler's mob at fourteen and began to exercise royal authority at about that time.

Edward V was already twelve; and, in the coming years, a cir-cle of adherents would gather around him, just waiting for their chance at power. Certainly, Elizabeth Woodville would continue to wield significant influence over the thoughts and decisions of her son. When Edward took power, whether in two years, three or even four, Richard would be at the mercy of the Woodvilles and his life would be at serious risk.

We have already touched on the fate of Duke Humphrey of Gloucester, who had been protector until Henry VI was crowned. In 1447, just two years after Henry's marriage to Margaret of Anjou, Humphrey was arrested without warning. Five days later, it was announced that he was dead—supposedly of a stroke. Richard could have anticipated a similar fate if he did not some-how alter the situation.

Moreover, young George Neville died without heirs on May 4, 1483, reducing Richard's interest in some of his most valuable properties to a life estate and jeopardizing his status as the great-est of northern magnates. That loss, possibly foreseeable even in early April, could have given Richard still another reason to reach for the throne. Even his northern power base was in jeopardy.

Still, we cannot really know what Richard intended—and when. Characteristically, Alison Weir considers Richard's state of mind a matter free of any doubt. Richard, she says, was "undoubt-edly convinced" that he must "seize the crown as soon as possible."

Whatever Richard intended up to this point, the course of English history was now suddenly changed. In early June, proba-bly around the 8th, Robert Stillington, the bishop of Bath and Wells, revealed to Richard and the council the long concealed fact that, in 1461, three years before his secret marriage to Elizabeth Woodville, Edward IV had entered into a "precontract" to marry the Lady Eleanor Butler.

As we will discuss later, the precontract, to which Stillington said he had been a witness, had an effect in canon law similar to that of a formal marriage. If Stillington's report was true, Edward IV's marriage to Elizabeth Woodville was bigamous and their children, *including Edward V,* were illegitimate and could not inherit the throne.

Gairdner suggests that the execution of Clarence in February, 1478 may have been due to his having discovered the secret of the Eleanor Butler precontract, which, of course, posed a severe threat to the Woodville interests. This may well have been the case. Given Clarence's character, the Woodvilles could hardly trust him to keep such a secret, and, if they feared his spreading this story, his death would have been their only safe course. Edward IV had forgiven Clarence for even the most heinous crimes, such as treason and rebellion. Seemingly then, something even more threatening to the Woodvilles or to Edward and his heirs must have induced him finally to order his brother's execution. That, of course, could simply have been Clarence's spreading the story that Edward himself was a bastard, a charge referred to in Clarence's indictment.

But it may be significant that, in March 1478, shortly after Clarence's attainder and execution, Bishop Stillington was also arrested and imprisoned. The following June, he was pardoned. His pardon showed that his offence had been uttering "words prejudicial to the King and his State."

There is no official record of what Stillington's criminal utterance actually was. But, of course, there wouldn't be if what Stillington claimed was that the heir to the throne was illegitimate. Edward and his queen would want no record made of *that.*

The bishop's diocese lay within Clarence's lands, and the two were closely associated. Possibly it was Stillington, among others, who urged Clarence to change sides and support his brothers against Warwick in 1471. It is a reasonable inference that, in 1477, Stillington foolishly told Clarence the secret of the Eleanor Butler precontract, and that Clarence had begun to spread that dangerous report along with the tale that Edward himself was a bastard.

The king's charges against Clarence in 1478 referred to the latter claim, but did not mention the Eleanor Butler precontract.

The distinction would have made sense from Edward's point of view. He probably felt that he could mention the tale of his own illegitimacy with relative safety. It was an old item of gossip that had circulated for years. There was no significant danger that the people would believe that their popular king was really a bastard and that his mother, the dowager duchess, was an adulteress. Besides, even if it was true, who could prove it?

But the claim that the royal marriage was invalid created a more meaningful risk. There was an eyewitness—and a bishop at that. And wasn't it consistent with the conduct of Edward in his single days to promise marriage if that was the only way to get a pretty woman into bed? After all, isn't that how Elizabeth Woodville became queen?

Public examination into the existence of the precontract could well have destroyed the rights of the royal children or at least created serious doubt among the people as to their being legitimate. And such doubts could always serve as a rallying point to support a rival claimant to the throne, such as Clarence, himself, who would be next in line if Edward's children were declared bastards.

Eleanor Butler had died in 1468, but, at the time, Clarence was still alive, as was Bishop Stillington. If the matter was kept private, Clarence could be executed and Stillington controlled. But public controversy on the point could prove most embarrassing. Even if spreading the tale of the precontract had been the fundamental reason for the arrest of both Clarence and Stillington, it was sound policy to say nothing about it in either indictment and to avoid any public discussion of a matter that could become a lasting cloud over the Prince of Wales's claim to the throne.

In any event, Stillington was released after three months of imprisonment, perhaps because the Woodvilles believed that, unlike the unstable Clarence, the bishop could be trusted not to make the same mistake again. Moreover, executing a noble was one thing, even if he was the brother of the king. Executing a bishop was quite another and would have required papal consent.

Weir speculates that Stillington allied himself with Clarence only in spreading the story that Edward IV himself was a bastard.

This is possible. But Clarence would hardly have needed Stillington's help in circulating *that* tale. As Edward's brother, he would be far more convincing in revealing such a family secret than would the elderly bishop. On the other hand, Stillington, speaking as an eyewitness, would have been invaluable in convincing others of the existence of the Eleanor Butler precontract. If, as appears to be the case, Stillington disclosed the precontract to the council in 1483, it seems a fair inference that this was also the nature of the "prejudicial" utterance for which he was imprisoned shortly after Clarence's trial and execution.

Weir makes no reference at all to the possibility that Stillington shared with Clarence the secret of Edward's precontract. This is because, as discussed below, Weir is committed to the view that the story of the precontract was a total fabrication, desperately concocted at the last minute to justify Richard's usurpation.

If Stillington's imprisonment in 1478 was the result of his knowledge of the precontract, he said nothing about it for the next five years. This kept him alive and out of prison; and, in any event, there was no moral, religious or political need for disclosure. But in 1483, with Edward dead and the Woodville power diminished if not destroyed by the arrest of Rivers and Grey, the former queen's flight to sanctuary and Richard's control over the new young king, there was no reason to continue keeping this secret that could so critically affect the future of the realm. Indeed, the elderly prelate may have felt an obligation at that point to come forward with the facts.

The announcement of Stillington's disclosure must have created shock and consternation at court and in council. According to Markham, Bishop Stillington appeared at a meeting of the Lords Spiritual and Temporal on June 9 and "brought in instruments, authentic doctors, proctors, and notaries of the law with depositions of divers witnesses." The reference to "doctors, proctors," etc. comes from Hall's Chronicle, a sixteenth-century publication by Richard Grafton. It purports to quote verbatim a lengthy conversation between Buckingham and John Morton. In this conversation, the "doctors," "proctors" and "depositions" are described as having been brought in by Richard, and

Buckingham goes on to say that he believed this evidence at the time but realizes now that it was false. Grafton does not make it clear that the meeting at which the evidence was produced was on June 9. Probably, however, it was. In any event, the case was prepared to be laid before the full Parliament on June 25.

It appears, however, that a small, but powerful, minority in the council, led by Hastings and including Lord Stanley and Bishops Morton and Rotherham, had become disaffected by things they saw in Richard's government. The four began to have their own private meetings separate from the rest of the council. Perhaps they were generally alarmed at the prospect that young Edward and his brother would be eliminated from the succession. Or perhaps that was only a rationalization for carrying out a very different and personal agenda.

Morton, although a staunch Lancastrian, was willing to switch sides when necessary to advance his own fortunes. He had served Edward, but had supported the Woodvilles. Perhaps he had expected to receive higher offices from Richard and was disappointed that others were chosen. He was certainly no friend of Richard at any time in our story. Stanley had also had run-ins with Richard, and he and his family had shown a remarkable willingness to change allegiances whenever it suited their interests.

Hastings, the Lord Chamberlain, was another story. He had been Edward IV's closest friend and had been a loyal friend to Richard as well. He had shared the brothers' exile in 1470 and had fought by their side time and again. We cannot know for sure why he turned against Richard now—if he did.

When he first arrived in London, Richard appeared to defer to Hastings. But that situation seemed to be changing, and in a way not to the lord chamberlain's liking. Hastings had been at the very center of power during Edward's reign. He had been the leader of the barons who supported the royal house, and the closest of them to the king. At great personal risk, he had given Richard staunch support against the Woodvilles in the period following Edward's death. Now he appeared to be in the process of losing his central role.

Hastings had retained the offices he held under Edward, but

Richard had not given him increased power such as that bestowed on Buckingham and on Lord Howard, a skilled admiral and warrior and head of a great East Anglian family. More and more, Richard appeared to counsel with and rely on Buckingham and Howard, while the great lords of Edward's reign, like Hastings and Stanley, seemed relegated to lesser roles.

And Hastings may have had other concerns. He had undoubtedly heard that Richard and Buckingham had publicly blamed Edward's disreputable associates for destroying the late king's health and his will to govern. Certainly this referred to the Woodvilles and particularly to the marquess of Dorset. But Hastings may well have believed it included him as well, since he had regularly shared Edward's carousing and, apparently, his mistresses.

Perhaps seeing the growing importance of Buckingham and Howard and Richard's lack of deference to the small group of nobles who had dominated Edward's reign, while discerning Richard's somewhat puritanical views and sensing his disapproval, Hastings concluded that his prospects of favor in a Ricardian reign were slim—and growing slimmer. Or perhaps he really was angered that Richard seemed about to supplant his late friend's son.

Whatever his reason, it seems likely that Hastings did, in fact, turn against Richard at this point. Along with Morton and Stanley, he may well have sought an alliance with the Woodvilles, whose future had been placed in severe jeopardy by Stillington's disclosure.

It cannot be considered farfetched for Hastings to have turned to the Woodvilles in this situation. While he had feuded publicly with Dorset, opposed Rivers for the Calais appointment and had been an obstacle to Woodville plans in the early days following Edward's death, Hastings had a long record of generally amicable coexistence with the family during Edward's reign. And if he was plotting to betray Richard, he would need all the help he could get.

If Hastings did conspire with the Woodvilles, the go-between was probably Jane Shore. Jane, whose true name was Elizabeth, had been the favorite mistress of Edward IV. Later she was the mistress of Hastings and apparently of Dorset as well. She seems to have been an extraordinary woman, possessing charm and intelligence, in addition to physical beauty.

More cautions that "some shal think this woman too sllight a thing to be written of and set amonge the remembraunces of great matters." Still, he gives us the following elegant description of Jane and of her relationship with Edward IV:

> Proper she was & faire: nothing in her body yt [that] you would have changed, but if you would have wished her something higher. Thus say thei yt knew her in her youthe . . . Yet delited not men so much in her beauty, as in her plesant behaviour. For a proper wit had she, & could both rede wel and write, mery in company, redy and quick of aunswer, neither mute nor ful of babble, some-times taunting witout displesure and not witout disport . . . For many he had, but her he loved, whose favor to saithe trouth . . . she never abused to any mans hurt.

It may seem odd that Elizabeth Woodville would accept her late husband's mistress as a go-between, but the selection was probably not hers. She may have been willing to accept *any* go-between who offered the possibility of improving her situation; and, whatever their personal differences, the former queen may have felt that Jane's loyalty to Hastings and Dorset would make her reliable.

Up to this point, letters and grants had been issued "by the advice of our Uncle Richard Duke of Gloucestershire, Protector and Defender." But, on June 9 and again on the 12th, Hastings and Morton openly issued royal commands without the protec-tor's name. Apparently, they also issued secret orders instructing members of Parliament not to assemble on the 25th, as they had been directed.

Evidently Buckingham gave Richard ominous and repeated warnings of a conspiracy between Hastings, Morton and the Woodvilles. To serve his own purposes, Buckingham may have exaggerated the conspiracy and the conspirators' goals. Others may have warned Richard as well.

Certainly Richard created the impression that he considered

himself in danger. On June 10, he sent a letter to the City of York asking that northern troops be sent to protect and support him "against the queen, her bloody adherents and affinity, who have intended and daily do intend to murder and utterly destroy us and our cousin, the Duke of Buckingham."

Weir, here again certain about Richard's state of mind five centuries earlier, states that "Gloucester's real motive in summoning troops from York was the intimidation of possible opposition to his intended seizure of the throne. The concocted tale of a Woodville conspiracy was just an excuse to raise an army, and one he knew the citizens of York would respond to."

But York was a good five-days' ride from London. It would take Richard's letter at least that long to reach there, plus more days for York to raise a body of troops and still more days to move those troops to London. If intimidation was Richard's goal in writing to York, he could not have expected that intimidation to take effect for quite a long time.

Besides, with only twelve thousand inhabitants, the substantial majority of whom were women, children, aged or infirm, York could hardly be expected to supply enough trained fighting men to intimidate London. Its troops might be loyal, but they were not likely to be numerous.

In fact, the York civic records show that on June 15, probably the day Richard's letter arrived, the city authorized Thomas Wrangwish and others to assemble two hundred horsemen "defensibly arrayed" and to move them to Pontefract to join the earl of Northumberland, who presumably would bring them to the capital in aid of Richard's cause.

Evidently Richard intended Northumberland to supplement the men of York with other northern troops and to bring them all to London. Such a combined force did arrive in July, but they were not particularly formidable; and Richard seems to have placed no reliance on them in designing his strategy. Indeed, as we will see, Richard made his decisive move against the conspirators on June 13, just three days after sending his letter to York and long before any northern army could possibly reach the capital.

Perhaps the Woodvilles were not conspiring with anyone. It is impossible to be sure about such things. But, Hastings and

Morton do appear to have been up to something—and it certainly appears to have been something contrary to Richard's interests. Morton and Stanley were plainly capable of plotting Richard's death or imprisonment. Rotherham would have gone along. And, whether his motives were self-serving or noble, it may be that Hastings had reached that point as well.

Whatever their aims, the conspirators—if that's what they were—were finally exposed by Sir William Catesby, a young associate of Hastings. Richard had appointed Catesby to the council on Hastings's recommendation; and the young man was sufficiently trusted by Hastings that he was told what was being planned. He immediately warned Richard. More writes that Catesby merely told Richard that Hastings would not go along with his usurping the throne and that he had heard the lord chamberlain speak "terrible woordes" when the subject was raised. But whether Catesby exposed a plot to kill or imprison Richard or simply reported that Hastings had voiced opposition to displacing Edward's son on the throne, Richard acted with characteristic decisiveness.

On June 12, he ordered that there be two separate meetings of council members the following morning. One group, including Bishop Russell, was to meet at Westminster. The other meeting was to take place at the Tower. It was to include Hastings, Morton, Stanley and Rotherham, as well as Richard and Buckingham.

On June 13, the latter group assembled in the Tower at nine o'clock in the morning. In a description of the scene that probably comes from Morton himself, More tells us that, on arriving, Richard asked to have some strawberries brought from Morton's garden, and Morton sent his servant to fetch them. This seemingly irrelevant incident was probably included by Morton to add a note of verisimilitude to his account. Richard then absented himself for about an hour. When he returned between 10:00 and 11:00, his demeanor was changed, and his expression was upset and angry. He was "knitting the browes . . . and knawing on hys lippes."

According to More, Richard then asked, as if rhetorically, what should be done with those who plotted his destruction.

Hastings replied that such persons should "bee punished as heighnous traitors." The others agreed. Richard then accused Elizabeth Woodville and Jane Shore of casting a spell that had suddenly caused his arm to wither.

At this point, according to More, Richard rolled up his sleeve to display his newly withered arm. More pronounced this absurd, asserting that everyone present knew Richard's arm had been withered all his life, and that the deformity had not been caused by any Woodville sorcery. The absurdity, however, would have been in More's believing that Richard ever said or did any such thing. As we will discuss later, Richard's arm was never withered, and this part of More's scene is palpable nonsense.

Withered arm or not, More reports that Richard suddenly turned on Hastings, angrily calling him "traitour" and loudly pounding the table. At this signal, someone outside the chamber cried "Treason!" The door was flung open and armed guards rushed in—"as many as ye chambre might hold." After a brief struggle, Hastings and Morton were arrested, as was Bishop Rotherham. Lord Stanley, who was injured in the melee, was confined to his London home.

Hastings was charged with treason and quickly condemned and executed, probably without a trial. According to More, Richard told him "I wil not to dinner til I see thy hed off." When it was done, royal heralds announced in the streets that, by authority of the council, Hastings had been executed for plotting to kill the protector and the duke of Buckingham.

More claimed that the heralds were in the streets within two hours of Hastings's execution, and that the parchments from which they read could hardly have been prepared in such a short time. If true, this would indicate that Richard planned the arrest and execution even before the council meeting. It would not, of course, rule out the existence of a plot by Hastings, Morton and others.

As Mancini put it, Hastings was "killed not by those enemies he had always feared but by a friend whom he had never doubted." Maybe. But maybe, as Richard charged, Hastings had formed a conspiracy with the Woodvilles, those very "enemies he had always feared," against Richard, the "friend whom he had never doubted."

Hastings' swift execution has been characterized as an act of terrorism by Richard designed to deter any further resistance. However, unless he had significant evidence of Hastings's guilt, it is unlikely that Richard would have chosen him for such a brutal example. If some innocent man were to be chosen for that purpose, Hasting's prestige, his high office as lord chamberlain and his formidable body of private guards would not have made him a sensible candidate.

Moreover, Hastings had been a lifelong friend of Edward IV. He had also befriended Richard, faced battle by his side and, at great peril, took his part against the Woodvilles. Even John Morton, a dedicated enemy of Richard, has been quoted as saying "Undoubtedly the protector loved him [Hastings] well, and was loath to have lost him."

It is also difficult to square Hastings' swift execution with Weir's thesis that Richard's June 10 letter to York was designed to bring an army to the capital for the purpose of intimidating his foes. If intimidation was Richard's goal and Hastings was not conspiring against him, why not wait until the troops from York were in London, or at least well on their way, before making him an example?

Richard had Hastings' body borne to Windsor and interred there in the Chapel of St. George near the tomb of his old friend, Edward IV. He soon restored the rights of Hastings's children, granted his forfeited estates to his widow, and liberally rewarded his brother for past and subsequent services. These were strange acts if Richard's aim had been to set an example through terrorism.

Whatever Richard's reason for executing Hastings, his reason for doing so swiftly may have been the threat posed by Hastings's private army. Many nobles in this period maintained their own military forces, and Hastings's large body of armed men posed a formidable threat, given Richard's somewhat vulnerable position. Had Hastings been confined awaiting a trial, that force might well have intervened—a risk Richard may have prudently wished to avoid.

Those arrested in London for conspiring with Hastings were treated with surprising leniency, a characteristic of Richard that was sometimes foolish and even reckless. After being briefly confined to his home, Lord Stanley was soon free to go about, was pardoned for his participation in the plot and was restored to his seat on the council. He played a prominent role in Richard's coronation on July 6.

Bishop Morton, a key organizer of this plot and many others, was released from the Tower and placed in the charge of the duke of Buckingham, probably at the duke's suggestion. He was to remain at Brecknock, Buckingham's estate in Wales, suffering no significant punishment at all. Bishop Rotherham, after a brief detention, was allowed to return to his diocese.

Jane Shore was initially arrested and imprisoned for acting as the liaison between Hastings and the Woodvilles. Richard soon released her, requiring only that she do public penance as a "common harlot," walking through the streets clad only in a kirtle and carrying a taper. This was undoubtedly humiliating; and More tells us that "her great shame won her much praise among those that were more amorous of her body than curious of her soule." But, considering that she could have been executed for treason, her punishment was mild indeed.

Later, Richard wrote a letter to the bishop of Lincoln consenting to Jane's marriage to Thomas Lynom, his solicitor general, even though, in the letter, Richard indicated that he considered Lynom mad to marry such a woman. The letter illustrates Richard's dry humor as well as his magnanimity. He refers to Lynom as "marvelously blinded and abused" by Jane, but adds that if, after the bishop tries to "exhort and stir him to the contrary," Lynom "to our full great marvel," is still "utterly set for to marry her," we "would be sorry" but would agree to the marriage.

Charles Ross, in his biography of Richard III, creates the erroneous impression that Richard refused his consent to the marriage. He quotes only that part of the letter in which Richard says that Lynom is being "marvelously blinded and abused" by Jane and that he would "be sorry" if the man wished to proceed. Ross leaves out the next lines of the letter in which Richard expressly says that, notwithstanding this, he will consent to the marriage. Ross adds the statement that "Bishop Russell's exhortations to Lynom to give up his marriage plan proved unavailing, *despite the disapproval of his royal master.*"

In a sense, Richard did express "disapproval," albeit in a light-hearted vein. But leaving out the fact that, in the same letter, he expressly *consented* to the marriage creates an impression that is quite inconsistent with the truth.

Perhaps, as has been claimed, Richard's aim in executing Hastings was terrorism, but he considered his point was sufficiently made with Hastings's death and felt no need to take draconian measures against the other conspirators. Other explanations seem more likely. Lord Stanley was the head of one of the four great magnate families of the time, along with the Staffords (Buckingham), the Percys (Northumberland) and the Howards (Norfolk).

Unlike Hastings' personal guard, which was in London but had no leader other than Hastings, the large body of troops retained by the Stanley family may have worked in Lord Stanley's favor. Those troops were in the North, a long march from London, so that there was no need to make a hasty decision. And, unlike Hastings's men, they would not have dispersed on Stanley's death, but would have been commanded by his brother, Sir William Stanley, and his son, Lord Strange. Led by an outraged brother and son, this formidable array could well have descended on London, creating a serious risk to Richard's still vulnerable position. Thus, the execution of Lord Stanley may not have seemed a prudent course.

Morton and Rotherham may have been spared because Richard considered himself unready to confront the church; and, in any event, papal consent would have been required for their executions and would have been granted only on a charge of heresy.

The Woodvilles were now beaten and gave up all further resistance to Richard's government. On June 16, Elizabeth Woodville, urged by Cardinal Bourchier, the archbishop of Canterbury, allowed her younger son, Richard, to leave sanctuary and join his brother Edward in the Tower. Bourchier reportedly argued to her that Edward was lonely and would be comforted by his brother's company. The former queen, remained in sanctuary with her daughters, possibly as a means of negotiating better terms. Certainly, Elizabeth knew of Hastings's execution only three days before. Her agreement to release Prince Richard has been taken as an indication that, while she may have feared and despised Richard, she did not consider him a terrorist or a serious threat to her younger son.

On the other hand, the former queen's decision may not have been entirely voluntary. More purports to quote a long speech by Buckingham to the council in which the duke argues that a child could not lawfully seek sanctuary and that removing someone to "dooe hym good" was not a breach of sanctuary. Kendall reports that the council was divided on the question, but that on the morning of the 16th, a number of council members went with Bourchier and that they were accompanied by a "body of armed men" who surrounded the sanctuary while Bourchier pleaded his case.

Almost certainly, Elizabeth was aware of this and it must have influenced her decision. Perhaps she assumed that if she did not consent, the prince might be taken by force. Still, she was a strong-willed woman, not reluctant to take a stand. If she had serious fears for her son's safety, why not withhold her consent and call the council's bluff? After all, what did she have to lose? If the boy was forcibly removed, she would seem in no worse position than if she handed him over voluntarily. And, if the council backed down—as they might well have done, given the religious significance of sanctuary—she would have won the day.

More and Vergil lessen the significance of the former queen's releasing Prince Richard by placing the release *before* Hastings's execution. This allows them to argue that Elizabeth was unaware of Richard's proclivity to kill when she agreed to deliver over her younger son. Their reports seem plainly wrong in this regard, as they are in others.

Why was Richard so concerned about removing Prince Richard from sanctuary if he already knew of Stillington's assertion that both princes were illegitimate? Did he still expect the coronation to proceed and want it unmarred by the absence of the king's younger brother? Was he really concerned about the older prince feeling lonely in the Tower? Both explanations seem unpersuasive.

Perhaps Stillington's disclosure was not made until after Prince Richard's release—say, on the 17th or 18th of June. But this seems less likely, as will be discussed below.

If the precontract had come to light on or about June 8, it is highly probable that, by June 16, Richard expected to take the throne himself. Most likely he realized that, precontract or not, if either prince remained in England and outside his control, his own rule could never be secure.

In fact, Richard and his advisors had been consulting with influential members of the nobility, clergy and commoners as to the very issue of what course to take in light of Stillington's disclosure. Buckingham and others had strongly urged Richard to claim the throne. With Hastings gone and the Woodvilles in disarray, there had been no opposition. It is likely that Richard had already agreed to the plan.

It has been asserted that, in this period, Richard rode through the streets in regal style, showing himself to the people as if he were already the king. Perhaps he did. Perhaps he was seeking to gauge public reaction to his claiming the throne.

On Sunday, June 22, 1483, Dr. Ralph Shaa, brother of the Lord Mayor, delivered a sermon at St. Paul's Cross in London, a place often used for political orations. Evidently, Buckingham and a number of dignitaries were in attendance. Even Richard arrived toward the end of the sermon. Shaa, a doctor of theology from Cambridge and a highly regarded orator, took as the subject of his sermon "Bastard slips shall not take deep root" from Wisdom 4:3. He told the people of the invalidity of Edward's marriage to Elizabeth Woodville, of the illegitimacy of Edward's sons and of Richard's consequent right to the throne. The duke of Buckingham made a similar speech at London's Guildhall on Tuesday, June 24. This appears to have been Buckingham's first public address.

There is some controversy as to whether Shaa and Buckingham referred only to the illegitimacy of Edward's children or claimed, in addition, that Edward himself was illegitimate, so that Richard was the rightful king on that score as well. The claim of Edward's bastardy may or may not have been made. This could be another charge trumped up by the Tudors to show that Richard's greed for the crown was so great that he accused his own mother of adultery.

Fabyan, who was in London at the time of the speech, described Shaa as referring only to the illegitimacy of Edward's children, not of Edward himself. The Croyland Chronicle does not refer to Shaa, but describes the princes' disqualification as based on the claim that the precontract to Eleanor Butler made Edward's later marriage invalid. Mancini says that "corrupted preachers" made the claim that Edward was "conceived in adultery," but that Buckingham argued to the peers that, when Edward married Elizabeth Woodville, he had already been "legally contracted to another wife" and that he had "espoused the other lady by proxy."

According to More, Shaa was instructed that the illegitimacy of Edward's children was to be "openly declared and inforsed to the uttermost," while the more inflammatory charge of Edward's own bastardy was to be handled not "plain and directly" but only "touched a slope craftely, as though men spared in yt [that] point to speke al the trouth for fere of [Richard's] displeasure."

More has Shaa carry out these instructions. First, says More, Shaa declared "that King Edward was never lawfully married unto ye quene," because he was "before god" married to another. Then, almost as an afterthought, More has Shaa "signify," rather than say outright, that neither Edward nor Clarence was considered "surely" to be the child of the duke of York, since they did not resemble him.

According to More, when Buckingham spoke at the Guildhall on Tuesday the 24th, he reminded the crowd that Shaa had openly charged that the two princes were not legitimate, because Edward "was never lawfully married unto ye Quene, their mother," having another wife at the time. Then the duke, again referring the crowd to Shaa's sermon, reminded them that there were "other thinges" which Shaa had "rather signified then fully explained" for fear of incurring Richard's displeasure.

Polydore Vergil reports that the only charge made by Shaa was that of Edward's bastardy and that Richard's mother complained bitterly about "the great injury" which Richard had done to her. This is highly doubtful. Richard had been living with his mother at Baynard Castle, her London home; and even after his wife arrived and they rented Crosby Hall, he continued to hold important meetings at his mother's home. He received at least one delegation of citizens there; and Walpole places Richard's first council meeting there. Every indication is that Richard and his mother were on the best of terms and continued so even after Shaa's oration.

Vergil's reliability on this point is questionable. He was Henry VII's official historian, and, as we will see, Henry was obsessive about supressing any reference to the invalidity of Edward IV's marriage, since his wife was a daughter of that marriage and since his claim to the throne was otherwise quite weak.

Vergil acknowledges "a common report" that Shaa claimed that Edward's children, rather than Edward himself, were "basterdes" but adds that this rumor "is voyd of all truthe." He makes no mention of the claim of a precontract invalidating the marriage, and his ground for asserting that Shaa did not call the children "basterdes" is that Richard's mother complained that she had been called an adulteress. This, of course, does not exclude the possibility that the children's illegitimacy was *also* claimed. Indeed, Vergil's acknowledging that claim as "a common report" indicates that the belief that Shaa did call the children "basterdes" was so widespread that Vergil felt the need to acknowledge and deny it (albeit on spurious grounds).

Charles Ross quotes the passage from Vergil about Duchess Cecily complaining that Richard had labeled her an adulteress, adding that "the same story" had "been around earlier." Most readers would take this as a reference to Vergil's "story," which Ross had just quoted—i.e., that Richard's mother complained bitterly about his charging her with adultery. Ross cites Mancini as his authority for the proposition that this "story" had "been around earlier." He then quotes Mancini as reporting that Richard's mother even fell into "a frenzy." Thus, Ross appears to be telling us that Duchess Cecily fell into "a frenzy" when she learned, in June 1483, of Richard's causing Shaa publicly to charge that Edward IV was illegitimate—"the same story" Vergil had reported and Ross had just quoted.

But the duchess's "frenzy" to which Mancini referred took place almost twenty years earlier and was over an entirely different matter. It occurred in 1464, when Duchess Cecily learned, to her astonishment, that Edward had married Elizabeth Woodville. Contrary to the impression created by Ross, the duchess's "frenzy" had nothing to do with a June 1483 accusation of Edward's bastardy. What Mancini wrote was that, in 1464, when the duchess first learned *of Edward's Woodville marriage,* she fell into a frenzy over this unseemly match and that *she* threatened to announce publicly that Edward was not legitimate and therefore not worthy of the crown.

It seems unlikely that the duchess made this threat and even more unlikely that she would have ever carried it out, even though she need no longer have feared her husband's reaction, since he had been killed at the battle of Wakefield in 1460. If, however, Mancini's report was true, it is conceivable, although unlikely, that the duchess was prepared to see the charge of Edward's illegitimacy resurface after his death in order to aid Richard's cause and frustrate the Woodvilles.

Weir asserts with absolute certainty that the *only* claim made by Shaa in his June 22 sermon was that Edward IV himself was a bastard, and that he said nothing about the invalidity of Edward's marriage. She provides no evidence to support that unequivocal assertion; and it is contrary to other, seemingly more reliable accounts of what Shaa said, including even More's. The charge of Edward's own illegitimacy may have been added to that of the precontract, or, as More put it, "touched a slope craftely" and "rather signified then fully explained." But it seems extremely unlikely that the *only* charge made was that Edward was a bastard and that the precontract was not mentioned at all.

It is essential to Weir's thesis that Shaa said nothing about the precontract. She claims that it was only after Richard realized that Dr. Shaa's June 22 sermon had not successfully convinced the public that Edward IV was a bastard, that Richard "had it put about that Edward IV's marriage to Elizabeth Wydville was invalid because he had, at the time, been contracted to another lady."

By moving the disclosure of the Butler precontract from the first to the last part of June, Weir is able to argue that it was a complete fabrication, desperately concocted at the last minute, when the claim of Edward's own illegitimacy was not embraced by the populace. It also permits her to argue that, between June 13 and 22, when Richard sounded out various nobles about becoming king and rode through the streets as if he were royalty, he was contemplating a naked act of usurpation, rather than acting upon knowledge that the precontract eliminated Prince Edward as a legitimate heir to the throne and left Richard himself as the logical and lawful successor.

Weir's contention is flatly inconsistent with More, who, as we have seen, reports that Shaa was instructed to charge openly that the princes were illegitimate because Edward had been married to another woman, that Shaa did make that explicit charge on June 22 and that Buckingham reminded the crowd of that charge two days later. Yet Weir, who generally treats More's account as gospel, says that none of this happened.

More even goes into detail about the precontract and how it was first claimed. He names the wrong "other woman," referring not to Eleanor Butler but to Elizabeth Lucy, a courtesan and sometime mistress of Edward, whom no one would be inclined to believe Edward would marry or even promise to marry. As will be discussed below, More adds the evidently fabricated story that an official inquiry confirmed the validity of Edward's marriage to his queen, and that Elizabeth Lucy publicly admitted that she had no precontract with the King. But it was Eleanor Butler, not Elizabeth Lucy, with whom Edward entered into the precontract.

Wrong woman or not, More's account cannot be squared with the theory urged by Weir that the *only* charge made by Shaa was that Edward himself was a bastard.

Could Edward IV really have been illegitimate? There is little evidence to support the charge, even though such gossip had been around for some time. Edward, who was born in France, did not resemble his father, the duke of York, while Richard, "a true son" and one born in England, bore the late duke a close resemblance. Clarence's appearance fails to shed any light on the issue. Evidently he was fair like Edward, but an examination of his bones at Tewkesbury Abbey revealed that he was only about five feet five inches, closer to Richard's height than Edward's six feet three. Of course, human experience tells us that brothers are often vastly different from each other in size and appearance.

At the time of Edward's birth, Cecily and Richard of York were living in France. There is no known record of her having had a relationship with anyone other than her husband, but, of course, such a record would be unlikely. Louis XI enjoyed calling

Edward "Bleybourgne," a reference to the French archer Louis liked to claim was Edward's true father. There is simply no way of assessing the probability of Cecily's having had an adulterous affair with M. Bleybourgne or anyone else.

Edward IV's charges against Clarence in 1478 included the claim that Clarence spread the tale of Edward's bastardy. If the story had been true, Clarence could claim that he was not merely the rightful heir, but the rightful king. Apparently Clarence had at least hinted in private circles that Edward was illegitimate and may have threatened to turn those hints into public charges. That, of course, cannot be considered evidence that the charges were true.

In any event, whether Shaa charged in June of 1483 that Edward IV was illegitimate or only that his children were, the opinion was now voiced that the Princes were not entitled to the crown and that Richard should be king.

According to Kendall, at about this time, Richard sent word to delay the arrival of the northern troops he had requested on June 10th. Presumably he did not want to create the impression that he had any forcible intent.

Now, however, Rivers, Grey and Vaughn were charged with treason. Although the fact has been disputed, they appear to have been found guilty by a court presided over by the Earl of Northumberland.

Whether or not there really was a trial, the three were beheaded on June 25th, perhaps on the direct order of Sir Richard Ratcliffe, an aid closely associated with Richard. The brilliant and scholarly Rivers had become highly involved in religion and religious thinking in his later years. At his death, he is said to have been wearing a hair shirt beneath his outer garments. The story may be apocryphal.

More has Rivers, Grey and Vaughn executed "the self same day" and "about the selfsame hower (hour)" as Hastings was beheaded in London. This is simply wrong. Hastings was executed on the 13th, Rivers, Grey and Vaughn on the 25th. More also reports that Hastings was delighted at the prospect that his old enemies, Rivers and Grey, were to be executed. More was wrong about the date of Hastings' execution, but he may have been correct that, before he was killed, Hastings knew Rivers and Grey faced execution and was in favor of the move.

Weir argues that the three beheaded on the 25th could not have been guilty of treason in plotting against Richard, because Richard was merely the protector, not the king. This is questionable. Treason is an act of rebellion against the lawful government. If that government is, at the same time, a protectorship, it would seem plotting the protector's death would be a treasonous act. Of course, there could be no treason if Richard was not legally the protector when the three men were arrested, because he had not been approved by Parliament and the Council. But, as we have seen, that proposition is also a questionable one.

Whether or not there was a trial, the execution of Rivers, Grey and Vaughn has been described by traditionalists as predetermined and directed by Richard well before they were charged and any trial was held. This may very well have been the case; but such predetermined judgments, while hardly justified, have not been rarities in any century. The guilt or innocence of the three men would seem a more significant question.

It is not easy to make a good case that the three were guilty of plotting with Hastings and Morton during June. While Elizabeth Woodville may well have joined in such a conspiracy, there appears to be little likelihood that Rivers, Grey or Vaughn did so while they were held in three separate northern castles.

On the other hand, it is not improbable that they did plot against Richard in April prior to their arrest. Almost certainly, they were involved in the Woodville decisions at that time to seize and retain power contrary to the will of Edward IV.

It may be that those earlier acts were the true basis for the executions. Richard had asked that the three men be charged with treason at the council meeting of May 10, less than a week after his arrival in London. The council would not give its assent, but the accusation had been made. It was, of course, a different situation and a differently placed Richard who successfully made the same charge in late June.

Interestingly, Rivers himself had enough confidence in Richard's integrity to name him supervisor of his will made on June 23, when he knew he was facing execution. Apparently,

Rivers had relied for some time on Richard's sense of justice, having agreed, in late March 1483, to submit a significant property dispute to Richard's arbitration.

Did Rivers feel that he had conspired against Richard prior to his arrest and that this justified his punishment? Probably not. But naming Richard the supervisor of his preexecution will does suggest that, even if he did not consider his sentence justified, he at least understood its rationale and did not allow it to shake his faith in Richard's general probity. Characteristically, Weir mentions that Rivers made a will, but omits any mention of this significant provision.

Dorset successfully escaped from sanctuary around the time that Rivers, Grey and Vaughn were executed. Possibly hearing of their deaths led him to fear for his own life, notwithstanding his claim to sanctuary.

Perhaps if the former queen had known on June 16 that the relatives were to be killed, she would not have released her youngest son into Richard's control. Her conduct after their execution does not suggest this, but we cannot know for sure.

On June 25, the same day as the execution of Rivers, Grey and Vaughn, the Lords Spiritual and Temporal (i.e., the representatives of the church and the nobility) assembled in London along with the Commons. In substance, this assemblage of the three "estates" (the church, the nobility and the "commons") amounted to a Parliament. But history has not considered it to have been a Parliament "in fourme."

Parliament had been duly summoned to convene on June 25 by order of Edward V issued in May, when he was accepted by all as the new king. Did the subsequent claim that he was illegitimate retroactively deprive the assembly of its legal status as a Parliament? Apparently not. The defect appears to have been that there was no king to *open* the session, even though a king had called it. Edward IV was dead. His sons, now perceived as illegitimate, could not open Parliament. Clarence's son had been attainted. Richard had not yet been acclaimed king; and, with young Edward declared illegitimate, Richard may have had no right to open Parliament as protector. In any event, he declined to do so.

Formal impediment or not, the three estates assembled as

they had been called. The proofs of Edward IV's precontract with Eleanor Butler were laid before the assembly by Bishop Stillington. It was formally decided that Edward's sons could not succeed to the throne for various reasons, including the precontract with Eleanor Butler. The supposed illegitimacy of Edward IV was not mentioned. Owing to the attainder of the duke of Clarence, his children could not succeed either. Although attainders had been reversed before, there was no attempt to reverse this one. Possibly this was because Richard's adherents dominated the proceedings. In part, it may also have been because Clarence's son Edward, the earl of Warwick, was only eight years old and no one was anxious for a minority reign.

Under the circumstances, Richard was considered the legal heir and the only logical candidate for the position. Practical politics dictated the same result, even aside from the strength of Richard's position. Whether the princes were really illegitimate or not, crowning Prince Edward would mean either a restoration of unpopular Woodville dominance or a civil war—or both. And Richard was a proven military leader who was perceived to be the conqueror of the Scots and whose beneficent governance in the North had been widely acclaimed.

A resolution of the three estates was passed stating the facts that supported Richard's right to succeed and directing that a "Rolle" be presented to Richard setting out those facts and calling upon him to accept the crown.

As was the general custom at the time, the "Rolle" went well beyond the specific charge upon which the disqualification of the princes was really based. It not only specified the Eleanor Butler precontract as a reason for their disqualification, it spoke of sorcery and the violation of God's laws and the evils of the Woodvilles. In addition, it rather stridently attacked Edward's reign, charging that while he ruled, "the ordre of all poletique Rule was perverted" and the land "ruled by selfwill and pleasure, feare and drede, all manner of Equite and lawes layd apart and despised." According to the "Rolle," this occurred because those governing the kingdom, "delityng in adulation and flattery and lede by sensuality and concupiscence, followed the counsaill of personnes insolent, vicious, and of inordinate avarice."

It seems apparent that Richard consented to this attack on his brother's reign. It probably reflected what Richard really believed about the last years of that reign. Nevertheless, he can be accused of exhibiting uncharacteristic disloyalty in allowing the point to be made in a public document, when it was hardly necessary to do so.

The action of the assembly of the three estates on June 25 makes Weir's view of the chronology of events seem most improbable. She places the very first mention of the precontract not only after Dr. Shaa's speech of June 22 but also after Richard reached the conclusion that Shaa's speech had not convinced the public.

As we have already discussed, this contradicts the description of Shaa's address given by More and others. It also seems improbable as a matter of timing. Buckingham did not address the crowd on the subject of the precontract until Tuesday, June 24. That might suggest that, if Weir's thesis were correct, it took Richard a full day or two to assess the public's reaction and decide to change the basis for his claim from Edward's illegitimacy to that of his children.

But, even assuming that Richard's assessment of public reaction was made on the 22nd itself or the very next day, there were still only two or three days left before the assembly of June 25. In that brief period, Weir would have Richard concoct, for the very first time, the rather complicated story that Edward IV had entered into a precontract with Lady Eleanor Butler, check into the facts about Lady Eleanor sufficiently to assure himself, as would have been essential, that there was nothing about the story that could readily be disproved, convince Bishop Stillington to go along with a fabricated tale and spread that brand new tale among the populace, once again assessing their reaction. Then, after all that was accomplished, he would have had to assemble spurious evidence of the precontract to present to the assembly of the three estates, and convince that large and diverse body of peers, churchmen, knights and county landowners to accept this startling new story as the truth and as the basis for disqualifying the royal heir. Moreover, while still acting in that extremely short period, he would have to have prepared a detailed written Rolle confirming the assembly's decision to accept the Eleanor Butler precontract as making the children of Edward IV illegitimate and asking Richard of Gloucester to accept the crown. Possible?

Maybe, but highly unlikely.

It seems far more probable that the precontract was disclosed around June 8 or even earlier; that, sometime thereafter, probably on June 9, the disclosure was informally presented to a gathering of the Lords Spiritual and Temporal; that supporting evidence was either found (or, if the traditionalists are right, fabricated) for presentation to a more formal assembly of the three estates and that Richard sounded out other barons and rode through the streets in regal splendor and Dr. Shaa and Buckingham made their speeches, only substantially *after* it had been revealed by Stillington that Prince Edward was illegitimate by reason of the Eleanor Butler precontract.

Weir argues that, after what she calls the June 9 council meeting, Simon Stallworth wrote a letter saying that there was nothing of special interest to report. Based on this assumption, Weir concludes that the precontract could not have been disclosed to the council on or before June 9 and that, therefore, it was only concocted much later that month.

Stallworth's letter, although ambiguous in some respects, does not support Weir's conclusions. Stallworth was the servant of Bishop Russell. He was writing to Sir William Stonor, a friend in the country, on the same day as the June 9 meeting. If, as is virtually certain, Russell was at the meeting that day, the chancellor may not have revealed to his servant something as sensitive as the precontract and the possible disqualification of Prince Edward. Or perhaps Russell intended to inform Stallworth what occurred that day but had not yet had the opportunity to do so. Or it is possible that Russell did tell his servant, but Stallworth felt it was not the kind of thing he should put in writing or perhaps disclose at all to his friend, Stonor.

Some of what Stallworth wrote does suggest that something very special was occurring on June 9. In describing the meeting that day, Stallworth seems to be describing a gathering beyond a normal meeting of the council. He speaks not of a council meeting, but of a meeting *in the council chamber* of Richard and Buckingham together with *all other Lords Spiritual and Temporal.* That was the term commonly applied to the assembly of two of the three estates that made up Parliament.

If Stallworth meant what he said literally and was not merely referring to the religious and secular members of the council, this gathering was indeed an unusual event. Even if it included only those Lords Spiritual and Temporal who happened to be in London at the time, it indicates a broader assembly than the council itself and one indicative of some important issue. It would not be a Parliament, since the Commons was not convened. But it would certainly suggest a happening of uncommon significance.

Moreover, Stallworth wrote that the assembled peers and prelates had been at the meeting from ten until two. We do not know the hour in which Stallworth wrote his letter, but his language suggests that the meeting might still have been going on as he wrote. But, even assuming that the meeting ended at two and did not resume later, it lasted four hours, once again suggesting that a matter of considerable importance was being discussed. Gairdner calls it "a remarkably long sitting"; and even Colin Richmond, who firmly believes in Richard's guilt, notes that the meeting of June 9 lasted four hours and concludes that "[i]t is likely that something of consequence" occurred.

In an ambiguous passage, Stallworth adds that "[t]here is great business against the coronation," which he says is scheduled for a fortnight later. Does "*against*" mean *in opposition to?* It could be that Stillington's disclosures had led to such opposition or at least the view that the coronation should be postponed while the matter was investigated. Perhaps, however, "against the coronation" only meant *in anticipation of* that ceremony. That would seem an unusual construction of the words; but it is not impossible.

In any event, even if Stillington's account was not presented to the council or the Lords Spiritual and Temporal on June 9, it may still have been disclosed to Richard at or about that time, which squares with most of the subsequent events and with Richard's behavior.

Russell's draft of a speech intended for the opening of Parliament on June 25 urges a continuation of Richard's protectorship. This suggests that when the speech was drafted, Russell did not know of Stillington's disclosure. Yet Russell, as chancellor, would seemingly have been among the first to have heard the news. Of course, Russell may have started drafting his speech the first week in June or earlier, even if it was not intended for presentation until June 25.

It might also be argued that Richard's pressing for release of the younger prince from sanctuary on June 16 suggests that he did not yet know about the precontract. However, even if he knew of the princes' illegitimacy, Richard would have wanted both boys in his own control, since either could serve as a rallying point for opposition or rebellion.

Whatever the timing of Stillington's disclosure, the "Rolle" prepared by the assembly on June 25 did expressly refer to the Eleanor Butler precontract and to the princes' illegitimacy. Although it criticized the debauchery and corruption that prevailed in Edward's reign, it made no mention of Edward himself being illegitimate.

The Rolle was presented to Richard the next day, June 26, by a delegation of citizens in a ceremony at his mother's home. This seems a strange place to hold the ceremony if Richard had just caused the making of a public charge that his mother was an adulteress and Duchess Cecily was enraged over that insult.

After Buckingham read the petition, Richard indicated to the assembled citizens his consent to assume the throne. He then rode from his mother's home to Westminster Hall, where he took the royal oath and occupied the traditional royal chair in King's Bench. Although not yet crowned, he was now greeted by the crowds as King Richard III.

Richard has been accused of stage-managing the assembly of the three estates, as well as the citizens' appeal that he accept the crown. The charges are probably true. At least there was an assembly and an appeal, however, and not, as in other cases, such as with Henry IV, Edward IV and Henry VII, simply a seizure of the throne by force.

Even Gairdner, who must certainly be classified as a traditionalist, pointed out that Richard obtained "a declaration of inherent right to the crown first by the council of the realm, then by the city, and afterwards by Parliament—proceedings much more regular and punctilious than had been observed in the case of Edward IV."

VIII

♚ USURPER OR RIGHTFUL KING?

Dominic Mancini's account of the events leading to Richard's accession has been given the English title "The Usurpation of Richard III." Mancini used the Latin word "*Occupatione,*" which does not necessarily mean "usurpation" or imply the absence of right. But that is almost surely what Mancini intended. Numerous historians have referred to Richard as a "usurper." Is that characterization warranted?

Richard's right to replace Edward V as king depends on the answers to two separate questions. First, was the report of the Eleanor Butler precontract true? And, second, did the existence such a precontract bar the two princes from the succession?

Assuming, as appears to be the case, that it was Stillington who told Richard of the precontract, was he speaking the truth? Edward IV certainly engaged in numerous affairs before (and after) his marriage to Elizabeth Woodville; and he seems to have been the kind of man who would be ready to promise marriage (or anything else) in order to bed an attractive woman. Indeed, that was how he came to marry his queen, the difference being that Elizabeth, unlike Eleanor Butler, held out for a wedding, rather than just a contract.

Edward had generally treated Stillington well, and the timing of certain royal favors may be significant. For example, in late 1461, the year of the precontract, Edward granted Stillington a substantial annual salary; and, in early 1465, shortly after Edward announced his marriage to Elizabeth Woodville, Edward made Stillington a bishop. Eighteen years later, in 1483, did the prospect of further advancement give the Bishop a possible motive to slander the late King or his children? By that time, Stillington was over sixty, and generally in poor health. Seemingly, he had little to gain from Richard; and, indeed, he gained nothing. He had previously served as chancellor under Edward, but had resigned and appears to have had no particular ambition to serve in that office again. In any event, Richard gave the position to John Russell.

There is no record of Stillington being considered deceitful, corrupt or even unduly ambitious. Nor is there any other evidence that his report of the Eleanor Butler precontract was not the truth.

Edward's marriage to Elizabeth had occurred nineteen years before Stillington disclosed the precontract to Richard and the council. Where had Stillington been all this time? Why had he not come forward before this? There is a credible explanation. The person with standing to attack the validity of Edward's Woodville marriage in an ecclesiastical court would have been Eleanor Butler, not Robert Stillington. So long as Lady Eleanor remained silent, why should the bishop take it up on himself to declare that the reigning king and queen were living in sin and that their children were bastards?

Indeed, during Edward's life, Stillington dared not speak out. As we have already discussed, one explanation for Clarence's execution and Stillington's arrest in 1478 is that they knew of the invalidity of Edward's marriage and were therefore a serious threat to the Woodville succession.

Perhaps, after his release from prison, the elderly bishop intended to take his secret to the grave. But, on Edward's untimely death, the situation changed dramatically. At that point, if Stillington realized the danger of a minority reign, grasped the public sentiment for Richard, and believed that an illegitimate child was about to take the throne instead of the legitimate successor, he may have felt compelled to come forward with his news.

Of course, the possibility exists that Stillington simply made up the story. Apparently there were no other eyewitnesses. Edward IV was dead. So was Eleanor Butler. According to legend, she retired, brokenhearted, to a convent, where she died in 1468. But the absence of other witnesses is not in itself an indication that Stillington's report was false.

James Gairdner, no supporter of Richard, found reason to accept the precontract story, although he reached no definite conclusion on the point. Gairdner considered it "highly probable" that, as Sir George Buck reported, Eleanor Butler even had a child by Edward before retiring to the convent. But Buck may not be correct in this. If the child was alive when Stillington made his disclosure, and if Edward's Woodville marriage was invalid, the child would have been the rightful heir to the throne. This fact could hardly have escaped notice by Richard, the council and anyone else who knew of the child's existence. Of course, the child may have died by 1483 or its existence kept secret.

Alison Weir does not agree with Gairdner that the precontract story may well have been true. She states flatly that the Stillington disclosure was a complete fabrication, created as a last minute cover for Richard's usurpation of the crown. Like so many hypotheses in this ambiguous situation, Weir's scenario is not impossible. But her arguments fall short of supporting the absolute certainty with which she presents her conclusion, and, as we have discussed, the chronology she insists upon is highly improbable.

Among contemporary writers, only de Commynes identifies Stillington as the man who revealed the precontract. But its existence was also reported in the Croyland Chronicle; and, Mancini wrote that, before his marriage to Elizabeth Woodville, Edward IV "was contracted to another wife."

Moreover, the fact of a precontract between Edward and Eleanor Butler was embraced and confirmed in June 1483 by the entire convocation of the three estates, and once again in January 1484 by the full Parliament. In each instance, it was recorded in a detailed written instrument that can be seen even today.

Weir is not clear as to whether she claims that (1) Richard concocted the entire "disclosure," when, in fact, Stillington told him nothing of the kind, or (2) Stillington made up the story and convinced Richard of its truth or (3) the two worked together to fabricate and spread the tale of a precontract with Eleanor Butler.

The possibility that Richard made up the entire concept and that Stillington told him nothing is difficult to square with the known facts. We know, for example, that, with the council's approval, the assembly of the three estates enacted a Rolle embracing the story of the precontract.

Yes, Richard must have had considerable influence with the assembly as he did with the council and the representatives of the city. But it is unlikely that any of these groups would have acted as they did without at least a prima facie case to support the precontract claims. *Someone* must have claimed and testified before the council and the assembly, in a reasonably convincing manner, that Edward IV had entered into such an agreement. There is no reason to believe that de Commynes was misstating things when he identified Stillington as that person. And Richard at least *claimed* that his information came from Stillington. He *had* to have been assured of the bishop's cooperation. How else could he have hoped to convince the council or the public that Stillington had told him of a precontract rendering Edward's children ineligible for the throne? How else could he have hoped to persuade the assembly of the three estates to accept the precontract story and displace the new young king? Plainly, Stillington's public denial of the story would have wrecked the entire enterprise.

Henry VII's historian, Vergil, denied that the children of Edward IV had been called bastards and was understandably silent about any claim of a precontract. During the reign of Henry VIII, however, Stillington was identified as the man who charged that Edward had "espoused another wife" before he married Elizabeth Woodville. Later historians, even traditionalists like Gairdner, have accepted the conclusion that it was Stillington who made the disclosure.

Stillington's arrest and imprisonment for unspecified utterances "prejudicial to the King and his state" near the time of Clarence's execution supports this view. So does the fact that one of Henry VII's first acts, immediately after his victory at Bosworth Field, was to order the bishop's arrest. Why else would the victorious new king rush to arrest a relatively obscure old cleric?

Under the circumstances, it seems a reasonable conclusion that *if* the account of the precontract was untrue, Stillington supported the account, either concocting the story alone or cooperating with Richard in creating and advancing it.

But why would the elderly prelate risk his neck to invent a story that would so radically affect the kingdom and the royal family? Riches? Career advancement? He got neither and seemed uninterested in getting them. There seems to have been no motivation for the bishop's coming forward with the account or supporting it before the council and the three estates unless he believed it. And if Stillington, who claimed to be an eyewitness, did in fact believe the story, it is difficult to resist the conclusion that it was true.

Weir argues that Stillington's failure to receive significant offices or riches from Richard indicates that his disclosure was a fabrication. But, since it appears that Stillington at least supported Richard's account, one would expect his reward to be greater if the story were false than if it were true. A modest reward might be appropriate for a bishop who presented a true account to the council and the assembly of the three estates. A far richer reward would ordinarily be paid to induce the bishop to present and actively support a complete fabrication before those august bodies. Contrary to Weir's reasoning, the absence of a material reward argues for the truth of the precontract disclosure, not its falsity.

Was Stillington a man of little character who could easily be persuaded to go along with whatever Richard wanted? Nothing in his past suggests that. On the contrary, in 1473, when sitting as chancellor, Stillington sharply questioned Richard's claim to the lands signed over to him by the countess of Oxford. It was only through the ruling of another chancellor that Richard's title was confirmed.

True, Richard was not the king when his case came before Stillington. But he was the king's favorite brother and a man of enormous power. The independence of mind shown by that episode suggests that Stillington would not have been easily persuaded to support a fabricated tale of a precontract.

And, if Richard was seeking a corruptible "witness" to support a concocted story, would he have turned to Stillington, the man who had given him such difficulty in the Chancery proceedings? Surely there were other, more pliable men available in the kingdom.

Weir argues that the very timeliness of Stillington's disclosures "undermines their credibility." But a disclosure is not necessarily false because it is made at a time when it is most relevant and most helpful to the recipient. There are seemingly cogent reasons why Stillington spoke up when he did and not before.

For example, Weir points to the fact that Stillington did not come forward with his revelation in 1464 when Edward IV married Elizabeth Woodville. But the Woodville marriage was a secret one, almost certainly unknown to Stillington, as it was to the council. Months later, in 1465, when the marriage was finally revealed, the Woodvilles had already accumulated power and influence with the king. Disclosure of the precontract while that power and influence remained would likely have resulted in the bishop's imprisonment, as it apparently did at the time of Clarence's attainder and execution in 1478. Besides, if Eleanor Butler, who had standing to attack the king's marriage in an ecclesiastical proceeding, elected not to do so, why would Stillington, who had no such standing, risk his neck and his career by making such an accusation?

Certainly Stillington's silence between his imprisonment for disloyal "utterances" in 1478 and Edward's death in 1483 is understandable. And, even after Edward's death, an early disclosure could have been dangerous, if not fatal, while the Woodvilles still held significant power.

Stillington appears to have made his disclosure in the early part of June. Richard did not gain control of Edward V and arrest Rivers until the end of April. Before those blows to Woodville power, and, indeed, before Richard arrived in London in May, Stillington would have taken an enormous personal risk in announcing the disqualification of a Woodville heir and the illegitimacy of Elizabeth's children. Even after that, he took a significant risk in being the only eyewitness to an event that could end the Woodville line. The apparent ability of the Woodvilles to align themselves with such powerful figures as Hastings and

Stanley shows that attacking their vital interests, even in June, was dangerous business.

Moreover, when Stillington was freed from his 1478 imprisonment, he may have been forced to take an oath not to "utter" such "words" again. If so, the aging prelate may have had considerable soul searching to do before he went to Richard with his disclosures. For all of these reasons, waiting from May until early June before speaking out would not seem unreasonable or to undermine his credibility.

Charles Ross reaches the same conclusion as Weir, but offers no further evidence to support it. His arguments are no more persuasive than hers. Ross says that "Richard's claim [that the princes were illegitimate] inevitably lacked conviction, since no firm evidence, as distinct from innuendo, could be produced in support of his allegation." No "firm evidence?" Only "innuendo?" How about an eyewitness? Certainly Stillington's testimony itself, whether believed or not, must be considered evidence and not mere innuendo.

Perhaps Ross means that there was no *written* evidence. Even here, he may be wrong. As we have seen, Hall's Chronicle as published by Grafton described a conversation in which Buckingham told Morton that Richard presented "instruments, authentic doctors, proctors, and notaries of the law with depositions of divers witnesses." According to Grafton, Buckingham told Morton that, when this evidence was presented, he believed it to be "true," but that he later realized that it was "fayned." Whether Buckingham considered these documents "true" or "fayned," they would have constituted written evidence—assuming, of course, that Buckingham and Morton really had any such conversation.

If such documentary evidence had existed, it may well have been destroyed by Henry VII, just as he destroyed every copy of the act of Parliament that referred to the precontract. Or such documents could have been destroyed by others, such as Polydore Vergil, who has specifically been accused of destroying documents that did not fit with his point of view, which, of course, was the same as Henry's.

Ross treats the precontract story as palpable nonsense that was understood by the people and the nobility to be an obvious fiction. But he cites no evidence that the peers and the public considered the story patently false, and what indications we have seem to contradict that view. For example, Henry VII seemed far from optimistic about what his subjects believed on this score. Otherwise, why would he order the immediate arrest of Stillington and (as we will discuss below) the destruction of every copy of the parliamentary act that accepted and documented the precontract story?

The vehemence with which Henry VII set out to destroy every copy of that act and his reluctance to make an explicit public charge against Stillington even after he was arrested or to have a public inquiry into Stillington's testimony tend to show Henry's concern that the people might accept the precontract story as true. Moreover, they point to his recognition that an inquiry into its truth could be dangerous and that the bishop's testimony might be difficult to disprove.

Ross points out that the parliamentary act contained other grounds for deposing Edward V besides his illegitimacy. It also refers to the failure of Edward and Elizabeth Woodville to marry in public, to sorcery and to the debauchery of Edward IV's court. But those matters could not conceivably serve as valid grounds for disqualifying the heir and were plainly not the reason the young king was deposed. Nor were they the reason Henry VII later destroyed every copy of the act. After all, a private marriage did not make one's children illegitimate, and the charge that sorcery and debauchery occurred in the reign of Edward IV hardly threatened the interests of Henry Tudor.

As we will discuss, the *only* thing in the act that threatened Henry was the claimed illegitimacy of his own wife, who was a child of Edward IV. And, of all the matters alleged in the act, it was the precontract alone that rendered her illegitimate. The essential point of the parliamentary act, and very clearly the only reason Henry had it suppressed, was its confirmation of the Eleanor Butler precontract, not such charges as sorcery and debauchery in a prior king's reign.

Even after the act was suppressed, Stillington's story continued to be accepted in at least some quarters. For example, during the reign of Henry VIII, Charles V's ambassador to England reported that people "say" Charles had a better claim to the English throne than did Henry VIII, since Henry could claim only through his mother, and she "was declared by sentence of the Bishop of Bath [i.e., Stillington] a bastard, because Edward had espoused another wife before he married the mother of Elizabeth of York."

Ross asks, if the precontract story were true, why wasn't it raised by Warwick and Clarence in 1470 when they were seeking to overthrow Edward IV? There are at least two reasons. First, the king they needed to depose was Edward himself, not his children. Illegitimacy of the princes would not have been a persuasive reason for rebelling against the reigning king. Second, Clarence probably did not learn of the precontract until around 1478, when he and Stillington were imprisoned.

Ross also asks, if Richard thought Edward's children were illegitimate, why did he want to marry Princess Elizabeth on the death of his wife? The answer is that we do not *know* that he wanted to marry Elizabeth, although it is possible. We do know that he publicly denied any such intention. Of course, that denial may have been false. Richard may, indeed, have been attracted to the young, attractive princess. But, if he did want to marry her or even considered that prospect, it would probably have been to prevent Henry Tudor from doing so. Henry had announced his intention to marry the princess; and that marriage, uniting Lancaster and York, was Henry's best hope for attaining the throne.

Assuming that there really was a precontract with Eleanor Butler, did it actually invalidate Edward's marriage to Elizabeth Woodville? Probably, although some have argued to the contrary.

Mortimer Levine has written both an article and a book dealing with the subject, concluding generally that Richard was not legally entitled to the throne. Mary O'Regan has written a brief but well-reasoned analysis disagreeing with Levine.

In the fifteenth century, canon law governed such issues, and that body of law treated an oral precontract to marry as an effective marriage for most purposes. This was true not only if the precontract included statements by the couple that they *were* married, but also if it involved only *promises* to marry in the future, if those promises were followed by sexual intercourse. It is not clear whether Edward and Eleanor actually said they were married or merely recited a promise to marry. But it would make no difference, since no one doubts that as de Commynes reported, they went on to have a sexual relationship. To Edward, that was the entire point; and, as we have seen, Eleanor Butler may even have had a child by Edward.

Under earlier canon law, if one of the parties married in good faith in a public ceremony, the children of the marriage could be considered legitimate, even if the other party turned out to have already been married. It seems clear that when Elizabeth Woodville wed Edward IV, she knew nothing of his precontract with Eleanor Butler and therefore married him in good faith. However, this exception may no longer have been applicable in the fifteenth century; and, in any event, it only applied if the good faith marriage was a *public* ceremony. Edward and Elizabeth's marriage, of course, was private and, indeed, secret.

Moreover, even if there had been an exception to the law that made a child legitimate for ordinary purposes, such as the inheritance of property, that exception might not have been applicable in deciding the different issue of their right to succeed to the throne, an issue governed by entirely different considerations.

Levine argues that the two princes were not illegitimate, because Eleanor Butler died in 1468, before either prince was born. According to Levine, her death "terminated" the precontract. But this misses the point. Edward's "marriage" to Elizabeth Woodville took place while Eleanor Butler was alive, so that the precontract was still extant. Accordingly, that marriage was invalid—nonexistent in the eyes of the law. Under canon law at the time, a formal, public marriage between Edward and Elizabeth *after Eleanor Butler's death* would probably have legitimized the children born after she died. But no such marriage took place.

Professor Ross, like Levine, seems to accept the view that because Edward *could have* married Elizabeth Woodville in a formal ceremony after Eleanor Butler's death, Edward V and Prince Richard were not illegitimate. Here again, the argument misses the point. Yes, Edward *could have* remarried his queen after

Eleanor Butler died; and yes, this probably *would have* legitimized the two princes and possibly all of their children. But the
fact is they *did not* remarry, formally or even informally. Their
ability to have done so has no relevance.

Why didn't they remarry? Until 1478, it is almost certain that
Elizabeth Woodville was wholly unaware of any impediment to
her marriage, and Edward was not about to tell her. In 1478, she
probably learned that Clarence was talking about the existence of
a precontract that would invalidate her marriage and was claiming that Bishop Stillington could prove it.

Edward probably assured his queen that the claim, although
dangerous, was false. Besides, to legitimize their children, they
would have to go through a formal, public ceremony. The mere
announcement that they intended a second wedding would obviously be an admission that their first one was bigamous, that they
had been living in sin and that their children were, at least for the
moment, bastards.

Indeed, under canon law, their daughters born before Eleanor
Butler's death in 1468 would likely remain bastards despite any
formal public wedding. And canon law was not totally clear even
as to the effect of such a public wedding on children born after
the death of the first "wife." Nor was it clear that the ordinary
rules of canon law would govern succession to the throne. They
might have gone through the humiliating and undesirable step of
publicly remarrying only to find that not only their older daughters were illegitimate but that even the two princes' right to the
throne remained in doubt.

Edward and Elizabeth would have been very reluctant to take
such a public step. Probably, the king and queen determined that
the more prudent policy was to arrest and execute Clarence and
to imprison Stillington, make him take an oath of silence and
threaten him with death and eternal damnation if he spoke out
after his release.

Could it be argued that the children were legitimate even if
the marriage of their parents was void? Not according to the logic
of canon law as it stood in 1483. If there was no valid marriage,
there could be no legitimate offspring. Modern social policy calls
for the legitimacy of children to be governed by a different and

more flexible rule than that governing the validity of marriage. But it is doubtful that such a policy-based argument would have found acceptance in a fifteenth-century ecclesiastical court.

Both Ross and Levine argue that Parliament and the public accepted the marriage of Edward and Elizabeth for many years until Stillington's disclosure in 1483. But public acceptance would not give the marriage legal or canonical validity for purposes of determining succession to the throne.

Assuming that there was a precontract between Edward and Eleanor Butler, it is probable that an ecclesiastical court would have held Edward's marriage to Elizabeth Woodville invalid and the princes illegitimate. With Clarence dead and his son attainted, Richard would have been the rightful king.

The revisionists contend that Parliament settled the issue in 1484 by passing an act declaring the princes illegitimate and Richard the rightful heir. They point out that, according to Blackstone, if the throne becomes vacant, it is Parliament that decides who is to be king. But whether the throne was, in fact, "vacant" is a different question. If Edward V was not illegitimate, there was no vacancy; and who then was to decide the issue of his legitimacy?

Levine argues that matters of legitimacy were within the exclusive jurisdiction of the ecclesiastical courts, not Parliament. This may be correct where the issue of legitimacy goes only to status—i.e., was a child legitimate or not? It may not be correct where the issue was the right to occupy the throne, even where that issue turned on legitimacy. England's great jurist, Lord Coke, wrote that "the power and jurisdiction of Parliament is so transcendant and absolute, that it cannot be confined either for causes or persons within any bounds. It can regulate or new model the succession to the crown."

In any event, Levine's argument goes only to the procedural question of whether Parliament acted in excess of its jurisdiction in deciding the issue, not to whether its decision was substantively correct. That is, Levine's point goes only to the issue of whether the princes' illegitimacy was decided in the wrong forum. It has nothing to do with whether, applying the substantive rules governing the issue, they were, in fact, illegitimate.

If there was a significant doubt as to Parliament's jurisdiction, why didn't Richard seek an ecclesiastical ruling? Gairdner takes a very pragmatic view of that issue. As he puts it, "[t]his was a question which properly it did not become a secular court to entertain. Yet to have referred it to a spiritual court, from which an appeal might have been carried out of the realm to Rome, was a course fraught with manifest inconvenience. . . . However bad in fact the King's title might be, and however objectionable in theory was the reference to Parliament of a question that should have come under the cognisance of a spiritual court, the peace of the Kingdom required that his title should be confirmed; and the fears of new invasions or disturbances completely overruled all other considerations."

Possibly, as Gairdner suggests and Levine asserts, the decision by Parliament was a legal nullity. But that did not make the princes legitimate for purposes of succeeding to the throne. Either they were bastards for that purpose or they were not, regardless of whether a proper forum (or any forum) adjudicated the matter. If they were illegitimate for that special purpose, they were disqualified, and Richard was the rightful king, even if neither the church courts nor Parliament decided the issue.

After all, rules of law can be applied to ascertain legal relationships in the absence of a court ruling. A competent lawyer can state whether A has a contract with B or whether X is entitled to inherit Y's estate, even though the matter has not been adjudicated by any court. Similarly, we can seek to apply the substantive rules that probably governed such matters to determine the legitimacy of the two princes, even without adjudication by a court.

While we may not be able to reach a certain and unqualified determination of that issue as a matter of fifteenth-century law, if we consider the probable rules then controlling such matters, we can at least conclude this: Assuming that there was, in fact, a precontract, Richard's assertion that the princes were disqualified as rulers and that he was the rightful king was not only a colorable claim, but a strong one. If so, should we not be somewhat less ready to brand him a ursurper?

A. J. Pollard argues that Edward V could have been legitima-

tized by the act of coronation. Perhaps this was an option available to the protector, the council and the assembly of the three
estates. But, even if Pollard is correct, legitimization of a royal
bastard was certainly not mandatory. If the boys were bastards, it
was also a lawful option to leave them in that state and to make
Richard king.

Given the choice between crowning a proven military leader
with an excellent record of governance, on the one hand, and an
unproven and illegitimate twelve-year-old boy dominated by the
Woodvilles, on the other, the choice would have been an easy
one.

Not surprisingly, after disclosure of the precontract there
appears to have been no more support for legitimizing Prince
Edward by coronation than there was to reverse the attainder of
Clarence and crown his eight-year-old son.

Russell's draft of a speech for the scheduled opening of
Parliament on June 25 urged that Richard's protectorship and
governance of Edward V be continued until the young king was
of an age to rule. But the draft was almost surely prepared before
the council learned of the precontract and cannot be taken as an
indication that Russell wanted or expected Prince Edward to be
crowned even if he was illegitimate.

♔ THE CORONATION

On July 4, 1483, Richard III and his wife, Anne, moved to the royal lodgings in the Tower, where both of the princes were now residing.

Clarence's son, Warwick, had also lived in the Tower after his father's attainder in 1478, having been ordered by Edward IV to remain there in the custody of the marquess of Dorset. After the loss of Woodville power, however, young Warwick's status had changed. According to Mancini, he was placed in Richard's own household. It appears that, throughout Richard's reign, he was considered free and was treated with respect if not deference.

There is no indication that the two princes were ill treated in the period between their being declared illegitimate and Richard's coronation. It was Richard's stated intention to raise them as honored members of the royal family. Bishop Morton said that Richard "promised that he would so provide for them and so maintain them in honorable estate as that all the realm ought and should be content." Did Richard mean to keep that promise? The claim, of course, is that he did not and that the boys never left the Tower alive.

In early July, the reinforcements Richard had summoned from York on June 10 finally arrived in London. There were four or five thousand of them, many more than the two hundred horsemen supplied by York. But their appearance was shabby, their equipment rusty and their demeanor pacific. This seemed to relieve the Londoners who had feared the onset of a menacing northern host. The army bivouacked in a field outside the city, where Richard reviewed them and received their cheers.

The coronation of Richard and Anne took place on Sunday, July 6, 1483, at Westminster Abbey. The aristocracy of England, both Lancastrian and Yorkist, was fully represented, and it appeared that factional strife was finally at an end.

A Woodville bishop was in attendance; and even Lady Stanley, the mother of Henry Tudor, bore the new queen's train. Buckingham played a significant role, carrying Richard's train. The proud duke also carried the staff of the lord high steward, although John Howard, who had been made duke of Norfolk, had also been appointed lord high steward and should have had the honor of carrying the staff.

Despite this, there is conjecture that Buckingham felt that as first peer of the realm and a descendant of Edward III, his role in the coronation should have been even more prominent, and that others were given roles of too much significance.

Richard had tried to spread the honors around. Howard, for example, while denied the staff of steward, was permitted the honor of carrying the crown. The earl of Northumberland carried the blunt sword of mercy, and Lord Stanley bore the constable's mace, even though he was not constable, an office soon bestowed on Buckingham.

Lavishly robed, Richard and Anne entered the abbey walking barefoot, as was the custom. Before the high altar their robes were removed and, bare to the waist, they were anointed with holy oil and re-dressed in cloth of gold. Cardinal Bourchier then placed the crowns on their heads, as the imposing sound of the great organs filled the abbey. They were now formally confirmed as king and queen.

X

👑 "A RUMOUR AROSE"

Two weeks after the coronation, Richard set out on a progress through England accompanied by a large royal party, including Clarence's son, Warwick. Lord Stanley was a member of the party, perhaps not so much for the pleasure of his company as to keep an eye on him.

Richard may have felt more comfortable in leaving the capital knowing that the great French schemer, Louis XI, was now mortally ill and not likely to make any new and aggressive moves.

What had happened to the two princes? Horace Walpole, in his "Historic Doubts," argues that the older of the two walked in Richard's coronation or at least was intended to do so. This, he said, proved that Richard treated young Edward with honor and respect, that the prince recognized Richard's right to the throne and that he was not murdered—at least not before the July 4 coronation. Walpole based his contention on an entry in what he called the "coronation roll," an accounting that listed the purchase of a large amount of fabric of various colors for "Lorde Edward, son of the late Kyng Edward the Fourthe" and his attendants.

Walpole believed that this entry referred to Richard's coronation, rather than young Edward's, since the entry appeared among others for Richard's ceremony, and since "Lorde Edward, son of the late Kyng Edward the Fourthe" would hardly have been an appropriate reference to a young man already acclaimed king and about to be formally crowned. It would, however, fit an illegitimate son of the late king, who was still an earl, and thus a "Lorde," in his own right.

Contemporaries of Walpole, particularly Dr. Jeremiah Milles, dean of Exeter and president of the Society of Antiquaries, argued that this document was not, in fact, Richard's "coronation roll," but only the "wardrobe account," a record of expenses of the royal wardrobe over a period of time. Milles contended that the entry Walpole found was out of order, making it appear, from its location, that it pertained to Richard's coronation when in fact it pertained to the coronation that had been planned for Edward V.

In a subsequent reply to Dr. Milles, Walpole conceded that he had given the document an incorrect name. He continued to assert, however, that the entries referring to "Lorde Edward" relate to Richard's coronation, not that planned for the young man himself.

Examination of the original wardrobe account tends to support Walpole's conclusion. A heading on folio eighty-eight refers specifically to the "DELIVEREE OF STUFF DELIVERED TO, FOR AND AYENST ... THE MOOST NOBLE CORONATIONS AWAL OF OURE SOUVERAYNE LORDE KYNG RICHARD THE THIRD AS OF OUR SOUVERAYNE LADY THE QUENE." This is followed by a large number of consecutive pages listing the materials and items of clothing to be worn by the king, the queen and numerous members of the nobility at *Richard's* coronation. There are various subheadings, all referring to the coronation of the "KYNG" or the "QUENE" or both. Those referring to the "QUENE" list costumes and materials for the female attendants at the ceremony such as the "Duchesse of Suffolk" and the "Countesse of Rychemonde." Of course, at the planned coronation of twelve-year-old Edward V, there would have been no "QUENE."

At folio 115, continuing the list, with no apparent change of subject, is the subheading in smaller letters "yit the deliveree off sylkes and also other stuff." This is followed by materials for lesser persons such as "two chamberers of our said souverayne Lady the Quene" and "many dyverse persons" for whom materials have "in haste" been commanded by "my Lorde of Bukkingham."

Again, the reference to the "Quene" excludes the possibility that the coronation referred to is that of Edward V.

On folio 115, immediately following this list of materials for lesser persons in connection with Richard's coronation is the entry entitled "To Lorde Edward, son of the late Kyng Edward the Fourthe, for his apparaill and array . . . " This designation, seemingly impossible as a reference to a new young king, is followed by an extensive list of apparel on folio 115 and continuing over onto 115b and 116. This, in turn, is followed on folio 116 and 116b by a list of apparel for the "henxemen of the said Lorde Edward," once again using that manifestly inappropriate title for a young man already king and about to be formally crowned.

The next entry, on folio 117 is a heading referring to the "DELIVEREE OFF DIVERS CLOTHES OFF GOLD AND SYLKES" delivered by commandment of the king unto "KNYGHTES AND OTHER DIVERS PERSONS AYENST THE SAIDE MOOSTE NOBLE CORONATION OF OURE SAID SOUVERAYNE LADY THE QUENE"—still necessarily the coronation of Richard and Anne. Among the "DIVERS PERSONS" provided with such gold and silks "FOR OURE SAID SOUVERAYNE LORDE THE KYNGES MOOSTE NOBLE CORONATION," folio 117 shows yards of blue cloth of gold for the "DUKE OF BUKKINGHAM." Thereafter, the coronation list continues—finally ending on folio 118b. Once again, we cannot be talking about the coronation of Edward V, because of the references to the "QUENE."

The next entry moves on to a different time period entirely. It starts with a heading stating that it delineates "stuff" delivered "between the coronations of the kynge and quene and the feeste of the purification." Here again, the reference to the "quene" precludes the notion that the entries are referring to the coronation of Edward V.

Given the placement of the entries pertaining to "Lorde Edward" and the manner in which he is described, it seems extremely unlikely that these entries referred to apparel for his own coronation. A king, even before his coronation, would be called "the Kyng," just as Richard was called "the Kyng." He would not be called "Lorde Edward, son of the late Kyng Edward the Fourthe."

Nor is it likely that a king would be attended at his coronation by other young chums or "henxemen." That phrase seems far more consistent with an honored young earl attending his uncle's coronation with a number of youthful friends as attendants.

Moreover, it seems highly improbable that, somehow, an out-of-place entry referring to material previously delivered for young Edward's scheduled coronation was fitted between all the numerous entries for the coronation of Richard and his "Quene." Was a space left in the middle of the list for Richard's coronation that turned out to be a convenient place to put an entry relating to a totally different and earlier coronation that never took place? It seems most unlikely. Nor is it much more likely that this entry, found among all the others relating to Richard's coronation, refers to items delivered to Edward for some other occasion entirely, as has also been suggested.

Dr. Milles argued that the wardrobe account was only prepared in 1484, after Richard occupied the throne and that it would have been imprudent to have referred then to the displaced prince as "Kyng Edward V." This might explain why Edward was not referred to as the king, but it does not satisfactorily explain why the entries pertaining to the boy's robes and those of his "henxemen" were placed in the middle of the orders for Richard's coronation, rather than preceding them.

Milles concludes that Peter Curtys, who prepared the account, had no choice but to list the items for young Edward's coronation among those for Richard's, because if he had listed them at an earlier place, as materials for Edward's own coronation, he would have been required to call Edward the "Kyng," since that's what the boy was when his coronation was being planned.

But Milles's conclusion relies on the assumption that Curtys chose this strange and inaccurate means of recording the prince's entry, when he could have handled the matter in a straightforward, easy and accurate manner. If these were really materials ordered for Edward's coronation, rather than Richard's, and the entries were made in 1484, rather than in 1483, there is no reason why Curtys could not have listed them in their proper chronological order as stuffs ordered for the "intended coronation" of "the

Lorde Edward." By 1484, there was no need to call the young man "Kyng," even if he had been entitled to that appellation in the spring of 1483 when the materials were ordered. There would have been nothing improper in Curtys making the entries after Richard took the throne. He had no need to pretend that they were made a year earlier. Everyone knew that Edward had been scheduled to have a coronation. Mentioning it as the intended coronation of "the Lorde Edward" would hardly be an insult to King Richard.

Besides, if the aborted coronation was a sensitive matter, Curtys could have put the entries in their proper order, simply describing them as "stuffs ordered for the Lorde Edward" without mentioning any coronation at all.

What seems far more probable is what appears to have been the case from the pages themselves—that these materials, described in the midst of numerous entries clearly referring to Richard's coronation, were intended to be worn by Prince Edward at that event.

If so, it seems a fair inference that Edward was, at one time at least, expected to attend the coronation, that he was alive when the materials were ordered and that, at that point in time, he was still treated with respect. Indeed, the fact that he was to be permitted a number of richly dressed "henxemen" suggests considerable respect indeed.

The fact that Cardinal Bourchier set the crown on Richard's head at his coronation also suggests that the two princes were still alive at the time. Elizabeth Woodville had entrusted her younger son to Bourchier when she consented to his release from sanctuary. Would the cardinal have been willing to play this critical role in Richard's coronation if he knew or suspected that the princes had been murdered? Of course, Bourchier, even though charged with the well-being of the younger prince, may have been unaware of his death. It seems most unlikely, however.

Do these facts prove that the princes were not subsequently murdered? Certainly not. If Richard were really the scheming, dissembling monster portrayed by the Tudor chroniclers, why wouldn't he put on an outward show of respect for the young prince he intended to kill?

So far as can be determined, however, both princes were still alive and residing in the Tower when Richard left on his progress in the latter part of July. Mancini reported that, after the execution of Hastings on June 13, "all the attendants who had waited upon the King [Edward V] were debarred access to him. He and his brother were withdrawn into the inner apartments of the Tower proper, and day by day began to be seen more rarely behind the bars and windows, til at length they ceased to appear altogether."

According to Mancini, "the physician Argentine, the last of his attendants whose services the king enjoyed, reported that the young king, like a victim prepared for sacrifice, sought remission of his sins by daily confession and penance, because he believed that death was facing him."

Mancini left England in July 1483 and wrote his report in December of that year. "The physician Argentine" was Dr. John Argentine, who spoke Italian and whom Mancini encountered in Europe between July and December. Accordingly, what Mancini wrote in December 1483 about the plight of the young princes was not necessarily information he had been given before his July departure. It may represent what he was told months later by Dr. Argentine.

Argentine was highly disposed to the Tudor cause and later was appointed by Henry VII physician to Prince Arthur, the king's first-born son. Kendall suggests that, while in the Tower, the older prince may have been in poor health. If this was the case, it is not inconceivable that Mancini or Argentine, or both, misconstrued the boy's fear of death from natural causes as fear of death by violence. On the other hand, Argentine's assessment could have been correct. Prince Edward had been given no reason to trust his powerful uncle, whom he hardly knew and who had displaced him on the throne. He may well have had serious concern for his own safety.

Mancini's report is ambiguous as to whether the prince was actually deprived of attendants or whether the former attendants—undoubtedly staunch Woodville supporters—were simply replaced with attendants thought to be loyal to Richard. There certainly would be nothing sinister or even surprising if the latter was the case.

More wrote that Richard "removed also divers of the princes olde servantes from him, *and set newe aboute him.*" More also says that, on the night of the princes' murders, *all* of the servants had been removed except Will Slaughter, known as "Black Will," who was "set to serve them and see them sure." Although ambiguous, this suggests that, until that night, there had been various servants assigned to the princes' care.

Mancini reports that the two boys were moved to "the inner apartments of the Tower proper." They are commonly thought to have been moved to the Garden Tower, which was renamed the Bloody Tower in the reign of James I, for reasons having nothing to do with the princes. Until then, it was called the Garden Tower, because it adjoined the garden of the Tower lieutenant's lodgings.

It is possible that the princes were moved to the White Tower, the ancient central keep. This would seem more consistent with Mancini's words. The White Tower, more than any other structure, would likely be called "the Tower proper." Moreover, the Garden Tower was located even closer to the outer walls than the royal apartment, where the boys originally resided. It would seem less likely to be called the "inner apartments." Perhaps there were two moves, first to the Garden Tower and then to the more central White Tower. Both Towers had comfortable accommodations suitable for highborn occupants.

If Mancini's report is true, it is not clear why the boys were moved. It might have seemed more appropriate, now that they had been declared illegitimate, that they be moved from the king's apartments to other quarters. Confinement, of course, could be the reason—to prevent their being taken from the Tower against Richard's will. Another possibility is just the opposite—that their location was changed to mask their removal from the Tower grounds to another place entirely.

Some apparently feared the worst for the two boys from early on. Between 1483 and 1488 a citizen of London (or possibly a succession of citizens) kept a series of anonymous notes including reports concerning political struggles of the period. These "Historical Notes" refer to "a resistance made in the parlement tyme" by four servants of the king who were "hangyd at The

Towur Hill." "Parlement tyme" apparently referred to the assembly of the three estates on June 25, 1483, at which Richard's claim to the throne was accepted.

A cryptic letter written by Richard from Minster Lovell on July 29, 1483, to his chancellor, John Russell, refers to "certaine personnes" who have, "of late," engaged in a mysterious "enterprise" and have been "attached" and are "in warde." Richard directs Russell to issue such "letters of commission" as Russell and "our counsaill" shall determine "to sitte upon thaym and to proceed to the due execucion of our lawes in that behalve. . . ."

Was the "enterprise" to which Richard refers in his letter the "resistance" in late June mentioned in the anonymous "Historical Notes"? Maybe. But maybe not. Sometimes historians have a tendency to connect unconnected events or references because of their proximity in time. It is possible that neither the "resistance" nor the "enterprise" had anything to do with the two princes. However, Richard's letter may have had another relationship to the fate of the princes. We will return to that later.

Certainly, by July, there was some public concern for the princes' safety. Was it justified? Was Richard motivated to kill them? Motive is, of course, one of the primary factors to be considered in evaluating guilt or innocence. There are few motiveless murders. The seemingly senseless drive-by shooting of a gang member or his family is based on misguided notions of territory, allegiance and revenge. Even the serial killer has a "motive," albeit a psychotic, delusional one, difficult for the ordinary citizen to comprehend.

One of the principal arguments of the traditionalists is that Richard III had a strong motive to kill the two princes. Is that conclusion justified?

Revisionists ask why Richard would kill the princes when they had been declared illegitimate, removing them as rival claimants to the throne. The cynical and perhaps realistic answer is not difficult. Given the unreliability of the barons and the readiness of powerful self-serving nobles to coalesce behind any possible candidate for the throne, could Richard ever really feel safe while the princes were alive? Probably not.

The act that declared their illegitimacy could have been

reversed at any time. In fact, it was reversed by Henry VII. If colorable justification were needed for such a reversal, there was always the argument that Elizabeth's good faith in marrying Edward IV made the boys legitimate despite the Eleanor Butler precontract. But any sort of legal argument would suffice. Power, not law, would be the primary determinant of whether the act would be reversed.

If a sufficiently powerful group of nobles coalesced behind the Woodvilles and Prince Edward, they might overthrow Richard and place the young man on the throne. A reversal of the princes' illegitimacy would then come quickly and easily from a complaisant Parliament. As long as the princes were alive, that danger would remain. It had the potential to render Richard's reign unstable and to put his life at risk.

On the other hand, the death of the princes might not solve Richard's problem. Weir points to a Woodville plot in July 1483 to smuggle Edward IV's daughters out of England, so that they would be available to take the throne if their brothers were killed. Weir argues that this plot demonstrates that Richard could never be secure on the throne while the princes lived. In fact, the plot shows just the opposite. Richard's motive to kill the princes was lessened, not increased, by the potential claim of their sisters. If their illegitimacy was reversed, Edward IV's daughters could succeed him, even if his sons were dead. Why kill the princes, only to face the claims of their sisters?

It would be more difficult to rally support for a female candidate—especially a young one. But a female candidate could find a powerful husband, who might be considered a suitable king. As we will see, Edward's eldest daughter found Henry Tudor; and, some two hundred years later, Princess Mary, the daughter of James II, married William of Orange, enabling the pair to depose and replace her father on the English throne.

Even aside from the royal princesses, there were other candidates for the throne if the two princes were killed. There was Clarence's son, Warwick, whose attainder could have been reversed. There was the able and attractive earl of Lincoln, a son of Richard's sister. Finally, there was Henry Tudor, forever plotting in exile. Killing the princes could eliminate the most obvious and viable claimants, but it would fall short of putting an end to Richard's problem.

We cannot conclude, as has been claimed, that Richard had *no* motive to kill Edward V and his brother. He did. But, as will be discussed below, other "suspects" had similar, and seemingly stronger motives.

Even among those who believe that the princes were killed during Richard's reign, there is no clear answer as to *when* this occurred. On June 28, 1483, shortly after Richard was proclaimed king, John Howard was given the title duke of Norfolk, a title that had previously been held by the younger prince. Prince Richard had received the title only through marriage, pursuant to his premarital arrangement with his deceased child-bride, Anne Mowbray. By the normal laws of inheritance, the title would have been Lord Howard's. It was to revert to Howard's family if the prince died without heirs.

Does this mean that, as early as June, 1483, Prince Richard was dead? Not at all. Title changes by the king's decree may have been inconsistent with the normal laws of inheritance; but they were not uncommon. Even if not legally justified, there were cogent reasons for this particular change. With Prince Richard declared illegitimate, it may have seemed appropriate that Howard and his family get their title back without waiting to see if the prince died without heirs. It could also be argued that Prince Richard's premarital agreement had no validity because it had been procured by the fraudulent concealment of his illegitimacy.

Moreover, Howard had rendered loyal and important service to the king and to Edward IV before him. He had been one of the men on whose advice and aid Richard had principally relied in the critical days of May and June, 1483. The Norfolk title also carried with it the right to be earl marshal, giving the title holder an important function at Richard's coronation. Bestowing the title on Howard before the July 6 coronation cannot be considered reliable evidence that the younger prince was already dead.

An official warrant dated July 18, 1483, authorizes payment of wages to fourteen men for services to Edward IV and to "Edward Bastard late called King Edward the Vth." However, the services could have been rendered days before the warrant, and it does not necessarily show that "Edward Bastard" was still alive on the 18th.

Rous says the princes were killed three months after Richard took control of the young king. This would place their death at the end of July, after Richard had left London on his royal progress.

At this point, we might reconsider Richard's letter of July 29 to his chancellor, John Russell. Richard's cryptic phrases, such as "certaine personnes" who "of late" engaged in "an enterprise" of which the king doubts not Russell has "herd," suggests that, while Richard wanted the matter raised with the Council and wanted the accused men punished, he was reluctant to be explicit about who they were and what crime they had committed.

Why? The direction to consult with "our counsaill" suggests that, whatever was the offense and whoever were the offenders, the situation was an unusual and delicate one that warranted special consideration. Could Richard have just learned that "certaine personnes" had murdered the princes, believing, as in the case of Henry II and Thomas á Becket, that they were acting in the King's interest? This has been suggested. Like so many theories bearing upon Richard's conduct, it can neither be proved nor disproved.

More—who, of course, accuses Richard of procuring the murder—places it in August 1483, which would also be during the royal progress.

The Great Chronicle of London, written some thirty years after the fact, reports that, during the time Sir Edward Shaa was mayor, "the childyrn of King Edward were seen shotying and playying in the Gardyn of the Towyr by sundry tymes." Because Shaa's term in office continued from October 1482 to October 1483, this entry is not particularly helpful. The "shotying and playying" could have taken place any time between June 1483, when the younger prince was released, and October 1483, when Shaa left office. Besides, the Great Chronicle is generally unreliable on chronology, sometimes even placing events in the wrong year.

The reference to "playying in the Gardyn" seems to indicate a lack of close confinement, at least at that point in time. This, in itself, is not inconsistent with Mancini's report about the princes being moved to "inner apartments" of "the Tower proper." The move could have been after the boys were seen "shotying and playying."

Mancini wrote that "I have seen many men burst forth into tears and lamentations when mention was made of him [Edward V] after his removal from men's sight; and already there was a suspicion that he had been done away with. Whether, however, he has been done away with, and by what manner of death, so far I have not at all discovered."

This would indicate that the princes' move to the "inner apartments," Prince Edward's "removal from men's sight," the "lamentations" and the "suspicion" of his murder all occurred before July 1483, when Mancini left London. Of course, as Mancini himself indicates, that does not mean that either prince had actually been killed, then or ever.

Moreover, this aspect of the report was, on its face, only gossip and speculation that Mancini heard from others, such as the men he saw "burst forth into tears and lamentation." It may, however, have been true. Sometimes gossip is.

According to the Croyland Chronicle "a rumour arose" in the summer of 1483 "that king Edward's sons, by some unknown manner of violent destruction, had met their fate." We are not told how the rumor "arose" or why. P. M. Kendall translates the Chronicle's Latin as "a rumour was spread." But "spread" seems to go beyond what the chronicler said: "*vulgatum est dictos Regis Edwardi pueros quo genere violenti interitus ignoratur decessisse in fata.*" Nevertheless, it is unlikely that the rumor arose spontaneously. Most probably, it was in fact "spread" by the forces that were, even then, about to rebel against Richard's rule.

If it was John Russell, Richard's lord chancellor, who wrote or supplied the information for the Chronicle, it is significant that, even in 1486, *three years after the event, and writing under a Tudor King,* this consummate "insider" did not know or would not reveal the actual fate of the princes.

While referring to *the "rumour"* of their deaths, the chronicler makes no comment on the truth of that "rumour." Throughout his account, he avoids any statement as to whether, in fact, the princes were dead and, if so, who killed them.

Why does he limit himself to passing on a "rumour" of the boys' deaths? Why does he omit any positive statement that Richard killed them or even that they were dead? Does this imply that he considered the rumor to have been false? That he considered Richard innocent? That he thought the boys were still alive? That he did not know if they were dead or, if so, who killed them? Or, that he knew these things, but would not say?

If it was the last, why would the anonymous chronicler be reluctant to say that the boys were dead or that Richard had killed then, if he knew, or even believed, that this was the case? He was ready to attack Richard wherever he could, and certainly neither assertion would have displeased Henry VII, the new king in whose reign the account was written.

The Second Continuator does append to his own account a poem, which he says was written by someone else (a "certain poet"), about the three Richards of England. The unknown poet uses the words *fratris opprimeret proles* with reference to Richard III. Pronay and Cox translate this as "he supressed his brother's progeny." *Opprimeret* could also be translated as "smothered"; but the translation of Pronay and Cox is probably the correct one. This is as close as we can come to finding a comment on the subject by the Second Continuator. It is not very close.

Despite the "suspicion" and the "rumour," Sir George Buck wrote that the princes were "living freely and securely (and without question) long after their murder was said to be done."

Here, we encounter an example of the overenthusiastic interpretation of documents and events that all too often has characterized this controversy. It has been reported that at the end of 1483, John Kendal, Richard's secretary, was appointed "keeper of the princes' wardrobe within the city of London." It is difficult to conceive of any other "princes" to whom this could refer. The word "princes'" in the entry is reported to be *plural* possessive, and the writer adds that "Richard's own son, the new Prince of Wales, still lived in the North, and what other 'princes' were there?" The reader is left to infer that both princes must still have been alive.

Here is the actual entry for December 12, 1483, recorded in British Library Harleian Manuscript 433:

"We have gevene & graunted to oure trusty servant and secretarie John Kendale the keeping of the place called the prince warderobe/and have licenced him to dwelle in the same . . . "

The word "prince" is not plural possessive and, obviously "Kendale" was being authorized to live in a building named the "prince warderobe," rather than, as reported, being appointed to take charge of "the princes' wardrobe." The appointment provides no evidence whatsoever that the princes were still alive.

In January 1484, shortly after Mancini's report was submitted to Bishop Cato, Guillaume de Rochefort, the chancellor of France, made a speech to the French Estates General, publicly accusing Richard of having murdered his nephews. De Rochefort's speech cannot be taken as reliable evidence that the princes had actually been killed by that time or that Richard killed them.

There was, as we have seen, a "rumour" of their deaths, and de Rochefort would have been quite ready to embrace it as the truth. His intentions were probably more anti-English than anti-Ricardian. He charged that King Edward's "children, already big and courageous, have been slaughtered with impunity, and their murderer, with the support of the people, has received the crown." He also pointed out that England had experienced twenty-six rebellions since the time of William the Conqueror.

At the time, France was ruled by a minor king, Charles VIII, and governed by his sister as regent. Perhaps de Rochefort was creating a horror story about an English regicide in order to deter such an occurrence in France.

De Rochefort knew Angelo Cato, the man to whom Mancini submitted his report. De Rochefort's brother was a close associate of Cato's. Apparently, the French chancellor knew Mancini as well. At the time Mancini was completing his report at Beaugency, de Rochefort was in the same area.

As we have seen, Mancini referred to the existence of a "suspicion" among Londoners that Edward V, the older of the two princes, had been killed. Mancini added that he was unsure of the truth of this rumor. It is a fair inference that either Mancini or Cato passed on the rumor to de Rochefort and that this was the source of the French chancellor's public charge. Possibly, de Rochefort never learned of Mancini's uncertainty as to whether the rumor was true, or possibly he was told, but decided not to mention it.

It has been argued that *Titulus Regius,* a formal act of Parliament passed in January 1484, reconfirming Richard's right to the throne, refers to the princes in the present tense, indicating that the members of Parliament believed then that the princes were still alive. Possibly they did. But the act itself doesn't prove this. The portion of the act that arguably uses the present tense in referring to the princes is simply repeating and ratifying the "Rolle" enacted by the assembled three estates in June 1483, when the two boys were almost certainly alive.

Moreover, the parliamentary statement is that "All th' Issue and Chilren of the seid King Edward, been Bastards, and unable to inherite or to clayme any thing by Inheritance, by the Lawe and Custome of Englond." This probably is the present tense, with the word "been" used as "being." But the statement speaks of Edward's "issue and chilren," not his sons. The reference could have been to Edward's daughters, who were clearly alive in January 1484 and, but for their having been declared bastards, might have been considered heirs to the throne, even if their brothers were dead.

After referring to the princes' "shotying and playing in the garden" during Shaa's mayorality, the Great Chronicle reports that "all the wyntyr season" of the next mayor's term (which began in October 1483) "the land was in good Quyet, but after Estryn (Easter, 1484) there was much whysperyng among the people that the King had put the childyrn of Kyng Edward to deth."

Does this mean that the princes were alive until Easter, 1484? Not at all. A rebellion occurred in October 1483. When it was put down, the land may have been considered "in good quiet," even if the princes had were no longer alive. And, certainly, there could have been a substantial interval between their actual murders and the "whispering among the people."

The Great Chronicle has the "whispering" start after Easter, at least six months after the Croyland Chronicle's "rumour arose." Possibly the "rumour arose" among the nobility in the summer of 1483, but did not reach the ears of "the people" until the following Easter. Of course, the Great Chronicle may simply have gotten the dates wrong.

An ordinance regulating King Richard's household in the North, dated July 23, 1484, provides that "The children" are to be "togeder at oon (one) brakefast." Were these "children" the two princes? Had they been moved from the Tower to Richard's estates in the North?

The high rank of "the children" to which the ordinance relates is indicated by another entry, specifying that no livery is to exceed a stated allowance "but oonly to my Lord and the children." The "Lord" referred to was Richard's nephew, the earl of Lincoln. But who were "the children"? Except for these entries, there is no specific record of any high-ranking "children" being part of the King's Northern household on this date. But the ordinance may refer to how the household should be run in the future, and the reference could have been to young nobles, such as Clarence's son, Warwick, who arrived a few weeks later.

An entry in the Tower wardrobe account dated March 9, 1485, calls for the delivery of clothes to the footman of the "Lord Bastard." It suggests that the "Lord Bastard" was still alive. But who was he? Prince Edward remained a "Lord" even after being declared illegitimate. But the reference could also have been to Richard's illegitimate son, John, who, although not technically a "Lord," might have been referred to in that manner as a courtesy. Of course, as was so often the case with fifteenth-century records, this entry could also have been misdated.

Regardless of the time of the murders, the traditionalists are in general agreement as to *how* they happened. That popular version of the boys' deaths comes from More, who probably got it from Morton. It was adopted by Hall and Holinshed, put on the stage by Shakespeare and then accepted by most of the world.

There was not always such agreement. It had been asserted that the princes were poisoned, starved to death, thrown in the sea, drowned in malmsey, stabbed, pierced with venom, put to the sword and, as More reported, smothered with their bedclothes.

According to More's account, when Richard was on the way to Gloucester during his 1483 progress, he decided that the continued existence of the princes threatened his reign. This would have been at the end of July or early August. Having reached that conclusion, says More, Richard directed one John Grene to convey a letter to Sir Robert Brackenbury, who had just been appointed constable of the Tower. The letter ordered Brackenbury to kill the princes.

It seems unlikely that a man in Richard's position would have put such an order in writing. But perhaps he thought that only a written order would be obeyed.

More writes that Brackenbury, the new constable and a man widely known for his integrity, refused to carry out the king's order. Grene rode back and reported Brackenbury's refusal to Richard during the second week in August.

The king, by then at Warwick, cried out to a "secret" and unnamed page "Oh whom shall a man trust?" The page responded that there was a man lying just outside the door who would do whatever the king asked. That man was Sir James Tyrell, who wished to rise higher in the king's service. He had been held down by Sir Richard Ratcliffe and Sir William Catesby, who, according to More, were reluctant to share their power as the king's closest aides. More tells us that Richard, who had been sitting on the toilet during this history-making discussion (a nice Tudor touch), rose and confronted Tyrell. As the page had predicted, Tyrell agreed to do the King's bidding.

On the morrow, More writes, Richard sent Tyrell on his way to Brackenbury with a second letter. This one directed the constable to turn over the Tower keys to Tyrell for one night, so that he might accomplish what the king had commanded. Acting somewhat out of character, Brackenbury obeyed this second order and gave Tyrell the keys.

According to More, Tyrell planned the murder for the following night and enlisted the aid of two others to do the actual killing. These were Miles Forest, one of the jailers, "a fellowe fleshed in murther before time," and John Dighton, Tyrell's horsekeeper, a "big brode square strong knave."

Around midnight, the three carried out their deadly plan. More tells us that Tyrell waited elsewhere while Forest and Dighton smothered the two boys with their bedclothes and laid them naked on the bed. Then they fetched Tyrell, who had Forest and Dighton bury the bodies "at the stayre foot, metely depe in the grounde under a great heape of stones."

More reports, however, that when Tyrell told Richard where the princes were buried, the king would not allow them to rest in "so vile a corner," but "would have them buried in a better place because thei wer a kinges sonnes." Accordingly, More says, Brackenbury's priest dug up the bodies and secretly reburied them in a place known only to him, which, because of his death, remains unknown. As we will see in chapter 17, this passage from More about the reburial of the princes is highly significant and creates a serious problem for the traditionalists.

According to More, Richard was so pleased at Tyrell's performance that he knighted him on the spot. But this is demonstrably untrue. Tyrell had been knighted by Edward IV twelve years earlier, in May 1471, for his service in the battle of Tewkesbury.

Nor was Sir James in any sense the striving, ambitious young fellow depicted by More. Edward IV had named Tyrell sheriff of Glamorgan and given him control of substantial Welsh properties. These offices made Tyrell a wealthy man. Tyrell was also well known to Richard. He had fought beside Richard in Scotland, where, for his bravery in battle, Richard made him a knight banneret in July 1482. Tyrell was a capable, well-regarded man on whom Richard had long depended for important services. He held the prestigious post of master of the horse at Richard's court. There would have been no need for him to have been called to the king's attention by an unnamed page.

These facts could easily have been ascertained by More had he done any checking at all. Was he aware that he had his facts wrong in this and many other respects? Deliberate falsification doesn't square with history's view of Sir Thomas as a great man of unshakable integrity. Of course, he was a young man when he wrote, and perhaps politically ambitious as well. Is integrity a trait acquired early or a luxury affordable only when one becomes mature and successful?

Whether More was being intentionally deceitful or actually believed what he wrote, but had not yet taken the time or trouble to check on the tales he heard from his informants, we cannot put great stock in the accuracy of his report. Possibly he did finally check on those tales and found them to be false, and this is why he abandoned his "History" half done.

More's account was not written until 1513 and probably between 1514 and 1518. His nephew, the printer William Rastell, who published More's incomplete "History" in 1557, published his own chronicles in 1529, some sixteen years after More wrote his work.

Oddly, Rastell provided two versions of the princes' death and the disposal of their bodies, neither of which accord with More. According to Rastell, "the most commyn opinyon" was that one boy was smothered and the other had his "throte hole" cut with a dagger. Their bodies were then placed in a chest which was thrown into the sea. In Rastell's other version, the boys were told to hide in a large chest lest they be harmed. When they obeyed, the chest was locked, then buried in "a great pytte under a steyre, which cheste was after caste into the blacke depes."

It seems strange that More and his nephew would not have shared their views and information on this subject which appears to have interested both of them. Yet, in 1529, Rastell was either ignorant of the princes' fate as described by More in 1513, or else he knew of that account but rejected it.

According to More, Richard wrote two letters directing commission of the murders, and nine people actually knew of the crime. These were Richard, Grene, Brackenbury, Will Slaughter, the unnamed page, Tyrell, Dighton, Forest and the priest who moved and reburied the bodies. With two letters floating about and that many people knowing the secret, it was not apt to remain a secret for long. Yet, many years passed before anyone wrote describing the crime, and much more time passed before that description was published.

Brackenbury was a man well known for his integrity, but also for his loyalty to Richard. Would he have refused the king's initial order to kill the princes? Perhaps. Brackenbury may well have considered murdering children—especially a child some still considered the rightful king—to be far outside the scope of his duties, no matter how broadly construed and no matter how strong his loyalties to Richard.

Having refused the first order, would Brackenbury obey the second and deliver the keys to Tyrell? Again, it is possible. This was an order he could obey without the same degree of personal risk. Perhaps he could pretend, even to himself, that he could not be sure of the king's purpose in giving Tyrell one night's control of the Tower.

For a man of noted integrity, Brackenbury did not behave as if he believed Richard had murdered the young king and his brother. He remained Richard's loyal and effective servant and, having led a contingent of Londoners to the battlefield, died fighting for him at Bosworth Field.

Interestingly, More, writing in 1513, adds that some men "remain yet in doubt" as to whether the princes were "destroyed" in Richard's time. Bacon, writing even later, described rumors, even during the reign of Henry VII, that one or both of the princes were still alive.

As we have said, Mancini, who wrote his account in December 1483, reports only a "suspicion" of their death. And the Croyland chronicler, who wrote in April 1486, during the reign of Henry VII, and either was an "insider," or was informed by one, reports only that a "rumour" arose that the princes had been killed. He never accuses Richard of the crime.

De Rochfort made his public accusation of murder in France in January 1484. If the boys were alive at the time, why didn't Richard produce them? Perhaps they were not alive, or perhaps he was unconcerned about what the French claimed, and felt that he could always produce the princes, if ever the claims and rumors created a serious political problem in England. Or, perhaps, he wished to keep them alive in some secret place where they would not be harmed but would not be a menace to him, as they might well have been if they were perceived to be alive and in England.

If the boys had been killed, why didn't Richard produce their bodies, claiming that they had died of disease or some other natural cause, thus making clear his right to the throne? As was the case with the body of Henry VI, the public need not have been given a close enough look even to speculate as to the cause of death, particularly if there was no blood or obvious wound. Given the limited scientific skills of the day, it is doubtful that even a close examination would have been able to distinguish disease from smothering as the cause of death. Even if there was some suspicion that a murder had occurred, there would be no proof. Richard would seem to have accumulated sufficient power to survive.

One possible answer is that the princes were still alive. Another is that they had been killed, but that Richard was unwilling to risk the reaction of the nobles and the public to their deaths. Another possible explanation is that Richard wished to keep the matter ambiguous.

If it was believed that the princes might be alive, no conspiracy would be likely to form around any other potential rival, such as Henry Tudor or Clarence's son, Warwick. Young Warwick was barred from the succession by the bill of attainder issued against his father. But attainders were frequently reversed; and, but for the attainder, young Warwick's claim to the succession was better than Richard's, since Warwick's father, Clarence, was the older of the two royal brothers. Ambiguity as to the fate and whereabouts of the princes might serve to dampen any enthusiasm for rallying to such a cause.

XI

"THE MOST UNTRUE CREATURE LIVING"

Whatever may have been the status of the two princes in the summer of 1483, the royal progress traveled on to Oxford, then Gloucester, then Warwick. Richard arrived in Gloucester on July 29. It is there that More has him decide on the murders, and it is there that he was briefly joined by the duke of Buckingham. What occurred between them has not been recorded; but the duke left the progress soon after arriving and traveled, perhaps with intervening stops, to Brecknock, his Welsh estate. Awaiting him there was his "prisoner," the wily and persuasive John Morton.

Richard remained in Warwick from August 8th to the 15th. More has Richard send Tyrell from there to London with the fatal order to get the keys to the Tower and kill the princes. From Warwick the royal party traveled to Coventry, Leicester and Nottingham and spent a few days at the castle of Pontefract.

On August 30, 1483, England's old enemy Louis XI of France died, leaving a minor heir, Charles VIII, and the government, in the hands of Louis' capable daughter, Anne of Beaujeau, as regent.

That same day, the royal progress reached York. The people of that city were always staunch supporters of Richard, the one king who was considered a northerner. On this occasion, they vied with each other in the warmth of their hospitality.

The Two Princes Edward and Richard in the Tower, 1483, by Sir John
Everett Millais. Bedford and Royal Holloway College. Courtesy The
Bridgeman Art Library.

Richard III, artist unknown. Royal Collection, Windsor Castle.

Richard III, artist unknown. The Society of Antiquaries.

Richard III, The Broken Sword Portrait, artist unknown.
The Society of Antiquaries.

X-ray of The Broken Sword Portrait. The Society of Antiquaries.

Edward IV, artist unknown. The Society of Antiquaries.

Henry VII, artist unknown. The Society of Antiquaries.

Elizabeth Woodville, artist unknown. Queen's College, Cambridge.

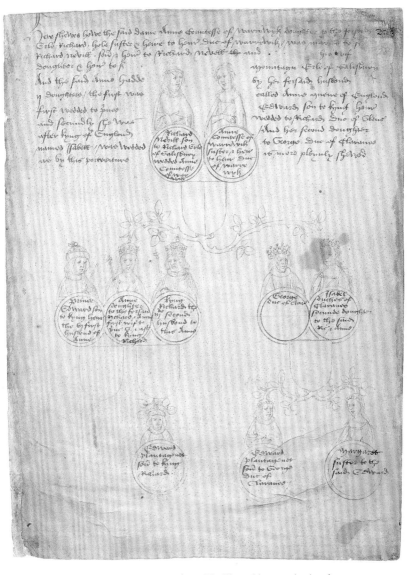

The Beauchamp Pageant. Anne Neville and her two husbands,
Richard and the Lancastrian Prince of Wales, artist unknown.
The British Library Department of Manuscripts.

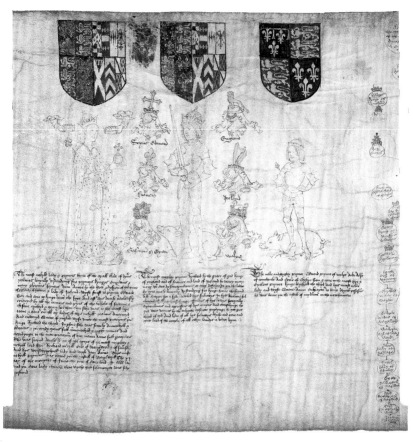

Rous Roll, Richard, Anne, and their son.
The British Library Department of Manuscripts.

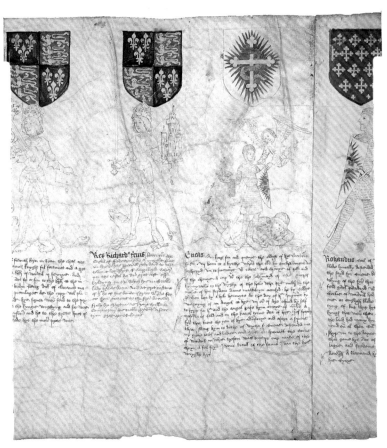

Rous Roll, Richard with sword and castle.
The British Library Department of Manuscripts.

The Family of Sir Thomas More, after Holbein.
The Thomas More Picture Trust.

Perkin Warbeck, artist unknown. Bibliotheque Municipale d'Arras.
Courtesy Art Resource.

The Battle of Bosworth Field. Richard III, wearing the crown, races across the field to get at Henry Tudor, whose horse rears at the oncoming charge. Richard slays Henry's standard bearer, Sir William Brandon, as Sir John Cheney rides forward to protect Henry. The red clad men of Sir William Stanley can be seen in the background. By Graham Turner. Courtesy of the artist.

Richard III and Anne Neville in Coronation Robes, artist unknown. The Duke of Buccleuch & Queensberry. Courtesy Weidenfeld Archive.

Richard III, James Butler. Courtesy Leicester City Council.

On September 8, Richard and Anne attended a splendid ceremony in York, creating their young son Edward Prince of Wales. This event has been described as a second coronation of Richard. It plainly was not.

At the castle of Sheriff Hutton, near York, Richard had ordered the establishment of his household of the North. Now he placed Clarence's son, Warwick, there in the care of his older cousin, the earl of Lincoln, Richard's loyal and dependable nephew.

Weir is certain that the princes were killed in September 1483, while Richard was at York. This conflicts with More, who has the murder occur in mid-August, while Richard was at Warwick. Weir calls this an error on More's part and blames it on the faulty memories of his informants.

Weir adopts a different time and place for the fatal order. She does this in order to make Tyrell's journey fit an entry in the wardrobe account. This entry indicates that Tyrell rode from York to London to collect costumes and wall hangings for the investiture of the Prince of Wales, which occurred on September 8. There is no record of Tyrell traveling between London and Warwick.

Using that entry to support her theory, Weir claims that the king's order to Tyrell was given at the end of August, and was given in York, rather than in Warwick. Because Tyrell had to arrive back in York by September 8 and because she says the journey between York and London took four days, she selects September 3 as the precise date of the murders. To Weir, everything flows from this. She has Tyrell leave York for London on August 30 or 31, arrive in London around September 3, kill the princes, pick up the materials and ride back to York in time for the investiture on September 8. All of this is inferred from the record of a trip by Tyrell from York to London to collect goods for the investiture.

Weir's theory conflicts not only with More, but also with the more reliable Croyland chronicler, who, contrary to both Weir and More, reports that the princes were still alive and in the Tower on September 8, the date of the Prince of Wales's investiture at York.

Sharon Turner's *History of England during the Middle Ages* also states that on August 31 the king dispatched orders to the wardrobe to send specified garments up to York. These entries do not, of course, show that the princes were killed at this time or that Tyrell killed them. In fact, the entry recording Tyrell's trip to London, possibly an innocent ride to pick up fabrics, may have been the source of the rumors that he killed the princes, rumors which Morton or others passed on to More as fact.

The festivities completed, the royal party left York on September 20 and proceeded to Lincoln. On October 11, the news suddenly reached Richard that his powerful ally and supposed friend, the duke of Buckingham, was leading a rebellion against him, that the Lancastrians, the former queen and the Woodvilles were involved and that the object of the rebels was, or appeared to be, placing Henry Tudor on the throne.

The Croyland Chronicle asserts that the conspiracy began in the South and West with the aim of releasing the princes from the Tower, presumably to place young Prince Edward on the throne. That is the point at which the chronicle states that "a rumour arose" that the boys had been put to death. The rebels turned to Henry Tudor, who was waiting in Brittany for just such a chance. Henry's mother, Lady Stanley, was undoubtedly ready to supply substantial aid and to persuade her husband's powerful family to go over to the rebels.

Elizabeth Woodville's participation in the conspiracy to put Henry Tudor on the throne suggests that she at least believed that the two princes were no longer alive. It would be hard to imagine the former queen or her family supporting Henry's claim, if they believed that either of her two sons were still living. If she believed them dead, however, her best chance for the recapture of her lost power would be to marry her eldest daughter to Henry Tudor and help him to take the crown from Richard.

This, of course, does not tell us that the princes were alive until the "rumour arose" or that, in fact, they were dead when the conspirators shifted their allegiance to Henry Tudor. While it would seem likely that the former queen would have had reliable sources of information about her sons' situation, she was still penned up in sanctuary at the time and may simply have been deceived by information flowing from Lady Stanley or other Tudor adherents.

We can also assume that the Croyland chronicler had reliable sources of information. Yet, as we have seen, even writing almost three years later in the reign of Henry Tudor, he does not report as a fact that the boys had been killed before the October rebellion, or ever—only that such "a rumour arose." Did Morton, Buckingham and Lady Stanley start that rumor for their own purposes? Did the former queen, closeted in Westminster, swallow that tale and support Henry in the belief that her sons were dead?

Apparently Richard had received information even before October 11 about a conspiracy involving the Woodvilles, the Lancastrians and Henry Tudor. It has been suggested that he even had prior knowledge of Buckingham's joining that conspiracy, and was carefully observing the mercurial duke's moves.

Whenever Richard first got information as to Buckingham's treachery, he must have been stunned. He had generously rewarded the duke with honors, power and wealth, giving him essentially the same authority Richard himself had once held to govern in Wales, plus vast powers in five English counties. Most recently, Richard had designated Buckingham constable of England for life, as well as lord chamberlain. He had accepted Buckingham's disputed claim to half of the enormously valuable Bohun estates, which had been held by the Crown ever since one of the two Bohun heiresses had married Henry IV.

The duke already owned half of these vast estates, which had come to him by reason of his direct descent from the other Bohun heiress. In July 1483, Richard approved his fervent request for the other half. Although Buckingham received a grant from Richard, final transfer of the title was made subject to the approval of Parliament. Perhaps Buckingham believed that Parliament would not confirm his full title and that Richard was not really going to fulfill his promise. Shakespeare has Richard sneeringly renege on his promise once he no longer needs Buckingham's support to seize the throne. This, very clearly, is incorrect.

Buckingham's father and grandfather died fighting for the Lancastrians, and it has been argued that he was always a

Lancastrian at heart. It seems most unlikely that this was the cause of his rebellion. The "rumour" that the two princes had been killed has also been given as the reason for Buckingham's decision to rebel. But, until shortly before the rebellion started, Buckingham either did not believe that the boys had been killed or pretended he did not believe it. According to Audrey Williamson, he wrote to Henry Tudor on September 24, 1483, urging his invasion of England and referring to the "liberation" of the two boys as one aim of that invasion.

Whether or not the duke believed that the princes had been murdered, it is unlikely that this was his motivation in rebelling. Not even More offers this as the explanation for his behavior.

Buckingham appears to have been an unstable and unprincipled man, full of vanity and self-importance. Evidently he was keenly envious of Richard's position. More reported that "as ye crown was first upon the protector's hed," some saw that Buckingham "could not abide ye sight thereof, but wried hys hed an other way." He seems also to have resented the significant role others were allowed to play in Richard's coronation; and he may have felt that, in leaving the matter of the Bohun title to Parliament, Richard was breaking his word.

Perhaps more significantly, Buckingham had been closeted at Brecknock with the sly and seductive Bishop Morton, who had been placed in his custody after Hastings' conspiracy and who was at the bottom of virtually every anti-Ricardian intrigue. More describes a series of conversations in which Morton plants ideas in Buckingham's mind, letting the duke believe they are his own. He has Morton feign reticence even to speak about Richard's kingship, but finally has the bishop "confess" his wish that God had given Richard the "excellente vertues mete for the rule of a realm" as He had "planted in the person of youre grace." In other words, the unctuous prelate says "Henry of Buckingham, you'd make a far better king than Richard. Don't you agree?" Obviously, Buckingham did.

If, as More indicated, Buckingham was filled with envy at Richard's wearing the crown and was resentful of Richard's conduct, such encouragement from Morton might well have ignited a spark of rebellion in the unstable duke.

Grafton goes far beyond More, providing, verbatim, page

after page of the supposed conversation between Morton and Buckingham. Since the duke and the bishop were alone, and since both died long before Grafton's work was compiled, the source of this extensive dialogue is a mystery. Perhaps this is one reason why More's nephew, Rastell, in the preface to the "History," refers to the version of More's account published by Grafton as "very much corrupte in many places."

Whatever was Buckingham's state of mind when he embarked on his revolt, we know Richard's. He was enraged at the duke's betrayal. He wrote to his chancellor, John Russell, that Buckingham was "the most untrue creature living," that "there never was false traitor better provided for" and that, before long, Richard would "subdue his malice."

It is here that Henry Tudor assumes an active role in our drama. The conventional wisdom is that Buckingham's aim was to depose Richard in order to put Henry on the throne. Certainly that is the impression Buckingham created. According to the Croyland Chronicle, "The duke of Buckingham, on the advice of the bishop of Ely, his prisoner at Brecknock, invited [Henry] to hasten into the kingdom of England as fast as he could reach the shore to take Elizabeth, the dead king's elder daughter, to wife and with her, at the same time, possession of the whole kingdom."

Henry had a weak claim to the throne. His father, Edmund Tudor, was the son of Katherine of Valois. Katherine was the daughter of Charles VI, the king of France who had made the treaty of Troyes with Henry V after that warrior-king had defeated the French at Agincourt and conquered a great part of France. Katherine had married Henry V; but he had died, leaving Katherine a young, attractive widow and mother of the infant king, Henry VI.

Edmund's father was Owen Tudor, a Welsh clerk in Katherine's household. A generation earlier, the Tudors had been even lower on the social ladder. Owen's father was the bishop of Bangor's butler.

Apparently none of this bothered the young French widow. While Owen was employed in Katherine's household, they had a clandestine affair. The result was Edmund, Henry Tudor's father.

Imprisoned after Katherine's death, Owen claimed that he and Katherine had secretly married before Edmund's birth. But there was no proof of this beyond Owen's word.

Thus, Henry Tudor's father, Edmund, was a half brother of Henry VI. But he may have been illegitimate; and, even aside from that potential defect, his connection to Henry VI was through their common mother, Katherine of Valois, rather than through any blood relationship to Henry V. Such a connection could not provide any significant basis for a claim to the throne.

Henry Tudor's mother was Margaret Beaufort. Here, as in the case of Richard's mother, Cecily Neville, there was a blood relationship to a member of the royal family. But here again, it was not one that gave Henry a solid claim. The Beauforts were descended from John of Gaunt, the duke of Lancaster, who was the second surviving son of Edward III. But they were the result of Gaunt's relationship with Katherine Swynford, his longtime mistress. Gaunt ultimately married Katherine; but, unfortunately, all four of their children were born before the marriage. Being illegitimate, they were given the name Beaufort. Henry Tudor's mother was descended from John Beaufort, the oldest son of Gaunt and Katherine.

The Beaufort family was legitimized by Richard II's Parliament, an act intended to please Gaunt, who was the powerful uncle of that unfortunate king. However, when Gaunt's only legitimate son seized the throne, making himself Henry IV, he had his Parliament permanently bar the Beauforts from the succession and thus from becoming rivals of the new king's own line.

There is controversy even today as to whether one Parliament can modify an act of legitimacy previously passed by another. The prevailing view appears to be that it can and that the Beauforts were lawfully barred from succeeding to the throne. If so, Beaufort descent provided no support at all for Henry Tudor's claim. Moreover, if the Beauforts were not lawfully barred, Henry's mother, Margaret Beaufort, Lady Stanley, would have had a better claim than Henry. Few Englishmen would have supported a female claimant at that time, although there was certainly no law against such a claim.

Richard III's maternal grandmother was also a Beaufort; but

that, of course, was never urged as a basis for Richard's claim. Richard was a Plantagenet, a direct descendent of Edward III through two of his sons, Edward, duke of York, on Richard's father's side and Lionel, duke of Clarence, on his mother's. Nor was there any hint of illegitimacy to mar his claim. Henry VI had been a legitimate descendent of John of Gaunt, another son of Edward III. He could match his claim against Richard's. Henry Tudor could not.

Even the king of Portugal and the queen of Castille, both of whom were descended from legitimate daughters of John of Gaunt, had a better claim to the English throne than either Henry Tudor or his mother.

Although she provided her son with a flawed claim to the throne, Henry's mother, Margaret Beaufort, was a fascinating woman. In 1455, when she was only twelve, she was given in marriage to Edmund Tudor. The following year, Edmund died, a prisoner of the Yorkists against whom he had fought. In January 1457, three months after his father's death, Henry was born at Pembroke Castle in Wales. His mother was only fourteen. Evidently she had an eye for political opportunity even then, naming her son after his godfather, Henry VI.

Margaret next married Sir Henry Stafford, a Lancastrian, who switched sides and backed Edward IV and the Yorkists. Following Stafford's death, she married her third husband, Lord Stanley, the wealthy and powerful nobleman who, along with his brother, Sir William Stanley, was to play a critical role in the lives of both Richard III and Henry VII.

Henry Tudor was Lady Stanley's only child, and her treasure. For many years, she devoted herself to his advancement and, of course, to the possibility of his becoming king.

Henry spent his first years at Pembroke Castle with his mother and his Uncle Jasper Tudor. When Edward IV took the throne, Jasper, who had fought on the Lancastrian side, fled to the Continent. Young Henry was placed in the care of Lord Herbert, a Yorkist who had been given the ownership of Pembroke. Henry continued on at the castle, spending much of his youth there.

During the Lancastrian restoration, with Henry VI again on

the throne, Henry Tudor was presented at court by his Uncle Jasper, who had returned from exile. He became, for a time at least, a student at Eton. In 1471, when the Lancastrians were defeated at Tewkesbury, Henry was but fourteen. Fleeing England with Jasper, he was shipwrecked in the territory of Duke Francis of Brittany.

For the next thirteen years, Henry was a "guest" and well-treated prisoner of the Breton duke. During the reign of Edward IV, Henry's mother, by then Lady Stanley, sought to ingratiate herself with Edward in an attempt to procure Henry's safe return from exile and his acceptance at the Yorkist court. Meanwhile, Henry was trying to persuade Duke Francis to support or at least permit a Lancastrian invasion of England. The duke, for his part, tried to use Henry as a bargaining chip in his dealings with both England and France.

In August 1483, Duke Francis, threatened by war with France, advised Richard that if he did not supply Brittany with four thousand archers for six months, with another four thousand in reserve, the Bretons would be defeated and the French would gain control of Henry Tudor, in which case they would provide him with the aid he needed for an invasion of England.

Richard took no action; and Duke Francis himself began to assist Henry in preparing his invasion. Presumably he needed English aid to fend off French aggression and apparently, having lost faith in the likelihood of receiving that aid from Richard, he decided to back another candidate for the English throne. The duke was not alone in his support for Henry. Massive sums of money were dispatched from England, enabling Henry to gather troops and prepare for a Channel crossing. Apparently the money came from his mother and other Lancastrian supporters, perhaps with Woodville aid as well.

But why would the duke of Buckingham support Henry's plan? Buckingham had his own claim to the throne, and a better one than Henry's. His mother, like Henry's, was a Beaufort. More significantly, Buckingham, like Richard and Henry VI, was a direct descendant of Edward III. He was the great-great-grand-son of Thomas of Woodstock, duke of Gloucester, the youngest surviving son of that prolific king. Given the illegitimacy of the two princes and the attainder of Clarence's heirs, only Richard and his young son appeared to bar Buckingham's path to the throne.

Possibly the duke believed he needed the support of Lady Stanley, the Lancastrians and the Woodvilles and felt he had no chance of winning that support unless he agreed to back Henry Tudor's claim. Perhaps his scheme was to use Henry Tudor and his allies to strike down Richard and then to seize the crown himself, especially if Henry happened to be "killed in the fighting," which might always be arranged.

The Tudor historians asserted (and others have espoused the view) that Henry, like Buckingham, set out to depose Richard because he had murdered the two princes. But Henry had schemed to take the throne well before any rumor of the princes' death began to circulate; and, while he may have used the rumor to gain support, it was hardly the motivating force behind his plans for the rebellion.

And the October 1483 rebellion was planned. It was by no means a sudden, spontaneous event. The planning may have occurred earlier than is generally believed. On June 20, 1483, just days after Hastings' execution, Simon Stallworth wrote to his friend Sir William Stonor that "[a]ll the Lord Chamberlain's [i.e., Hastings'] men are switching allegiance to the Duke of Buckingham."

Clearly, by the fall of 1483, all the Lancastrian and Woodville supporters had been contacted and their efforts had been coordinated with those of Buckingham. The money had been sent to Henry, and his invasion was planned for October 18. At the appointed time, simultaneous uprisings were to take place in the South, while Buckingham was to lead his force eastward across the Severn from Wales. Significantly, the northern counties were not involved.

When Buckingham announced the rebellion, Dorset and the Woodville forces attacked as planned. Henry Tudor sailed across the Channel from Brittany with an invasion force of Bretons and Lancastrian exiles.

As usual, Richard moved swiftly and decisively. Considering London well protected by troops under the reliable John

Howard, he gathered a sizeable force and moved to head off Buckingham's forces approaching the Severn from Wales. Meanwhile, Richard's allies attacked Buckingham's Welsh estates and harassed the duke on his march, cutting off his lines of communication and destroying the bridges across the Severn.

Now nature proved a significant ally to Richard and his loyal adherents. Heavy rains created a massive flood that rendered the Severn impassible in the absence of bridges. It also swept away corn, livestock and any other form of food and prevented the arrival of provisions from the English side of the river. Hungry and discouraged, Buckingham's men began deserting, and his army evaporated.

Most of Henry's ships, scattered by a storm, returned to Brittany. Henry, however, arrived off Dorset with a small part of his fleet. A handful of English soldiers tried to lure him ashore with the tale that Buckingham's rebellion had succeeded. Evidently Henry's advisors were too experienced to fall for that ruse, and the small fleet sailed on to Plymouth. Finally, hearing the news that the rebellion had utterly failed, Henry turned his ships and sailed back to Brittany.

Shakespeare, taking extraordinary dramatic license, has Henry land his ships in Wales, march across England and, in single combat, slay Richard at the battle of Bosworth Field. Of course, Henry sailed back to Brittany in 1483, when Buckingham's rebellion failed. Bosworth Field did not occur until 1485; and Henry, although present, took no part in the actual combat. Had he engaged the skilled and experienced Richard in single combat, he would have had virtually no chance of survival.

In any event, with his army dispersed, Buckingham fled in disguise. Richard offered a huge reward for his arrest. Posing as a commoner, Buckingham took refuge in the Shropshire cottage of Ralph Banaster, a staunch Lancastrian. But the reward proved too tempting, and Banaster appears to have betrayed the fugitive duke. Buckingham was arrested by the sheriff of Shropshire with the aid of a man listed as "Sir James Tyler," who was probably Sir James Tyrell.

The duke was taken to Salisbury, where Richard and the royal forces were encamped. He asked to be brought before Richard, purportedly to ask his pardon. According to his son, however, his true intention was to rise suddenly and stab the king with a concealed knife. Richard refused the duke's request for an audience and, in doing so, perhaps saved his own life.

It has been claimed that Buckingham was executed without a trial. But subsequently discovered documents indicate that he was, in fact, tried before the vice constable, Sir Ralph Assheton, and duly condemned to death. There certainly was no doubt as to his guilt. He was beheaded at Salisbury on November 2, 1483.

Richard treated the duke's widow, who was a Woodville and a sister of the former queen, with his usual generosity. He granted her a substantial pension and paid Buckingham's debts lest she be forced to bear them. The duchess was then allowed to join her sister, the former queen, in sanctuary at Westminster.

Dorset and Bishop Morton escaped abroad. A few conspirators were caught and beheaded. Richard believed that Lord Stanley had not joined his wife in the conspiracy to put her son on the throne. Stanley was neither attainted nor even arrested. Pollard suggests that the reason he did not join the rebellion in aid of his son-in-law may have been a longstanding dislike for Buckingham. There may have been other reasons.

While there is no evidence that Richard had promised such things in advance, when the rebellion was put down Stanley was made constable of England for life, replacing Buckingham. He was also granted some of Buckingham's most valuable properties. Sir William Stanley, who like his brother was believed to have stayed clear of the conspiracy, was given great honors and offices in Wales.

A contemporary letter refers to Stanley's son, Lord Strange, going forth at the time of Buckingham's rebellion "with 10,000 men, whither we cannot say." Presumably they were intended to aid Richard—or at least Richard thought so. Lord Strange participated with his father in the receipt of numerous estates apparently for their service against the rebels.

Aside from Buckingham, none of the great magnates of the realm seem to have joined in the rebellion. Still, ninety-five rebels were named in the bill of attainder that followed its end. Many of these were ultimately pardoned. Lady Stanley, known to have been a leading member of the conspiracy, was among those attainted. Theoretically, her lands were taken; but in fact they were simply given to her husband. Her attainder was soon reversed, and she was merely placed in her husband's custody.

Richard had made Tyrell a commissioner of array to raise Welsh troops who would resist the rebels. Now Tyrell was given a share of Buckingham's wealth and made steward of Wales and the adjoining marches. This was ostensibly for raising loyal Welsh troops and possibly also for a role in apprehending Buckingham. Could it actually have been a reward for killing the princes?

Brackenbury was designated receiver general of all lands forfeited by Buckingham's attainder that were not specifically conveyed by the king to others. Would Brackenbury have been so well rewarded if he had just disobeyed the king's order to murder the two boys? Possibly—if he had obeyed the king's second order to give Tyrell the keys and was keeping the king's guilty secret.

XII

GOVERNING THE REALM

For the moment, Richard seemed to have crushed his opposition. But Henry Tudor had not given up his dreams of invasion. His position in exile was strengthened by the arrival on the Continent of many leading rebels, including the marquess of Dorset and the capable and dangerous John Morton. Perhaps it was on Morton's advice that, on Christmas Day, 1483, Henry took a solemn oath in the cathedral of Rennes to take the English throne and marry Princess Elizabeth, eldest daughter of Edward IV, thus uniting the houses of Lancaster and York.

Most of those pardoned for their part in the rebellion received back at least a substantial portion of their lands. But they must have realized that they were no longer considered dependable by the king and that their chances of advancement in a Ricardian reign were limited.

Moreover, Richard had created the appearance in the South that he had favored his loyal northerners in the redistribution of lands and positions following the rebellion. After the fighting, which had been concentrated in the South and West, Richard felt particularly dependent on what he considered his loyal and reliable northerners. Placing his trust in them, he gave them power and authority in the South, creating the kind of southern bitterness manifested in the Croyland Chronicle.

The Second Continuator was relatively open in expressing his regional bias and distaste for northerners and the North itself, which he described as the place from which "all evil spreads." As the chronicle puts it, having collected "great numbers of estates" by attainder, Richard distributed "all" such estates "amongst his northerners, whom he had planted in every part of his dominions, to the shame of all the Southern people, who murmured ceaselessly and each day for the return of their old lords in place of the tyranny of the present ones."

Despite bitterness in the South, the quiet hostility of former rebels and the continued threat of invasion, Richard turned his attention to governing the realm. There seems little doubt that he was an effective and beneficent king. He reduced corruption, introduced substantial legal and political reforms, granted relief from harsh taxation and improved the economy.

Richard provided financial assistance to towns, fostered foreign trade, eased the procedures for the presentation of petitions by commoners and prevented the seizure of prisoner's goods without trial. He confirmed the liberties and immunities of the clergy, while directing them to pay closer attention to their spiritual duties, to enforce discipline and to promote morality. He demanded detailed accountings of receipts and expenditures from fiscal administrators and continued the rebuilding of the navy that he had begun as lord admiral during his brother's reign.

Richard's proclamation to the people of Kent is an example of his demonstrated concern for the ability of the common people to protect their rights.

> The King's highness is fully determined to see due administration of justice throughout this his realm to be had, and to reform, punish and subdue all extortions and oppressions in the same. And for that cause will at his coming now into this his said county Kent that every person dwelling within the same that find him grieved, oppressed or unlawfully wronged do make a bill of his complaint and put it to his highness and he shall be heard and without delay have such convenient remedy as shall accord with his laws. For his grace is utterly determined

all his true subjects shall live in rest and quiet and peace-ably enjoy their lands, livelihoods and goods according to the laws of the land which they be naturally born to inherit.

Francis Bacon, hardly a Ricardian, described Richard as "a prince in military virtue approved, jealous of the honour of the English nation and likewise a good law-maker for the ease and solace of the common people." Similarly, Cardinal Wolsey wrote about Richard in 1525 that "although he did evil, yet in his tyme wer many good actes made."

In a private letter to the prior of Christ Church, Canterbury, Bishop Thomas Langton wrote:

He [Richard] contents the people where he goes best that ever did Prince, for many a poor man hath suffered wrong many days have been relieved and helped by him and his commands in his progress. And in many great cities and towns were great sums of money given him which he hath refused. On my trouth I liked never the conditions of any prince so well as his; God hath sent him to us for the weal of us all.

Even Rous, writing after Richard's death, pointed out that when Richard was offered money "by the peoples of London, Gloucester and Worcester, he declined with thanks, affirming that he would rather have their love than their treasure."

Richard established a council of the North presided over by the earl of Lincoln. The council functioned for the North much like Richard's council in London functioned for the nation as a whole. It greatly enhanced the king's ability to govern effectively in the northern part of his realm. In addition to its other func-tions, the council was directed to meet at York at least every quar-ter to hear, examine and order all bills of complaints. Unfortunately for Richard, his creation of this northern council may have alienated the earl of Northumberland, with disastrous consequences.

Along with their great rivals, the Nevilles, Northumberland's family, the Percys, had exercised vast power in the North before Richard himself became the principal magnate in that region. Northumberland apparently expected that when Richard became king he would cede his place in the North to the earl, and the Percys would regain their traditional power and status.

But, just as Edward IV had relied on Richard, rather than on Percys or Nevilles, to control the North, Richard, when king, was unwilling to return to the days of dependence on the great northern families to govern the region. He retained extensive northern estates and governed himself, through his council of the North, making his trusted nephew, Lincoln, its president. Northumberland was simply a member of the new council, and he may well have resented its existence and function. Perhaps most of all, he may have resented having to follow the directions of Lincoln.

Richard's only Parliament convened on January 23, 1484, having been postponed from an earlier date because of Buckingham's rebellion. Its first order of business was to pass the act of *Titulus Regius,* confirming Richard's title by converting into a formal act of Parliament what had been a resolution of the assembled lords, prelates and commons on June 25, 1483.

The new act noted that the three estates assembled in June 1483 were not "in fourme of Parliament," that this had led to "doubts, questions and ambiguitees" and that, to end any such doubt, the "Rolle" enacted by that earlier assemblage was now "ratified, enrolled, recorded, approved and auctorized." *Titulus Regius* then went on to repeat the substance of the "Rolle" of 1483, including the charge of the precontract between Edward IV and Eleanor Butler and the illegitimacy of Edward's children.

Richard's Parliament also passed considerable sound and beneficial legislation. One such act freed juries from intimidation and tampering. Another protected buyers of land from secret defects in title. Still another made bail available to persons accused of crimes. "Benevolences," an oppressive system of forced grants to the king, were abolished, and deceitful conduct in the manufacture of woolens was forbidden.

For the first time, Parliament's acts were published in English, so that they could be understood by at least that part of the population that was literate, rather than being confined to churchmen, educated nobles and the few others who could read Latin.

Lord Campbell wrote "We have no difficulty in pronouncing Richard's Parliament the most meritorious national assembly for protecting the liberty of the subject and putting down abuses in the administration of justice that had sat in England since the reign of Henry III."

Some modern historians have questioned whether there was anything really unique in the legislation enacted by Richard's Parliament and whether, in any event, he should be given credit for his Parliament's accomplishments. But, whether unique or not, the legislative program of the 1484 Parliament must be considered sound and beneficial. And Richard, who would have borne the blame for any harsh or ill-conceived enactments, must be accorded substantial credit for the new laws that benefited his realm and his subjects.

A significant part of those measures strengthened the position of the common people and the merchant class, who applauded them. On the other hand, they did not endear Richard to some of the barons, whose rights were correspondingly eroded.

At this point, Elizabeth Woodville was still in sanctuary with her five daughters. Richard promised that if her daughters would come out, he would treat them kindly and honorably as his kinswomen, marry them to gentlemen and give them suitable allowances.

Finally, in March 1484, Elizabeth agreed to these terms, which were set out in a written oath that Richard took and faithfully observed. The former queen not only came out of sanctuary with her daughters, but showed so much confidence in Richard's good faith that she wrote to her son, the marquess of Dorset, asking him to return to England and submit himself to the king. In fact, Dorset did attempt to leave the Continent, presumably in response to his mother's assurances. He was apprehended by Henry Tudor's adherents, however, and forced to remain abroad.

Later in March, the king and queen left London on another progress, reaching Nottingham on April 20. Here they received news that their only son, the eleven-year-old Prince of Wales, had died on April 9 of a sudden and brief illness. It is reported, without contradiction, that Richard and Anne were overwhelmed with grief. As the Croyland chronicler put it, "You might have seen the father and mother almost out of their minds for a long time when faced with the sudden grief."

It has been reported that after the death of his own son, Richard declared Clarence's son, Edward, earl of Warwick, heir to the throne. Perhaps he intended that ultimately Clarence's attainder would be reversed. Probably he did not intend this to occur in his own lifetime, since it would have made Warwick's claim better than his own. In any event, young Warwick was given precedence over other peers and graciously resided as a member of the king's household in the North.

Rous claims that the king changed his mind later, declared his sister's son, Lincoln, to be his heir, and imprisoned young Warwick. The claim of imprisonment is untrue. But Lincoln may well have replaced Warwick as the heir at some point; or he may, in reality, have been Richard's choice from the death of his own son.

There is some indication that young Warwick was retarded. By contrast, Lincoln was a sound and able man, mature, loyal and ready to fight for Richard's cause. Richard had placed Lincoln in charge of his council of the North and, perhaps more significantly, had designated him lieutenant of Ireland, a position the Yorkists traditionally reserved for the heir to the throne.

There are, however, some indications that young Warwick continued to receive preferential treatment over Lincoln at least until the spring of 1485. Possibly, as the danger of Henry Tudor's invasion increased, Richard finally recognized that the more able Lincoln should be his heir. Cynics might say that designating a mental defective as the heir created a powerful incentive to keep the king alive. But there is no evidence that Richard engaged in such thinking; and his designation of an incapable heir would provide the adherents of Henry Tudor with an additional argument. In any event, Warwick's feeblemindedness may have been exaggerated or, for that matter, a total fabrication.

Ironically, Lincoln was killed at the battle of Stoke in 1487, ostensibly fighting to establish his cousin Warwick as the rightful king.

Buck wrote that, in 1484, Richard ordered renovation of that part of the Tower "toward the Thames." Audrey Williamson suggests that this would have been a rash move if he knew the princes were buried there. Of course, the renovation, which apparently was in an area near "the sluice gate," may not have been anywhere near where the bodies were buried.

But, if More's account was correct, Brackenbury's priest had moved the bodies, and no one knew where they were—not even the king. If so, *any* digging in the Tower area would have created a serious risk. It would have been one thing for Richard to have produced the bodies of the two princes and to have announced that they had died of natural causes. He might well have carried it off. It would have been quite another matter for workmen to unearth their bodies, making it clear that they had been killed and secretly buried while in Richard's control. That could have caused a new rebellion.

By mid-1484, Lancastrian and Tudor supporters were again circulating gossip critical of Richard. Even his governance was attacked. In July 1484, a Tudor agent, William Colyngbourne, nailed to the door of Saint Paul's Cathedral a paper bearing the rhyme "The Cat, the Rat and Lovell our dog/Rule all England under the Hog." The "Cat" referred to Sir William Catesby, the "Rat" to Sir Richard Ratcliffe and "Lovell our dog" was Francis Viscount Lovell, Richard's lord chamberlain. They were all friends and staunch supporters of the king and had positions of power and authority in his reign. "The Hog" referred to Richard himself, whose personal badge was a wild boar.

It has become part of the Tudor legend that Colyngbourne was executed for what might seem only a mischievous prank. The fact is that he had attempted to send a message to Henry Tudor in France, urging him to launch a new invasion. This was undeniably treason, and he was executed for it. The offensive doggerel was added to the indictment as a second count. Undoubtedly it angered the king; but it is not likely that, in itself, it would have led to his execution.

Colyngbourne's execution, like that of every commoner executed for treason, was a horrifying process. Fabyan describes it: "[F]or him, was made a newe pair of gallowes upon whych, after he hadde hangyd a shorte season, he was cutte down, being alyve, and his bowellys rypped out of his belly and cast into the fyre there by hym, and lyved tyll the butcher put his hande into the bulke of his body; insomuch that he sayd in the same instant, 'O lorde Jesu, yet more trouble', and so dyed." Peers, even those who were convicted traitors, were not subjected to this kind of death. They were "entitled" to beheading, which at least was normally quick and painless.

Despite provocation from Lancastrian and Tudor adherents, Richard continued to earn generally high marks for his management of domestic matters. His handling of foreign affairs was less successful.

France and Brittany were plagued with internal power struggles and external conflict that could have been exploited to Richard's advantage. But, at least until late in his reign, Richard was not inclined to play one group or country against another when it conflicted with his own personal views or visceral reactions. Perhaps the problem was his lack of personal experience in international dealings and the absence of a shrewd adviser well grounded in the intricacies of foreign policy—a Richelieu, an Olivares or even a Morton.

As we have seen, Duke Francis of Brittany had previously asked Richard to supply four thousand archers. He argued that this would allow him to refuse French demands to turn over Henry Tudor and to resist the French invasion of his dukedom that he predicted would follow his refusal.

Richard might have struck a deal at that moment to supply the archers in return for the delivery of Henry Tudor to England as a prisoner, rather than to the French as a potential ally. Possibly he could have settled for three thousand archers or even twenty-five hundred. Even providing four thousand would have been a small price to pay to end the Tudor threat. But Richard did not pursue the matter. His failure to comply led Duke Francis to aid Henry's abortive invasion of October 1483.

Richard's response to this hostile act had been to launch a sea war against Breton shipping, a war that gradually extended to French and Scottish shipping as well. This naturally tended to promote an accommodation among the Bretons, French and

Scots and to cause each of them to look more favorably upon Henry Tudor as a potential occupant of the English throne.

Meanwhile, Duke Francis had become mentally ill and Brittany was controlled by his treasurer, Pierre Landlais. But Landlais had opposition from powerful Breton nobles; and, like Duke Francis, he feared that the duchy would be overrun by France.

In France, Louis XI had died and the capable Anne of Beaujeu was governing as regent in the name of her younger brother, Charles VIII. Like Louis before her, Anne had designs on Brittany. Also like Louis, she feared an English invasion and realized that supporting Henry Tudor's claim could be the key to eliminating that concern.

But Anne faced a serious domestic problem that prevented her taking more vigorous measures against Richard. The duke of Orleans was conspiring to overthrow Anne's government and hoped to organize a combination of Brittany, England and his own forces to achieve that end. So long as the Orleanist threat persisted, Anne was unlikely to provide significant backing for Henry Tudor's invasion of England.

It may have been in Richard's interest to provide whatever assistance was needed to keep the Orleanist threat alive or even to bring it success. But Richard appeared unwilling to make common cause with the duke of Orleans. Presumably doing so would have involved a pledge to support the duke's claim to the French throne; and Richard was probably unready to concede that anyone but the king of England was entitled to be king of France. Possibly he believed that, in the future, he would mount an invasion and press that claim himself.

At some point in 1484, Richard seems at least to have recognized the need for a less bellicose approach to the Bretons and Scots and for a preemptive move against Henry. He concluded a peace treaty with Scotland; and through a trusted emissary, probably Sir James Tyrell, he negotiated with the Bretons to deliver Henry into his hands. Accomplishing that would end, in one stroke, the principal threat to the peace and to his reign.

Toward this goal, Richard finally offered a substantial portion of the archers Duke Francis had requested the preceding year.

More importantly, he appears to have promised vast personal wealth to Pierre Landlais in exchange for the troublesome Tudor. Landlais and his Bretons were prepared to seize Henry and hand him over. Richard began recruiting the archers.

It appears, however, that the ever watchful John Morton, then living on the Continent and still possessing excellent sources of information, discovered Henry's peril and arranged for his escape to France and his welcome at the French court.

In September 1484, pretending to ride into the countryside to visit a friend, Henry left the road and entered the woods. There he switched clothes with a servant. Thus disguised, he raced for the French border, reaching his goal shortly before the arrival of the pursuing Bretons. Soon he was at the French court vigorously seeking assistance for an invasion of England.

Most of the exiled English rebels were still in Brittany. They were now in some peril and of little use to Henry. Remarkably, however, Duke Francis had a temporary recovery and consented to the exiles leaving Brittany and following Henry to France.

Richard was spared the need to deliver the archers and to pay anything to Landlais. But he was now faced with an enemy who might generate a far more potent threat. At the time, the French were more inclined than the Bretons to support Henry Tudor and were better equipped to help him mount an attack on England.

Anne of Beaujeu, the French regent, tended to follow the policies of the late king, Louis XI. Richard III was a bold and effective military leader. It seemed likely that someday he would aggressively press the Plantagenet claim to the French crown. Unlike his brother Edward, who could be bought off, Richard might not only invade France, but might indeed pursue a full-scale war to conquer the country and occupy its throne. Thus Anne's policy was to do what she could to replace the dangerous Richard with the less warlike and more controllable Henry Tudor. That policy was supported—even urged—by a sizeable group of Anglophobes at the French court.

Fortunately for Richard, Anne's hands were tied by the need to meet the threat posed by the duke of Orleans. But unless Richard supported Orleans, that threat could, at any time, be diminished or eliminated by an Orleanist defeat.

At the end of October 1484, Richard received another set-back. The earl of Oxford, England's most experienced military leader, escaped his imprisonment in Hammes Castle near Calais and joined Henry Tudor and the Lancastrian exiles at the French court. He was accompanied by a number of defectors from the Calais garrison. Oxford, long a dedicated Lancastrian and a vet-eran of many battles, was a fierce and capable enemy of Richard and the Yorkists.

Oxford, Tudor and the Lancastrian exiles meant to invade England—that much was clear. But with Anne of Beaujeau occu-pied with the duke of Orleans, significant French backing was questionable. In any event, with winter at hand, there could be no invasion for months.

Richard spent the Christmas of 1484 at Westminster. All was gaiety and splendor. Edward IV's eldest daughter, the tall, fair-haired Elizabeth, appeared richly attired in a dress similar to that worn by the queen. This led to gossip about a possible relationship between Richard and the young princess Henry Tudor had sworn to marry. Richard has been even accused of poisoning Anne in order to marry Elizabeth himself. This is almost certainly untrue.

What is true is that Anne, Richard's longtime companion who had shared all of the joys, sorrows, triumphs, and tragedies of his life, was seriously ill and slowly dying. She appeared to be suffering from the same devastating and incurable illness that had taken her sister Isabel.

The Croyland chronicler, in one of his nastier moments, reported that Richard "was completely spurning his consort's bed. Therefore he judged it right to consult with doctors." He implies that this rejection worsened Anne's condition. It is not at all unlikely that Richard did avoid sexual relations with Anne in the later stages of her illness, and that this was, in fact, by his doctors' advice. If, as seems probable, Anne was dying of tubercu-losis, there was serious danger of contagion; and, in any event, sexual relations would probably have been most inadvisable for a patient in her critical condition. For Richard to have been unkind about this or to have made it seem like a personal rejection would have been unnecessary, unwise (given the power and prestige of Anne's family) and totally out of character.

After Christmas, Anne's decline became more rapid, and she died on March 16, 1485. She was twenty-eight. Richard had her buried in Westminster Abbey. He is reported to have shed copious tears over her tomb.

Nevertheless, the story was soon spread, probably by Rotherham and others, at the direction of John Morton, that the king planned to marry his niece. Elizabeth was young and attractive, and Henry Tudor had taken an oath to wed her. Richard may have entertained the thought as a means of frustrating Henry's plans and of getting a male heir, but it is doubtful that he had actually decided to enter into such a marriage.

Ultimately faced with an increasing volume of such gossip, and the even more malicious tale that he had poisoned his queen in order to marry his pretty, young niece, Richard took the extraordinary step of publicly announcing, in early April, that he did not intend the rumored marriage.

The Croyland chronicle reports that this was done at the urging of Catesby and Ratcliffe, who argued that Queen Anne had been beloved in the North, where her family had long held vast power, and that Richard's previously loyal northerners would "rise against him" if he did not immediately and publicly deny any plan to marry his niece. With a Tudor invasion at hand, this was not a risk Richard could afford to take.

Gairdner suggests that Catesby and Ratcliffe had a different motive. He believes they pressed Richard to renounce the match because they feared a Woodville resurgence if he were to marry Elizabeth. The two aides, having played an important role in the executions of Rivers and Grey, would have had good reason to fear for their lives if the Woodvilles returned to power. There is no hard evidence to support this theory. But, if Gairdner is correct, it would indicate that, instead of simply being concerned about public perception, the two counsellors believed Richard was really considering such a marriage.

In late 1484, Richard sent Sir James Tyrell to Flanders on a secret mission "concerning greatly the king's weal." In January 1485, the king appointed Tyrell commander of the Castle of Guisnes, the fortification that shielded Calais. That same month, Richard paid Tyrell a huge sum at Calais. The sum was said to be as great as the annual royal budget. Was this related to his secret errand of the preceding year? Was it a reward for the murders? Did Richard want Tyrell to be handsomely paid, but away from England? We do not know. Other possible and intriguing explanations are discussed below.

In early 1485, Henry Tudor's fortunes received perhaps their most significant boost. The duke of Orleans, despairing of aid from either Brittany or England, started a rebellion on his own. By March, he had been soundly defeated by the royal forces. Now, with the Orleanist pressure removed, the resources of the French government could be turned against Richard and focused in support of Henry Tudor.

By the spring of 1485, it was obvious that, with substantial French backing, Henry and the Lancastrian exiles would soon launch their invasion. In June, a royal proclamation was issued declaring "Henry Tydder" a false claimant to the throne and branding Henry and a list of his adherents traitors and outlaws. Significantly, Elizabeth Woodville's son, the marquess of Dorset, was not on the list, even though the marquess had previously opposed Richard, and Henry had announced his intention to marry Dorset's half-sister, Elizabeth.

In light of the invasion threat, Princess Elizabeth was sent north to Richard's castle at Sheriff Hutton. The young earl of Warwick, who may still have been the heir, was there as well. The invading army was expected to land on the Channel coast in the South of England or else in Wales. The North was the safest place for Richard's charges.

The coming invasion created serious difficulties for Richard. Apparently he began to have doubts concerning some of the men on whom he had relied. In July 1485, he appears to have dismissed John Russell from his office as lord chancellor, an act that may have had a significant impact on the attitudes expressed in the Croyland Chronicle, since Russell, if he was not its author, was a likely source of its information about Richard and his reign.

Peculiarly, Charles Ross states at one place in his biography of Richard that another historian, Alison Hanham, "is wrong" in reporting that Russell was dismissed. Later in the same work, however, Ross writes that, in fact, the dismissal did take place. The later report appears to be correct.

Finances had been a problem throughout Richard's reign, since much of Edward IV's treasure had been taken by the Woodvilles and had never been regained. The charge made by More and others that he was profligate and wasted a vast royal treasure is simply untrue. Richard was prudent in fiscal matters, but what funds were there were drained by the cost of putting down Buckingham's rebellion in 1483, battling the Scots in 1484, meeting the many other fiscal requirements of his reign and preparing for the invasion of Henry Tudor.

In 1485, finding his funds nearly exhausted, Richard was obliged to resort to borrowing in order to raise the massive sums needed to prepare for the coming fight. He is accused of having restored the oppressive practice of "benevolences," which Parliament had previously declared illegal at Richard's own urging.

At least technically, the charge is unfounded. Benevolences were coerced "gifts" to the crown. Repayment was neither promised nor intended. Richard raised funds for defense against the coming invasion by arranging loans from wealthy subjects, for which he delivered "good and sufficyent pledges" of repayment in specified installments at specified times. Whether the prospective lenders felt free to refuse the king's request for a loan is another matter.

Meanwhile, the French regent, aided by the collapse of the Orleanist threat, had raised the necessary funds to enable Henry to outfit an expedition and had authorized a sizeable body of French troops to accompany him under the command of a French officer. The invasion was coming—and soon.

XIII

BOSWORTH FIELD

On August 7, 1485, Henry Tudor landed at Milford Haven in South Wales with a small force of diehard Lancastrian exiles, a troop of Scots and a sizeable group of Frenchmen. He had been away from England for fourteen years.

Despite the Scottish-English treaty of 1484, the Scots appear to have joined in the invasion with at least the tacit approval of James III of Scotland. James evidently shared the view of the French that Richard was a dangerous and aggressive opponent, and he believed that Scotland would be better off with Henry Tudor on the English throne.

The French contingent has been labeled "scum" and the refuse of French prisons. Apparently some of them were, but even these were fierce, if undisciplined, fighters. Most of the French, however, seem to have been experienced soldiers. Henry's forces were well led, not only by French officers but also by the highly skilled earl of Oxford. Henry himself had no military experience and intended to leave the tactics and the fighting to others.

Regardless of the experience of its troops and the skill of its leaders, the small invasion force was not likely to prevail against the massive army that Richard was expected to assemble. Only two things could win the day for Henry. His army could be joined by substantial numbers friendly to his cause, or Richard could be betrayed at a critical time by the troops on whom he relied. Henry hoped, and had planned, for both. His agents had roamed England in search of potential supporters, promising land and honors to former Lancastrian sympathizers and others who would join Henry in the coming fight.

Henry's original landing force was probably around four thousand men, of whom over two thousand were French and perhaps one thousand were Scottish. The balance were Lancastrian exiles. Being half Welsh, Henry planned to raise an army in Wales before moving onto English soil to attack Richard. To this end, Henry's agents made promises to Welsh chieftains and emphasized Henry's "Welsch" descent. As his standard, Henry wisely chose the red dragon of Cadwallader, an ancient symbol of Welsh kings.

To some extent, Henry's Welsh strategy succeeded. But he knew that his best—and perhaps his only—chance of success lay in persuading his stepfather, Thomas, Lord Stanley and Stanley's brother, Sir William, to add their powerful forces to his own.

The Stanleys were sworn to bring their sizeable forces to the aid of the king. But that was hardly a promise Richard could take to the bank. During the Wars of the Roses, the Stanley family was known for switching sides to promote its own advantage and for trying to keep the goodwill of both the Yorkists and the Lancastrians.

Lord Stanley himself had on at least one prior occasion refused to fight for a reigning monarch. His brother, Sir William Stanley, had actually fought *against* the reigning king (Henry VI) when Edward IV returned to England to recapture the throne.

The family strategy, in general, was to stay neutral until they could play a decisive role on one side or the other and thus earn rich rewards from the winner. Indeed, the two brothers had, on occasion, even taken opposing sides, although neither fought vigorously. The Stanley on the losing side had always been successful in begging forgiveness, in part because of his brother's support for the winner and, in part, because of his own demonstrable lack of vigor in supporting the loser.

The Stanleys had reason to resent Richard. In March 1470, Lord Stanley had been about to side with Warwick and the Lancastrians against Edward IV, when the unexpected arrival of Richard with a small band of Yorkist troops cut Stanley off from the Lancastrian forces and caused him to alter his plans and remain neutral.

Despite this incident, the Stanleys had expected that, with Warwick's demise, their northern power would be considerably enhanced. Instead, a grateful Edward IV had conferred the bulk of that power on Richard. Adding to the Stanleys' grievances, Richard had actively supported their opponent in a bitter four year dispute over Hornby Castle.

Even aside from their general proclivity to betrayal and their resentment of Richard was the very significant fact that Lord Stanley was married to Margaret Beaufort, Henry Tudor's mother. Lady Stanley had already been accused (and correctly so) of participating in Buckingham's conspiracy. Although Richard had not been harsh with her and had been most generous to Lord Stanley himself, it must have been obvious that Lady Stanley would support her son's bid for the throne and that this would necessarily influence her husband. Even the most loyal nobleman of the age would have been tempted by the prospect of seeing his stepson on the throne; and loyalty was hardly Lord Stanley's salient quality.

Stanley had been accompanying the king for some two years, ever since he had been forgiven for his part in Hastings' conspiracy. Possibly Richard felt that the shrewd and experienced noble would be able to provide sage advice. But he must have realized that Stanley's advice would be tempered by whatever course served his family's interests. It is just as likely that Richard wanted Stanley nearby in order to keep an eye on him, on the theory that it is better to keep your friends at a distance and your enemies near.

Just before Henry Tudor's invasion, Lord Stanley approached Richard, begging leave to return for a time to his estates. He claimed that his presence was required there and argued that, in his own domain, he would be in a better position to gather an army for defense of the realm. Richard granted Stanley's request, but he must have been suspicious. He insisted that Stanley's son, Lord Strange, be delivered to Richard to serve as an "aid" in the absence of his father. Stanley certainly knew that Richard was demanding his son as a hostage. Nevertheless, he agreed. Lord Strange was sent for and reported to the king.

Perhaps because he held Strange, Richard seemed ready to

believe that, in the battle to come, the Stanleys would remain loyal. Stanley had also been a comrade in arms during Richard's Scottish campaign, and Richard tended to place trust in those who had served with him in battle. Moreover, he had treated Stanley well, giving him honors and lands and the indicia of his own trust and respect.

What Richard did not know was that *both* Stanleys, acting characteristically, had already given assurances of their support to Henry Tudor. Probably Henry's experienced advisors were even more skeptical than Richard about these "assurances" from the Stanleys. But their position gave them even less leverage than Richard with which to force the elusive brothers into an open choice.

After landing, Henry's forces were joined by those of several Welsh chieftains, including Rhys ap Thomas. Rhys is said to have given bold assurances to Richard that Henry Tudor would have to pass "over his belly" to penetrate the country. But Henry promised to make Rhys lieutenant of Wales for life if he supported the Tudor cause. Supposedly, Rhys lay on his back under a Welsh bridge as it was crossed by Henry's army. In that way he could feel that he had kept his word to Richard. Henry's troops had indeed passed "over his belly." Rhys's was the first of such betrayals. It was not the last.

According to the Croyland Chronicle, Richard had established a system by which one mounted courier would be stationed every twenty miles so that messages could be carried swiftly across the entire kingdom. Richard's couriers, riding hard, reached him at Nottingham on August 11 with news of the invasion. Richard quickly rallied the troops at his disposal and sent word to his principal supporters, such as Norfolk, Brackenbury, Northumberland and Stanley to assemble their forces and join him at Leicester. There, he would be in a position to cut off any attempt on London by the invading army.

Henry crossed the border into England around August 15, 1485, with a force that probably numbered five to six thousand men, including his original force and his new Welsh allies.

Contrary to Tudor claims, the majority of English peers supported Richard, or at least made a show of supporting him.

Apparently, about twenty-five percent of the English nobles actually brought their men to the field to fight for the king. This was not significantly different from the percentage that came to fight for Henry VII at the battle of Stoke in 1487. And the invading forces at Stoke were at least nominally fighting for an obvious imposter, so that rallying support for Henry VII in 1487 should have been considerably easier than it was for Richard in 1485.

Some nobles on whose support Richard had counted decided to remain on their estates and not take either side. Henry faced the same problem. Much the nobility was wearying of the periodic wars between royal or would-be royal houses.

Most who remained on the sidelines probably preferred that Richard retain his crown, assumed he would have no trouble doing so and were not inclined to die for either side. It is highly doubtful that, as the Tudor writers claimed, there were sizeable defections from Richard's side because of the belief that he had murdered his nephews.

Richard's army was joined by a large East Anglian force under John Howard, the duke of Norfolk, whose loyalty had been proven again and again. Another group was on the way from London led by Sir Robert Brackenbury. Richard also awaited a large contingent under Henry Percy, the earl of Northumberland.

As we have discussed, Northumberland's family had dominated the North for centuries, and Richard may have aroused the earl's enmity by turning over administration of the area to a council of the North, presided over by his sister's son, Lincoln. If so, Richard seemed unaware of it. He relied on this powerful noble and appeared to trust him. Certainly he needed Northumberland's support in the coming battle.

On August 17, Henry met secretly with Sir William Stanley. Henry was again assured that both Stanleys were with him, but was also told that they could not yet go over openly to the Tudor side, particularly in the case of Lord Stanley, since his son was held hostage. Instead, they would fall back before Henry's advancing troops, ultimately placing their forces on Richard's flank, from which position they would destroy him at the right moment. This was not exactly what Henry had hoped for; but he was in no position to insist on anything more.

As Henry's army moved into the midlands, he drew some additional support, but nothing like the overwhelming change of allegiance that has sometimes been claimed. Indeed, given the proclivity of the English nobility to shift from side to side for short-term personal gain, the addition to Henry's army was thinner than might have been expected. It is probable that, if anything, Henry was disappointed in the failure of the English to rise up and support him and was seriously concerned that if the Stanleys failed to keep their promises, he faced almost certain defeat.

Lord Stanley maneuvered in the direction of the expected confrontation with a force of four thousand men. His brother, Sir William Stanley, accompanied him with two to three thousand more. Their ambiguous movements could be taken by either side as a sign of the Stanleys' support in the coming battle. More likely, both sides had their doubts.

It is always difficult to estimate the number of men who fought in any ancient battle. The figures vary widely from writer to writer, often reflecting a tendency to show that the victor faced overwhelming odds.

For example, the *Ballad of Bosworth Field,* apparently created for the Stanley family, numbers Richard's army at "40,000 and 3." De Molinet puts the number at "around 60,000." Diego de Valera made it "70,000." All of these estimates were hugely exaggerated.

Apparently Henry approached the area where the battle was to be fought with six to seven thousand men. Richard already had with him an army of approximately the same size. He counted on the addition of three thousand of Northumberland's men who were still on their way, as were more men from other parts of the kingdom. Maneuvering nearby were the six to seven thousand men brought by the two Stanleys.

If the Stanleys fought with Richard, his force would be more than twice that of Henry's. If the Stanleys stayed out of the fight, Richard still had a substantial numerical edge, assuming he could count on Northumberland. Apparently Richard thought he could. If the Stanleys' men went over to Henry, however, Richard would be outnumbered. Should Northumberland desert him as well, the situation would be desperate.

On the roads to the area, however, there were loyal men still moving in to fight for the king. Among them was a contingent from York. It was not until August 16 that York even learned of the invasion. By that time the two armies were already approaching each other. This inexcusable delay may have been attributable to the duke of Northumberland, whose responsibility as commissioner of array was to deliver the summons to York and to see that its men were brought to the field.

Even on the 16th, when they finally got the news, York had no orders. How many men were needed? How equipped? Where were they to go and when? The city sent messengers to Richard seeking instructions. Richard, who must have been stunned to see only two dusty messengers arrive from York instead of a band of armed men, sent back word that he did indeed need as many men as the city could provide. But it was late—probably too late. One of the York messengers stayed to fight beside Richard. The other started back for York. He arrived on the 19th, only three days before the battle.

At the time, the city was afflicted with the plague, creating a shortage of manpower. Its principal counsellors were in the countryside, where there was comparative safety from the contagion. It would take time to collect, uniform and equip a contingent of fighting men and to raise the necessary money. But there was no time. Certainly there was insufficient time to put together a sizeable contingent of foot soldiers and march them from York to Leicester. It was decided to send some eighty mounted men to fight for the king. It is doubtful that they reached the field on time.

Whatever faith Richard had in the Stanleys must have been shaken when, after an unsuccessful escape attempt, Stanley's son confessed that his uncle, Sir William Stanley, was in league with Henry Tudor. The young man insisted, however, that his father, Lord Stanley, was no part of the plot. Nevertheless, letters were sent to Lord Stanley reinforcing the threat to his son if he did not join Richard in the coming fight.

As the armies approached each other, Richard had some choices. He could delay the battle, awaiting the arrival of the loyal troops on their way to join him or still being assembled in various parts of the country. That alternative would give him a greater advantage in manpower that would substantially increase the likelihood of victory.

On the other hand, he could bring Henry to battle at once, without waiting for his forces to be at full strength. One fault ascribed to Richard is impetuousness, an inclination to make quick, bold decisions, to rush headlong into battle, to fall upon his enemy no matter what the odds or how great the obstacles. We can see some of that same impulsiveness in his father's behavior at the battle of Wakefield. There, the duke of York was taunted into leaving his castle and fighting against unfavorable odds, rather than prudently taking a siege and waiting for the reinforcements being raised by his son, Edward.

We see that trait in Richard's behavior at Bosworth Field. Even if he had complete faith in Northumberland, Richard must have known that the Stanleys' loyalty was shaky at best. He knew now that Sir William Stanley, whose two to three thousand men were still maneuvering between the two armies, was actually conspiring with Henry. And even with Lord Stanley's son as a hostage, Richard could hardly bank on Stanley's support. Giving immediate battle was taking a serious and seemingly unnecessary risk. Prudence called for waiting and maneuvering until he could be joined by the additional forces assembling and moving in from other areas.

Moreover, during the preceding year, Richard had assembled a powerful supply of artillery in the Tower, including large cannons of formidable caliber and range. Richard had some artillery with him, but the big guns in the Tower might have provided him with a more powerful defensive position. Before the battle, a contingent of men arrived all the way from London, led by the ever loyal Brackenbury. Had Richard ordered it, they could have brought the big guns with them. But Richard had not asked for them. Nor would he wait for their arrival.

Richard was a proven military leader and warrior—a veteran of many battles. He considered Henry Tudor a pretender and a weakling. Perhaps he felt no need for more troops or heavier guns.

At this point, the movement of Henry's forces may have

forced the issue. On August 18, the invading army appeared to change direction and move toward the main road to London. Even if his forces were not yet at full strength, this threat to the capital probably made up Richard's mind. He would bring Henry to battle immediately with what he had, personally directing his men as he had done before, time after time. He would cut the invader off from London and drive him from the realm or, better still, kill him.

The decision made, Richard left Nottingham for Leicester, where he was joined by Norfolk, Brackenbury and finally Northumberland. After meeting with his commanders and reviewing his troops, Richard led his combined forces out of Leicester on the 21st in the direction of the invading army.

He drew up his men opposite Henry's forces near Market Bosworth and Sutton Cheney in Leicestershire. Richard's troops occupied fairly high ground on Ambion Hill overlooking Redemoor Plain, now called Bosworth Field. His left flank was protected by an extensive marsh on the south side of the hill. His right was reasonably secured by the steep grade of the north side.

The traditional account has the battle take place on the plain just below Ambion Hill. More recently, it has been argued that, while Richard's troops may have occupied Ambion Hill, the battle was actually fought off to his left, on the more southern part of Redemoor Plain nearer Crown Hill and the town of Dadlington. Weapons have been found in that area, and the battle may have ended there after a pursuit by the victorious army. But most of the fighting appears to have taken place near the foot of Ambion Hill, where the traditional account places it.

As the two armies moved toward the battlefield, the Stanleys' men continued to maneuver between them, leaving their intention ambiguous. Like his brother, Lord Stanley met secretly with Henry before the battle. Evidently, Sir William was again present. Lord Stanley said that he could not align his army with Henry's before the battle began and that he would be unable to enter the fight at all, at least in its early phases. Probably his excuse was that his son was held hostage. Nevertheless, in true Stanley style, he continued to assure Henry of his unqualified support.

William Stanley, on the other hand, said he was still prepared to enter the fight on Henry's side. He remained unwilling, however, to have his men join openly with Henry's until the right moment.

Henry and his advisors almost certainly realized that the two Stanleys were still playing their old double game. They gave assurances of support, and they probably did want a Tudor victory. After all, Lord Stanley was Henry's stepfather. But by now it must have become evident that they would wait out the battle and then come in decisively on what appeared to be the winning side—even if it was Richard's.

Evidently Richard did not know of these meetings; or, his fighting blood aroused, he no longer cared. If it was the latter, he was not merely impetuous, but reckless to the point of being suicidal. It is also possible that, with the Tudor forces seeming to move in the direction of the capital, Richard felt he had no choice but to engage them no matter what the Stanleys intended.

Shakespeare tells us that Richard had hideous nightmares the night before the battle, suggesting that he was conscious of his overwhelming guilt. The Croyland Chronicle says "it was reported" that Richard had such dreams and adds that, in the morning, the king, who "was always drawn," was "ever more pale and deathly." We have no eyewitness account and cannot be sure.

There was, however, further evidence of treachery. Reportedly, a message was affixed to the duke of Norfolk's tent. It read "Jocke of Norfolk, be not too bold, for Dickon thy master is bought and sold." "Dickon" was a nickname for Richard used by his family and friends.

Lord Stanley had avoided meeting Richard before the battle, claiming to be suffering from the "sweating sickness," a common ailment at the time. By the morning of the battle, August 22, 1485, Richard had lost patience. He sent a final message to Stanley ordering him to join the royal forces at once if he valued his son's life. Stanley is reported to have replied that he had other sons and was not ready to come to Richard's side. Depending on whose account is accepted, Richard either ordered or contemplated the execution of Lord Strange, and either his men failed to carry out the order or Richard decided to let the outcome of the battle determine the man's fate.

As the day of battle dawned, Richard's men were concentrated on the high ground of Ambion Hill. The duke of Norfolk commanded the front under his banner of the silver lion. Richard himself was just behind Norfolk in the center. Northumberland's men were in reserve. Their mission was to move up should any part of Richard's front be weakened. Northumberland himself had proposed this position, arguing that his men were tired from their long march and that, from a reserve position, they could swing around and attack Lord Stanley's flank, should he go over to Henry Tudor. Richard accepted the suggestion.

Richard stood beside his own white boar banner. Over his helmet he placed the royal crown, as Henry V had done at Agincourt. Richard was warned that the gold circlet would make him a prime target. He was not deterred. He was the king of England.

Gairdner reports that Richard gave a stirring address to his assembled army. He referred to Henry Tudor as "a Welsh milksop, a man of small courage and less experience in war" who "never saw army, nor is able of himself to guide one." And "as for the Frenchmen and Bretons, their valour is such that our noble progenitors and your valiant parents have vanquished them oftener in one month than they at first thought possible to do in a whole year." Then, he exhorted, "dismiss all fear, and like valiant champions advance forth your standards. Every one give but one sure stroke, and the day is ours."

Henry's troops were now directly in front of Richard's in the valley below. His vanguard was commanded by the veteran earl of Oxford, with Sir Gilbert Talbot on the right and Sir John Savage on the left. Henry, no warrior, was in a protected position in the rear of the left flank. Next to him was his standard-bearer, carrying Henry's huge white banner with the red dragon of Cadwallader.

As the morning drew on, the Stanleys' men were arrayed on the plain forward of Richard and on his right toward Market Bosworth. Both Stanleys were now lined up closer to Richard's side of the field than to Henry's, which could have been taken as a sign favorable to Richard if one were grasping for such a sign.

The area is not much changed today. The visitor can still stand on Ambion Hill and look out over the plain, just as Richard did that summer morning over five hundred years ago. One can almost see Henry's forces in battle formation at the foot of the hill and the Stanleys' men off to the right, with Market Bosworth behind them in the hazy distance.

The fighting began with rather ineffective artillery barrages on each side. Next, Oxford's men started up the hill. Richard's archers rained arrows on them, causing the first serious casualties and slowing the assault. Then, with a rousing cry, Norfolk led his men in a charge down the hill into the midst of Oxford's forces. Ferocious hand-to-hand combat ensued. As time passed, the tide of battle flowed back and forth, with the Stanleys still playing no part.

To offset Norfolk's greater numbers, Oxford formed his men into a wedge. This created a difficult situation for Norfolk's center, but it allowed his wings to press in on Oxford's flanks. Seeing that this posed a serious danger, Oxford briefly broke off the engagement and regrouped his forces. Norfolk allowed him this respite, probably content to strengthen his own line.

Now, Oxford launched a fierce and concentrated attack on Richard's center. The fighting was brutal and bloody. Suddenly a cry went up. The intrepid Norfolk had been killed. This posed a serious problem for Richard. Fifteenth-century troops were typically fighting not so much for the king or his opponent as for their own lord, who had brought them to the field. The Welsh who came to Bosworth with Rhys ap Thomas were primarily fighting for Rhys, rather than for Henry Tudor. The duke of Norfolk's men were fighting primarily for Norfolk, rather than for Richard.

When Norfolk fell, his son immediately assumed command of the center and tried to rally his men. But the loss of their lord was demoralizing, and Richard's entire line seemed in peril. Slowly but steadily his men were being pushed back up Ambion Hill.

At this critical point, Richard called on Northumberland's reserve. This was just the situation in which a fierce attack by the reserve could turn the tide of battle and even win the day. But Northumberland ignored Richard's order. The reserve failed to attack. Like Norfolk's men, they were essentially there to serve the lord who had brought them to the field. When Northumberland gave no order to attack, they simply held their positions.

Richard was urged to flee. This was only one battle. He was still king. He could gather many more men and fight another day. A ballad of the Stanley family records Richard's defiant reply:

One foot will I never flee,
Whilst the breath is my breast within.
Give me my batell axe in hand
and sett my crowne on my head so hye,
for by him that made both sea and land
King of England this day I will dye!

Grasping the extreme difficulty of his situation, Richard decided on a bold throw of the dice. He spurred his horse forward, racing down Ambion Hill and across the plain directly toward Henry Tudor, hanging back under the red-dragon flag. A hundred or so loyal knights joined Richard in this fierce, headlong charge. Henry had taken no part in the fighting; and Richard's plan was to engage his rival in personal combat and kill him, ending the battle with a single stroke.

Richard's plan, while bold, was risky. His charge required him to lead his charging knights directly across the front of the Stanleys' massed troops. Undeterred by the risk, Richard and his men thundered across the plain and smashed into the host of Lancastrian nobles surrounding and protecting Henry.

Even according to Tudor historians, Richard was courageous and highly effective. Attacking ferociously first with his lance and then his battle-ax, he killed Henry's standard-bearer, Sir William Brandon, who was within a few yards of Henry himself. Moving forward, he unhorsed the famed giant Sir John Cheney, a powerful and experienced warrior who had come forward to aid Brandon. Then, his blood aroused, Richard made straight for Henry Tudor, who was certainly no match for him in individual combat.

At that moment, Sir William Stanley's men attacked. Three thousand men in Sir William's blood-red tunics fell upon Richard from his unprotected right flank. Soon he was surrounded by hostile red-coated troops in overwhelming numbers.

With his small escort quickly cut down, Richard stood his ground alone, swinging his weapon in all directions, knowing that death was certain, but intending to take as many of the traitors with him as possible. There was no hope. Wounded over and over again by the hostile throng pressing in on him from all sides, Richard at last sunk to the ground, slain.

Why had he made this risky charge, rather than holding the high ground and personally rallying his troops as he had time and again? Riding across the front of the Stanley forces, he was literally putting his fate in their hands. If they attacked his small force on its unprotected right, he and his men would almost certainly be killed.

How could he have believed that the Stanleys would not take this extraordinary opportunity to kill him and put Henry Tudor on the throne? In Richard's eyes, both Stanleys had betrayed him before the battle started. The Stanleys knew this. They knew that if Richard won, they faced the loss of their power, their lands and probably even their lives. On the other hand, if Henry won, especially through their intervention, they could look forward to rich rewards.

Surely Richard must have realized this. Perhaps he believed he could get to Henry and kill him before the ever cautious Stanleys would decide to intervene. Perhaps he felt that the demoralization caused by Norfolk's death and Northumberland's refusal to fight had created an irreversible situation, so that, even holding the high ground, he would necessarily lose. Perhaps he believed that the obviously disloyal Northumberland was about to attack his rear. Perhaps, as has also been suggested, he saw Henry riding toward the Stanleys' position, evidently to urge them to enter the battle now that Richard's force seemed in disarray. If so, he may have considered it essential to prevent that meeting. We can never know.

What we do know, even from his enemies, is Richard's remarkable bravery in the last moments of his life. Vergil, Henry's official historian, reported that "kyng Richard alone, was killyd fyghting manfully in the thickkest presse of his enemyes."

Even Rous, eager, once Henry took the throne, to say the worst of Richard, wrote that "he most valiantly defended himself as a noble knight to his last breath." The Croyland Chronicle joined in praising the courage of the slain king, "As for King Richard he received many mortal wounds and, like a spirited and most courageous prince, fell on the field and not in flight."

Did Richard lose because Englishmen were disgusted and ashamed to fight under a murderer's banner? Shakespeare said so. But it is almost certainly untrue. He had enemies, of course; and was far less revered in the South than in the North. Many nobles may have remained on the sidelines unwilling to risk death for either side. But Richard's defeat was not caused by the lack of popular support. There was ample support available, and it could have been brought to bear successfully at another time and place.

His defeat was the result of betrayal by the Stanleys and Northumberland, and of his own decisions—first, to fight before his forces were at full strength and without all his available weaponry and then, when Norfolk fell, to launch a risky personal attack across the menacing front of Sir William Stanley's massed force, rather than to rally his troops on the high ground and continue the battle, or else to flee the field, raise another army and fight again.

With its king slain, Richard's army disintegrated. Most of his men attempted to flee to their left toward the town of Dadlington. Many were impeded by the marsh. Most were ridden down by Henry's men and killed. Soon the battle was completely over. It had lasted only two hours.

True to form, Lord Stanley had hung back from the fighting. Only his brother's forces had descended upon Richard's exposed flank. They were more than enough. Now, with the battle over and the victor safely established, Lord Stanley approached Henry and placed Richard's crown on his stepson's head.

With Henry's knowledge and concurrence, Richard's body was stripped and mutilated, thrown over the back of a horse and ridden into Leicester, where it was publicly displayed for days. Finally, Richard was buried by monks in the Church of St. Mary at Leicester. He was only thirty-two. Both the church and his grave have since disappeared.

The entire North grieved at Richard's death. Despite the power and menace of the new Tudor regime, the following entry was made in the York register: "He [Richard] was piteously slain and murdered, to the great heaviness of this city."

XIV

♛ "INFANTS BLOOD"

The twenty-nine year old Henry Tudor was now Henry VII, King of England. His character had been formed and hardened by adversity. Born posthumously, he was denied a father. As a boy, the defeated Lancastrians fled to the Continent, leaving Henry in England among his family's Yorkist enemies. After Henry VI's brief and unsuccessful restoration, he was forced into a youthful exile in Brittany. There he remained for thirteen years, constantly intriguing, constantly in fear that the Bretons would sell him to his enemies, constantly and desperately imploring the Bretons and the French to support the invasion of which he had dreamed for so long.

Unlike Richard in many ways, Henry had become shrewd, greedy, calculating and careful. Sir Francis Bacon, generally pro-Tudor in his views, described Henry as "A dark prince and infinitely suspicious," who "kept a strict hand on his nobility, and chose rather to advance clergymen and lawyers who were more obsequious to him, but had less interest in the people." Indeed, Bacon says that Henry kept watch on everyone around him through "his secret spies, which he did employ both at home and abroad, by them to discover what practices and conspiracies were against him."

So far as the two princes are concerned, Henry's conduct is even more ambiguous than Richard's. It raises more questions than it answers. Certainly it is suspicious.

A few days after his victory at Bosworth Field, Henry entered

London and took control of the Tower. Where were the princes? If they were missing, why didn't Henry send out a hue and cry seeking them everywhere? There is not the slightest indication that he did anything of the kind. It has been claimed that Henry did search the Tower, but there is no record of this, and it seems unlikely that if the search had been widespread and thorough, we would have some indication of its having taken place. Nothing was said publicly about the princes. There was no announcement that they were dead or even that they were missing.

There could be several explanations. Henry could have found the princes dead or found them missing and assumed they were dead. Perhaps he believed that everyone whose opinion counted was already convinced that the boys had been killed by Richard. If so, why do anything to cause further discussion?

Perhaps, for his own reasons, Henry wanted to keep the nobility and potential rivals guessing as to whether the boys were alive or dead. If it was thought that Henry might still produce the live princes, what was the point of rebellion in favor of some other claimant whose right to the throne might be considered inferior to theirs?

On the other hand, if Henry found the princes missing when he took the Tower and thought they could still be alive, announcing their deaths (or even their absence) could be embarrassing if the Yorkists then produced them from hiding. And, even if he thought they were probably dead, he may have been content simply to leave the matter ambiguous.

Henry had lived among the Bretons and the French. He was aware of the European view of England as a violent and unstable place. Conceivably, as the new ruler, he felt that his own prestige depended on avoiding further public discussion of that violence and instability.

Finally, as has been argued, Henry could have found the boys alive and had them put to death. If they were alive when he took the Tower, he had a strong motive for killing them—considerably stronger than Richard's. And, unlike Richard, he had no ties of blood or loyalty that would make him hesitate before committing such a crime.

One of Henry VII's earliest acts was cancelling *Titulus*

Regius, the January 1484 act of Parliament that had declared the children of Edward IV illegitimate by reason of the Eleanor Butler precontract. Evidently Henry took the unusual step of having the act abrogated without its even being read in Parliament.

The customary summary of an act being repealed was not included in Henry's act of 1485. Only the opening words were quoted (which, of course, gave no hint of the precontract or the illegitimacy of Edward's children), followed by a statement that the earlier act was repealed "for the false and seditious imaginacons and untrouths thereof." Indeed the repealing act of 1485 ordered that *Titulus Regius* be removed from the Parliament roll and burned.

And Henry took an even more remarkable step. He ordered that before Easter 1486, every single copy of *Titulus Regius* in the realm must be turned in to the chancellor for destruction, on pain of imprisonment, "so that all thinges said and remembred in the said Bill and Acte thereof maie be for ever out of remembraunce, and also forgott."

Henry's cancellation and suppression of *Titulus Regius* supports the inference that he knew, or at least believed, both princes to be dead. Otherwise, his conduct would have legitimized them along with their sisters. It would have made Prince Edward the rightful king if he was still alive, or made Prince Richard the king if his older brother was dead.

If, on the other hand, both princes were dead, Henry could establish their legitimacy without fear of the claim that he was as much a usurper as Richard. If Henry thought that one or both princes might still be alive, would he have taken that risk?

Perhaps. Henry may have been compelled to take the risk of eliminating *Titulus Regius* in order to establish the legitimacy of the Princess Elizabeth, Edward IV's daughter and Henry's intended wife. Under *Titulus Regius*, she was as illegitimate as her brothers.

As we have seen, Henry's claim to the throne was exceptionally weak. Flawed on both his father's and his mother's sides, his claim was clearly inferior to Richard's and to that of his own intended wife. Later, Henry tried to bolster his title by vague ref-

erences to descent from King Arthur. He appointed commissioners to investigate his relationship to the ancient kings of Briton.
As might have been expected, the commissioners dutifully
reported that Henry was descended not only from King Arthur,
but also from Brutus, an even more ancient king. This was almost
certainly untrue; but it was appealing to the still lingering anti-
Norman feelings of the populace, particularly among the Welsh.

Although it was a fact he detested, Henry's best chance to
establish the entitlement of his own line to the throne was
through Elizabeth, as the daughter of a king and a direct descendant of Edward III. If Elizabeth was not legitimate, that chance
was gone. Even Henry's publicly committing himself in
Christmas 1483 to marry Elizabeth, uniting the houses of
Lancaster and York, was thought to have significantly bolstered
his cause. In 1485, Elizabeth's legitimacy must have seemed critical. Thus, *Titulus Regius* had to be reversed and suppressed.

Despite Henry's draconian attempt to destroy every copy of
that act, one overlooked copy was found in the seventeenth century. Its contents had also been summarized in the Croyland
Chronicle, which similarly lay undiscovered for many years.

This is one of the strange things about the chronicle. Its
author wrote in the reign of Henry VII, after Henry had ordered
every copy of *Titulus Regius* destroyed. The author certainly knew
that, if his account was discovered, it would be political (if not
actual) suicide to have written about the Eleanor Butler precontract and the illegitimacy of Edward IV's children. He clearly had
no desire or motive to help the reputation of Richard, whom he
harshly criticized, or to harm that of Henry, whom he reported
was held to be "an angel sent from heaven."

Yet, amazingly, the chronicler was completely open in
describing the "Parchment roll" proclaiming that "King Edward's
sons were bastards" because "he had been precontracted to a certain Lady Eleanor Boteler before he married Queen Elizabeth."

One of the interesting facets of Henry's conduct is his treatment of Bishop Stillington. Obviously Henry considered the
bishop a threat. On the very day of his victory at Bosworth Field,
Henry had an immediate warrant issued for Stillington's arrest.
The cleric was hunted down, found and imprisoned. Taken with

the arrest of Stillington at the time of Clarence's execution, for disloyal utterances, this rush to imprison the bishop as soon as the battle was over tends to confirm de Commynes's identification of Stillington as the man who disclosed the precontract and the conclusion of later historians to the same effect. Why else would the new Tudor king think immediately of arresting the elderly prelate who appeared innocent of any other "wrongdoing"?

Stranger yet, once imprisoned, the bishop was soon pardoned. He may have been interrogated; but, if he was, it was done privately, and no report of his responses was ever issued or found.

While trying to eradicate every record to the effect that the children of Edward IV were illegitimate, Henry had Parliament grant a full pardon to the man who told Richard, the council and Parliament that they were, and who claimed to be the sole eyewitness to the precontract on which that assertion was based. And Henry appears to have done so without calling for any inquiry into the truth of Stillington's claims.

Stillington's act of pardon refers to the bishop's "horrible and heinous offences," but it carefully avoids specifying what those offences were. The pardon is easier to square with the inference that Henry actually believed Stillington's story about the precontract than with the view that Henry thought it was a lie. It is difficult to believe that Henry would so quickly pardon a man for concocting and selling to the council and Parliament a tale that led to the exclusion of the rightful king and the usurpation of the throne by his scheming uncle. Harsh punishment, rather than a pardon, would have seemed called for if Henry really thought the bishop had engaged in that fraudulent and treasonous conduct.

On the other hand, even if he thought Stillington had lied, Henry might conceivably have pardoned him simply to avoid giving the matter notoriety. Obviously, Henry could have obtained a coerced statement from Stillington to the effect that there had never been a precontract. But issuing such a statement would have led to public speculation and perhaps disbelief. After all, Parliament had officially and publicly acknowledged the existence of the precontract, and there may well have been other evidence of its existence. Possibly Henry opted for keeping the matter as quiet as possible. The less said about the precontract, the better.

Following his accession, Henry caused Parliament to attaint Richard and twenty-eight of his followers for "treason." Treason? How could that be when Richard, rather than Henry, was the reigning king at the time of the battle? Henry pressed this unique charge based on a measure that shocked much of Parliament, but which its members dared not oppose. He simply dated his own reign from the day *before* the battle, so that Richard and his men were fighting against the king, rather than for him.

Later in his reign, Henry realized that this kind of ex post facto attainder for treason could make men afraid to fight on *his* side against rival claimants. Accordingly, Parliament enacted a bill establishing that it was not treason to fight for a reigning king, whether or not his claim was rightful.

The bill of attainder against Richard in 1485 sets out Henry's charges against his late rival. It is frequently cited by revisionists as strong proof that Richard did not kill his nephews. William Snyder puts the revisionist case as follows: "In enumerating the crimes alleged against Richard III, the most important charge Henry could have made to blacken Richard and strengthen his own weak title to the throne would have been to charge that Richard murdered the two young sons of his brother, Edward IV. This the Act does *not* do."

Or does it? The bill charges Richard with "shedding of Infants blood." What "Infants" if not the two princes? Those revisionists who attempt to deal with this language at all tend to argue that it is just a vague and general reference, included in a list of varied crimes, and that if Henry thought that Richard had killed the reigning king and his brother, the charge of treason and regicide would have headed the list and would have been made explicit in order to generate public outrage at Richard's conduct.

Indeed, if "shedding of Infants blood" does not refer to killing the princes, there is no record of Henry's charging Richard with their murder for the next seventeen years.

But the revisionists may not be giving the bill of attainder a fair reading. "[S]hedding of Infants blood" is not merely one of a long list of crimes. Fairly construed, it is the *only* specified crime.

The one specific charge made against Richard in the actual text of the bill is that he committed "Perjuries, Treasons, Homicides and Murdres, in shedding of Infants blood." Beyond that, he is accused, only in generalizations, of "manie other Wronges, odious Offences, and abominacons, ayenst God and Man." The language of the bill does not charge Richard with a list of crimes *plus* "shedding of Infants blood." The charge is that he committed perjuries, treasons, homicides and murders "*in* (not *and*) shedding of Infants blood."

Two constructions of the this language are possible. The first is that Richard shed "Infants blood" and that this same act also constituted "Perjuries, Treasons, Homicides and Murdres." Since treason would require an act against the Crown, this construction of the language, charging Richard with treasonous conduct that shed "Infants blood," would very likely be a reference to killing the princes.

The second construction is that "in shedding of Infants blood" modifies only "Murdres" and not "Perjuries, Treasons and Homicides." If this was the intended meaning, Richard was accused of murdering infants, but the victims of his Perjuries, Treasons and Homicides could have been adults. This construction would avoid the conclusion that the "shedding of Infants blood" was also "Treason," leaving room for the possibility that Richard murdered some other, nonroyal "Infants." But whom? There is no record of Richard being charged with killing any other young children.

Modern punctuation rules would support the first construction, that "in shedding of Infants blood" refers to "Perjuries," "Treasons" and "Homicides," not just to "Murdres." But commas may not have conveyed the same meaning in 1485 as they do today. Perhaps the use of both "Homicides" and "Murdres" was intended to distinguish between "Murdres" that shed "Infants blood" and "Homicides" that involved the killing of adults.

Because there is no apostrophe in "Infants," we cannot be sure if it is singular or plural. Clearly it is used in the possessive sense; but, standing alone, it could refer to the blood of one or more than one infant. Since "Murdres" is plural, however, it would seem that "Infants" must also be.

Did capitalizing "Infants" signify that the children had royal status? Probably not. There is no consistent pattern of capitalizing words in the bill of attainder. "Offences" is capitalized, "abominacons" is not. "God" is capitalized, but so is "Man." Elsewhere in the bill, the word "virtue" is sometimes capitalized and sometimes not.

The document provides no definite answers to any of these questions. But we cannot rule out the possibility that "shedding of Infants blood" is a reference to killing the princes.

If it is, why was Henry not explicit in charging Richard with the heinous crime of killing the reigning king, who was still a child and was Richard's own nephew?

Perhaps a belief in Richard's guilt was already so widely held that Henry saw no need to be more specific in the bill. Perhaps, not knowing the truth, Henry was reluctant to charge Richard explicitly, since the boys could still have been produced from some hiding place. Perhaps, again, Henry hoped to keep the matter ambiguous. If the princes were thought to be alive, or even possibly alive, that would deter others from rallying to the cause of some other claimant. Or perhaps Henry knew that Richard did not kill the princes, because he had learned that Buckingham or someone else had committed the crime, or Henry had killed them himself or he knew they were still alive.

On January 18, 1486, five months after Bosworth Field, Henry fulfilled his pledge to marry the Princess Elizabeth. Plainly he was in no hurry to do so, and he appears to have gone through with the ceremony only reluctantly after that step was strongly urged by his advisors.

Henry would not permit Elizabeth's coronation for the first two years of their marriage. That delay might signify some problem between them. More probably, it indicates his own inclination to deemphasize both her importance to his rule and her own potential claim to the throne.

Certainly Henry realized that once Elizabeth was declared legitimate by the reversal and suppression of *Titulus Regius,* there was a strong argument that she, rather than he, was the true heir to the throne. If so, Henry would be ruling only through her title, not his own, and on her death there would be a serious question as to his continuing right to the throne. By deferring Elizabeth's coronation, Henry emphasized that he was ruling in his own right, not hers.

Probably for the same reason, when Henry finally allowed his wife's coronation to take place, he did not attend. Along with his mother, Lady Stanley, the king watched the coronation and the subsequent banquet discreetly hidden behind a latticework screen.

From the time of their marriage in 1485 until her death in 1503, Henry kept his queen very much in the background. Her function was to remain silent and beget male heirs. Elizabeth gave birth to a son in 1486. Consistent with Henry's claim to be descended from the ancient kings, the boy was named Arthur. Prince Henry followed in 1491. Arthur died in 1502. The younger prince went on to become the legendary Henry VIII, who ruled from 1509 to 1547.

After Bosworth Field, Henry VII richly rewarded John Morton, making him archbishop of Canterbury in 1486 and chancellor in 1487. Morton, who later became a cardinal, was widely detested as the originator of "Morton's Fork," a device he used to extort money for the Crown. If a potential "donor" lived on a lavish scale, Morton pointed out that he obviously could afford to give a great deal to his king. If, on the other hand, his target lived frugally, the wily bishop claimed that this modest scale of living necessarily left him ample funds to give the Crown.

Henry's relationship with the dowager queen, Elizabeth Woodville, is curious, considering that she had supported his claim and had become his mother-in-law. In 1487, at the time of Lambert Simnell's rebellion, Henry confiscated her lands and gave them to her daughters. As a practical matter, much of the forfeited property went to Henry himself as her oldest daughter's husband.

The former queen was dispatched to the convent at Bermondsey, rarely, if ever, emerging again. No official reason was given. It was said that Henry was incensed at the way she had cozied up to Richard. But Henry had known that from the time he first took the throne in 1485. Why did he wait until 1487?

One could speculate that if Henry killed the princes, and

their mother discovered the crime and could not live with her son-in-law's guilt, she would have posed a serious threat. Henry could, of course, have had her killed, but she was his mother-in-law, and it might have been a convenient compromise to banish her to the convent and threaten her with death if she spoke out about the murders.

But this is sheer speculation. Another and perhaps more likely explanation for Henry's action against the former queen is that in 1487 she supported the pretender, Lambert Simnell, a matter discussed later, along with the theory that Prince Richard may never have been killed at all.

Henry's treatment of James Tyrell is among the strangest aspects of his behavior. The Tower was occupied by hundreds of curious folk. If Richard wrote a letter to the Tower constable directing that the princes be murdered and then wrote a second letter directing them to turn over the Tower keys to Tyrell for one night, and Tyrell and his men had proceeded to take over the Tower, kill the princes, dig a deep hole under a staircase and bury them in it, and then a priest had come along, dug them up and reburied them, and at least nine people had known about all of this, one would expect that, when Richard was killed at Bosworth Field, someone would tell Henry Tudor about Tyrell's involvement, or at least that there would be considerable gossip implicating Sir James.

Yet, Tyrell was neither attainted nor apparently even investigated. At first, as a known Yorkist, he was deprived of certain offices given him by Richard. But these were soon restored by Henry; and, over time, Tyrell was given other coveted and lucrative posts by the King and appeared to enjoy Henry's favor.

A peculiar aspect of Tyrell's relationship with Henry is the matter of the pardons. On June 16, 1486 Henry issued Tyrell a general pardon for all crimes that he might have committed. This in itself is not suspicious. Such general amnesties were periodically granted to loyal and favored subjects, and it is of course possible that at this point Henry did not suspect that Tyrell had committed any crime.

But just one month later, on July 16, 1486, Henry issued Tyrell *a second general pardon*. This is a more unusual event. It suggests that in the four weeks between June 16 and July 16, Tyrell may have committed some serious crime approved or at least condoned by Henry. That crime *might* have been the murder of the princes. They might have been found alive by Henry when he took possession of the Tower in August of 1485 and kept in close confinement there or elsewhere until late June or early July 1486, when they were killed by Tyrell at Henry's request. The operative word is "might." We have no evidence that any such thing happened. The second pardon could have been for some entirely different and unrelated act, or it could have had some other purpose altogether.

The case can be made that killing the princes would not have been out of character for Henry. Neither he nor his son, Henry VIII, was reluctant to imprison or kill rival claimants and others who posed a danger. Unlike Richard, Henry imprisoned Clarence's son Warwick, and had him executed when he was twenty-four years old. He imprisoned the marquess of Dorset; and, in 1495, he even executed Sir William Stanley, who had saved the day (and Henry's life) at Bosworth Field.

Henry had no need to kill the faithless Northumberland, who had betrayed Richard when his reserve was so desperately needed at Bosworth Field. Northumberland was murdered by an angry band of northerners while on a tax-collecting mission for Henry. The Great Chronicle of London reported that the northerners "bore him a deadly malice for the dysappoyntyng of Kyng Rychard at Bosworth Field."

By the time of Henry's death in 1509, virtually every member of the House of York had been killed off, except the earl of Suffolk and Clarence's daughter, the countess of Salisbury.

On the other hand, despite this somewhat brutal record, Henry VII appeared reluctant to kill children. He deferred the execution of young Warwick until he was twenty-four, and, as will be seen below, he spared the rebel Lambert Simnell, possibly at least in part because of his extreme youth.

On his deathbed, Henry advised his son, who was about to become Henry VIII, to execute Suffolk. Upon occupying the throne, that filial son dutifully followed his father's advice. But, of course, Suffolk was not a child.

Henry VIII went on to make the elimination of potential rivals something of a Tudor policy. The execution of Suffolk was followed by that of the then-current duke of Buckingham, the marquess of Exeter, Lord Montagu and finally Clarence's daughter, the aging countess of Salisbury, who was beheaded (at age seventy) after being falsely charged with treason.

Traditionalists have argued that such Tudor successors of Henry VII as his son, Henry VIII, and his granddaughter, Elizabeth I, had no need to blacken Richard's reputation. Despite the weakness of Henry VII's own claim to the throne, these Tudor monarchs were also descended from Henry's queen, Elizabeth of York, a daughter of Edward IV. Thus, the argument goes, they could be secure in their title even though Henry VII could not.

But this overlooks the fact that *Titulus Regius* would have made Elizabeth of York as illegitimate as her brothers. Unless Richard's claim could be discredited, the subsequent Tudors had no better title than Henry VII—and that was a shaky title at best. Even James I, who succeeded Elizabeth, had to base his claim on descent from the eldest daughter of Henry VII and Elizabeth of York, and therefore was motivated to foster the Tudor view of Richard and his "usurpation."

XV

"PRETENDERS" AND "IMPOSTERS"

F rancis Bacon wrote in the seventeenth century that during the first year of Henry Tudor's reign there were "secret rumours and whisperings—which afterwards gathered strength and turned to great troubles—that the two young sons of King Edward the Fourth, or one of them, which were said to be destroyed in the Tower, were not indeed murdered, but conveyed secretly away, and were yet living." Bacon added that during the second year of Henry's reign "it was still whispered every where that at least one of the children of Edward the Fourth was living." Were these "rumours and whisperings" true?

In late 1486, a young man appeared in Ireland apparently claiming to be Clarence's son, Edward, duke of Warwick. He was not Warwick, of course. The real Warwick was in the Tower, having been imprisoned there from the time Henry took the throne.

The Irish were given to Yorkist sympathies ever since the popular Irish administration of Richard's father. They seem to have called the young man "Edwardus" and to have acclaimed him as "King Edward VI." If true, this is interesting in itself, since it implied that Edward V, the older prince, was dead. "Edwardus" was joined in Ireland by Warwick's cousin, the earl of Lincoln, who arrived from Burgundy with an army of German mercenaries supplied by his Aunt Margaret, the dowager duchess of Burgundy. Like Lincoln's mother, Margaret was a sister of Richard III and Edward IV.

On June 4, 1487, Lincoln's forces invaded England. Henry VII dealt with the situation with his customary shrewdness. To expose "Edwardus" as an imposter, he produced the real Warwick from the Tower. Then Henry raised an army and marched north to meet the invaders.

The brave and determined Lincoln met the royal army at the battle of Stoke on June 16, 1487. The royal forces were commanded by the veteran earl of Oxford, the victor of Bosworth Field. Lincoln had two thousand well-armed and well-trained German mercenaries, another two thousand English volunteers who had flocked to his cause, and four or five thousand Irish, who had no armor, no training and only clubs and other crude weapons. Oxford and Henry had come north with four to five thousand fighting men to which the Stanleys (evidently certain of the outcome this time) added five thousand of their own men.

Thus, the two armies were of approximately equal size. Gradually, however, superior weaponry told. The Irish fought fiercely, but were no match for Oxford's armored swordsmen. The German troops and Lincoln's English adherents put up a stiff fight; but, ultimately, Lincoln's forces were defeated and he was killed along with much of his army.

"Edwardus" was captured. He was identified as Lambert Simnell, the son of a common tradesman. It was reported that he had been coached to play Warwick by a priest. Henry was not vindictive toward Simnell. Supposedly, because of his youth, Lambert was spared, was put to work in the royal kitchens and later became one of the King's falconers. Perhaps Henry felt that it was clear to everyone that Lambert was an imposter and that whatever threat might lie out there to Henry's reign did not reside in that poor young man. Besides, if that threat did eventuate and another "pretender" appeared, Henry could point to Simnell and say "Look who the last one turned out to be. Well, here comes another."

After the battle of Stoke, Henry expressed regret that Lincoln had been killed, saying he was "sorie for the earl's death, because from him he might have known the bottom of his danger." This suggests that Henry, while not knowing the truth for sure, suspected that there was something or someone behind the rebellion that was far more dangerous to him than Lincoln, Warwick or Lambert Simnell. What other unknown and greater "danger" could Henry have feared was behind the rebellion?

Two scenarios come to mind, neither of which can be dismissed. Under both, the princes, or at least one of them, survived and was living secretly abroad. The first possibility is that Simnell was indeed an imposter and that Lincoln and Margaret used him as the focal point of the rebellion, intending to replace him with one of the princes if the rebels were successful. If that was the plan, the risk of failure would be borne by Simnell and Lincoln, while the true prince would be kept safe under Burgundian protection until the outcome of the rebellion was decided.

If Prince Edward was alive, he would have been seventeen. Prince Richard would only have been thirteen. If Richard was the only surviving prince, Margaret and Lincoln may have originally intended to wait until he was older before making their move. But the birth of Prince Arthur in September 1486 gave Henry VII a male heir. Possibly that event forced Margaret and Lincoln to take action earlier than they had planned. Even though Prince Richard was still young, the experienced and able Lincoln could serve as protector in the early years of his reign.

This may seem a romantic fantasy. On analysis, however, it may make more sense than the theory that Lincoln fought to put Lambert Simnell or the possibly retarded Warwick on the throne, or that Lincoln intended to seize the throne for himself.

Certainly, if Simnell was an imposter, Lincoln and Margaret knew it. If the two sons of Edward IV were dead, why would Lincoln risk his life supporting an obviously bogus claimant, rather than directly asserting his own legitimate claim? After all, Richard was dead, Clarence's attainder (and thus that of Warwick) had never been formally reversed and a good case could be made that if Edward's own sons were also dead, Lincoln, as the nephew of Edward IV, was the rightful heir to the throne.

Why would Margaret send troops in support of a youthful imposter, rather than to place her nephew Lincoln on the throne, where he lawfully belonged? And if the goal was to obtain the crown for the mature and popular Lincoln, why go through the charade of supporting a demonstrable phony, instead of directly fostering a rebellion in Lincoln's own name?

But, if Margaret and Lincoln knew that one of the princes was alive, it could make sense to support an imposter, with the intention of putting the surviving prince on the throne if the rebellion was successful, while keeping him safely abroad if it was not.

Support for this theory may be found in Elizabeth Woodville's apparent backing of Simnell's rebellion. We know that, in February 1487, Henry VII suddenly confiscated his mother-in-law's lands and dispatched her to the convent at Bermondsey, where she remained "in prison, poverty and solitude."

Henry trumped up the demonstrably false explanation that the former queen had turned her daughters over to Richard. But this had occurred years earlier, and Henry had known it all along. It was obviously not the true reason for his sudden and harsh treatment of his mother-in-law. Even Bacon, generally pro-Tudor in his views, considered it "very probable there was some greater matter against her, which the king, upon reason of policie, and to avoid envy, would not publish."

What was that "greater matter"? Henry's action against Elizabeth Woodville flowed directly from a council meeting in early February. The subject of that particular meeting was the threat posed by Simnell, who was in Ireland with Lincoln and his army waiting for spring to invade. What seems "very probable" was that Henry and his council believed the ex-queen was in league with Simnell and Lincoln.

With her daughter reigning as queen and her new grandson destined to succeed to the throne, would Elizabeth Woodville plot to enthrone an imposter or Lincoln or even the real Warwick, a son of the hated Clarence and probably feebleminded to boot? It makes no sense. But her support for the rebellion would make perfect sense if Simnell, Lincoln and Warwick were just "stalking-horses" for one of her own sons, who had not been killed after all but had been hidden abroad awaiting the moment when he could return and claim the throne.

The one thing that Elizabeth Woodville would have preferred to her daughter reigning as queen would have been her son reigning as king. Under Henry VII, the former queen had none of her former power and influence. Awaiting the rule of her grandson would take many years and, even if she survived, it is unlikely that, as an aged widow, her position at court would be significant. But her young sons had loved and respected her and had been completely under her influence and that of her family. If one of her sons were now to become king, her own powerful position and that of the Woodvilles would be completely restored—and at once.

This theory is further supported by Henry's action in imprisoning Elizabeth Woodville's older son, the marquess of Dorset, for the duration of the Simnell threat. That act strongly suggests that Henry feared the entire Woodville family was supporting Simnell's rebellion. Why would the Woodvilles support a rebellion against the husband of a Woodville princess, unless its aim was to put a Woodville prince on the throne? Like that of his mother, Dorset's position in the reign of one of his nephews, with a Woodville-dominated court, would be far greater than it could ever be under Henry VII, as a half brother of Henry's queen.

The other scenario as to the rebellion of 1478 has been suggested in a fascinating article by Gordon Smith in the December 1996 Ricardian. Smith's theory is that the "Lambert Simnell" put to work in the royal kitchens was, in fact, a commoner, but that the young man who appeared in Ireland and was called "Edwardus" was a different and considerably older youth who was, in reality, Edward V. Under this view, Edward was killed at the battle of Stoke, after which Henry VII substituted as his "captive" a young commoner who could be readily shown to be an imposter.

This theory would also explain the apparent support for the rebellion by Elizabeth Woodville and her family. Their aim was to place her son Edward on the throne that had been taken from him, even if it was then occupied by her daughter's husband, Henry VII.

The additional evidence in support of this theory is sparse. It consists primarily of two factors. Supposedly, the troops who fought for "Edwardus" at Stoke claimed that they were doing so to "restore" the king. That terminology, if it has been accurately reported, would only be applicable to Edward V, who had been proclaimed king even though his coronation had not taken place. Neither Warwick, nor Lincoln, nor even Prince Richard could be "restored" as king.

The second factor is what appears to have been a marked difference in age between "Edwardus" and Lambert Simnell. Irish chronicles refer to the young man who was the focal point of the 1487 rebellion as being at least fifteen. Vergil altered his "History" to change his description of the youth from a "boy" to an "adolescent," a term that usually means someone between thirteen and eighteen. Edward V would have been seventeen in 1487. Lambert Simnell was only ten.

Was Edward killed in the battle, after which Henry substituted a young commoner who, in fact, was much younger, and who could be kept on hand to remind everyone that the rebellion had been in support of the bizarre claims of an obvious imposter?

It is interesting that "Lambert" was Jane Shore's maiden name, that "Simnell" is a kind of grain used by bakers and that Lambert's father was reportedly a baker. Was the name simply made up by Henry's agents?

Despite these speculations, the "stalking-horse" scenario seems more likely than the "substitution" theory. But neither can be ruled out. Whether Simnell was a "stalking-horse" for one of the princes or was himself Edward V, it is difficult to find another explanation for Elizabeth Woodville and her family supporting the rebellion, and it is not easy to find any credible explanation for Henry's shutting away the former queen and arresting her son, Dorset, other than that they were at least suspected of supporting "Simnell's" cause.

In the fall of 1491, another and even more dangerous "pretender" appeared in Ireland. This one had the distinctive Plantagenet looks, was richly dressed and claimed to be Prince Richard, the younger of the two sons of Edward IV. He also claimed the right to the English throne. Later, Henry VII, distressed at the ability of this young man to captivate the crowned heads of Europe, sent out spies to investigate his background and claimed that he was, in fact, Perkin (or Pierrequin) Warbeck, a commoner from Tournai. Still later, after a rebellion in his name failed, "Perkin" supposedly confessed to the accuracy of Henry's claim.

The fact that the identity claimed by this pretender was not Edward V supports the inference that, by then, the older prince was known to be dead. If this were not so, Prince Richard would have had no claim to the throne. The rightful king would have been his older brother.

Perkin arrived in Cork Harbor on a Portuguese ship. Either then or relatively soon thereafter he spoke English fluently and displayed an intimate and detailed knowledge about the family of Edward IV, including facts that would only be known to members or close associates of that royal family. He appeared to be about eighteen, which fit with Prince Richard's age. He claimed that he had been smuggled out of England and had lived in Flanders until he was old enough to act. Now he had come forward to claim his rights.

Apparently, Perkin was generally vague about the fate of his older brother, but he certainly created the impression that Edward was no longer alive, and he wrote at least one letter stating that he had been told his brother had been murdered.

While most historians treat it as established fact that Perkin was an imposter, he was able to persuade a number of English and European noblemen of the validity of his claim. Indeed, most European rulers at least acted as if Perkin was the younger son of Edward IV and the rightful king of England.

Spain and France were exceptions to this, or at least sought to create the impression that they did not accept Perkin's authenticity. Ferdinand and Isabella were negotiating for the marriage of their daughter, Katherine of Aragon, to Henry VII's son, Prince Arthur. They had every reason to reject Perkin's claim to the throne. Spain also wanted Henry VII's aid in frustrating the French king's ambitions in Italy.

Interestingly, however, D. M. Kleyn points out that the Spanish monarchs, in corresponding with their own ambassadors, used a code in which the members of royal families were given a roman numeral. Although commoners were not assigned such cyphers, Perkin was. Despite their public position, in the private code used between Ferdinand and Isabella and their emissaries, Perkin was classified as royalty.

The French king, Charles VIII, had originally welcomed Perkin; but later political considerations, including the desire to keep Henry out of the league of Spain and other European powers aimed at stopping a French invasion of Italy, led the French, at least publicly, to speak of Perkin as a pretender.

On the other hand, Maximilian, "king of the Romans" and his son, Archduke Philip, gave Perkin substantial support and treated him as the duke of York and the rightful English king. Evidently they had their own reasons for doing so.

Probably no valid conclusion can be drawn from the public behavior of any of the European monarchs. Whether they supported Perkin or rejected him, they were acting out of political self-interest and not based upon what they really considered to be the truth.

There were two notable exceptions. One was Margaret, the dowager duchess of Burgundy, who would have been Prince Richard's aunt, and who appears to have been steadfast in her backing of Perkin. The other was James IV of Scotland. James not only welcomed Perkin to his court as Richard IV of England, he also supported him financially and militarily and allowed him to wed Katherine Gordon, a beautiful member of the Scottish royal family with whom Perkin was and remained deeply in love. Even after Perkin supposedly confessed that he was a commoner from Tournai, James would not renounce him and continued to refer to him as the duke of York and to hold the view that Perkin was entitled to the English throne.

Perkin was persuasive enough to cost Sir William Stanley his life. In 1495, Stanley, who had saved the day for Henry VII at Bosworth Field, made the mistake of saying that if Perkin was really Prince Richard, he would not fight against him. Given the Stanleys' proclivity for having one brother support a rebellion, while the other remained "neutral" or supported the other side, Sir William may actually have established a secret liaison with Perkin. If so, he was betrayed by Sir Robert Clifford. Clifford, a staunch Yorkist, had joined a group of conspirators at the court of

Margaret of Burgundy, saying that he had seen Perkin and knew him to be the true son of Edward IV. Soon Clifford became a leader of the conspiracy to put Perkin on the throne. But Henry's shrewdness and money prevailed. Clifford was given a pardon and a bribe of five hundred pounds to identify the conspirators in England and on the Continent. Whether Clifford merely quoted Stanley's remark or implicated him in the conspiracy, Clifford's report to Henry resulted in Stanley's arrest and execution.

Sir William's statement that if Perkin were the younger Prince, he would not fight against him, is interesting in itself. It shows his recognition—at least by 1495—that the two princes may not have been killed by Richard or anyone else, and makes it less likely that, as has been argued, the reason the Stanleys betrayed Richard at Bosworth Field was their horror at Richard's having murdered his own nephews.

Henry instructed his emissaries to spread the word of Perkin's low birth throughout Europe. Curiously, among the points he told them to make in support of this assertion was that the reason Elizabeth Woodville was attainted in 1487 was her having surrendered her daughters into Richard's custody.

Henry's making that claim in this context is strange and possibly significant. How did this seemingly incredible excuse for sending Elizabeth Woodville to a convent in 1487 argue against Perkin's authenticity? The two matters would seem wholly unrelated—unless Henry felt that there was a suspicion among European nobility that the *true* reason for Elizabeth's banishment had been her support for Lambert Simnell's rebellion.

In fact, that does appear to have been the cause of her banishment and attainder, as well as for the arrest of her son, Dorset, in the same period. And if the Woodvilles supported Simnell's rebellion, the Europeans would certainly have asked why. Probably there was gossip in Europe that the former queen and her family had supported the rebellion because "Simnell" had been a stalking-horse for Elizabeth's younger son, Richard, who was still alive and might well be "Perkin." Probably the Europeans could think of no other reason why the Woodvilles would have supported Simnell's rebellion, and no other reason why Henry had moved against both the ex-queen and Dorset when he did.

If so, Henry would have been anxious to make the case that supporting Simnel's rebellion was *not* the reason for Elizabeth's attainder, and so would have instructed his emissaries to provide an alternative explanation. It is difficult to think of any other reason for Henry's including this point about Elizabeth Woodville's attainder in the arguments to be made against Perkin's authenticity.

In 1496, Perkin, accompanied by a Scottish army, crossed into England. James IV personally led the Scottish forces in what was supposed to be an incursion to attract English support for Perkin's cause. Proclamations were issued to the effect that no harm was meant to England or Englishmen and that the true king, Richard IV, was simply asserting his legitimate rights.

Very little support was attracted. Perhaps this was because of the hatred and fear with which the Scots were regarded in the English border areas. What hope there was of attracting English support vanished entirely when the Scottish troops began to rape, pillage and burn everything in their path. What had begun as a campaign to put Perkin on the English throne was becoming simply a brutal border raid.

Perkin was appalled at the barbarous conduct of the Scots and appealed to James to stop it. James, who failed to share Perkin's sensitivity, replied that this was what war was like and that his men were simply taking what they considered their due. He also expressed his disappointment that no Englishman appeared ready to support the man who claimed to be their rightful king.

Perkin left James and the raiding army and returned to Edinburgh in a state of shock and disgust. He had never had military training of any sort. Nor had he seen even a mild skirmish, much less the kind of brutality he had witnessed in the Scottish invasion.

It has been argued that when James returned home he had lost faith in Perkin and pressured him to leave the country. This does not appear to be the case. While perhaps disappointed at Perkin's lack of martial spirit and depressed by the lack of enthusiasm shown by the English for Perkin's cause, James continued to be open and direct in supporting his new kinsman. He did however conclude, apparently with Perkin's agreement, that

Perkin must now move on and organize a true incursion into England.

In 1497, Perkin landed with a small force in Cornwall. He gathered some local supporters, but they were ill equipped and were soundly defeated by the royal forces. Perkin fled, but was captured when he was lured out of sanctuary by the suggestion that he would go free if he threw himself on the king's mercy and made a full confession. Supposedly this is what he did. He is reported to have appeared before Henry VII on October 5, 1497, and to have confessed his "true" identity as an imposter and a commoner. But of course he was not allowed to go free.

After a period of imprisonment in the Tower, Perkin unsuccessfully tried to escape. Later, he conspired to escape again, this time along with Clarence's son, Warwick, whom Henry had kept imprisoned there for years. The plot was exposed and both young men were executed in 1499. Warwick was beheaded, as befitted his rank. But Perkin, to emphasize his confessed status as a commoner, was hanged, drawn and quartered—the prescribed punishment for treason by a member of that class.

It is entirely possible that the "conspiracy to escape" was trumped up as an excuse to kill both Perkin and Warwick. It is reported that the Spanish refused to consider the match between Prince Arthur and Katherine of Aragon so long as any Yorkist claimants remained alive.

Perkin's confession itself raises as many questions as it answers. If there was a confession, it was not really voluntary, and it may have been false. Here again, "may" is the operative word. There probably was a confession, and, even if it was coerced, it may still have been true. Supposedly, Henry forced Perkin to repeat his confession in the presence of his wife, who had also been captured but who was treated with courtesy by reason of her rank. The confession has been "quoted" and "copied"; and its contents were published by Bernard Andre, Henry VII's official historian and a Tudor sycophant. But if there ever was a signed original, it remains undiscovered.

The Milanese ambassador said that Perkin actually signed such a document. Perhaps he did. If Henry could force Perkin to recite a confession and to repeat it in the presence of his wife, he could certainly force him to sign it. But, if so, where is it? It seems incredible that Henry VII and his descendants would allow such a critical document to disappear.

Naturally, Henry had many unsigned copies of the confession made and distributed. One purported copy was in the archives of the city of Tournai. Another is in the Library of Burgundy in Brussels. The actual archives of Tournai were destroyed by German bombing during the Second World War. A few limited entries had been supplied to James Gairdner by an informant named Weale. They are printed at the end of Gairdner's book, published in 1898. A more complete summary had been provided in an article by a Belgian historian, Count de La Hawardie. Unfortunately, Hawardie appears to have interspersed matter from other sources with the actual record entries, making it difficult to know just what was really taken from the official records.

Although history has come to call this pretender Perkin Warbeck, his "confession" describes him as the son of "John Osbeck," the controller of Tournai. It was supposedly even signed "Osbeck," rather than Warbeck. But the Tournai records (according to Hawardie) showed a "Pierrechon Werbecque" born to "Jehan Werbecque," and (according to Gairdner's informant) listed "Jehan de Werbecque" as the son of "Dieric de Werbecque." Neither summary of the records mentions the name Osbeck.

The following note appears to have been added by Hawardie: "The historian Lingard reports that according to a document— imperfect and unsatisfactory—'Perkin Warbeck' acknowledged that he was born in Tournai, that he was the son of JEHAN OSBECK and of CATHERINE DE FARO, names by which it is easy to see and recognize the father and mother given above." The Tudor historians were also untroubled by the difference between "Osbeck" and "Werbecque," asserting that they were similar enough to be recognized as the same. The contention is difficult to accept, especially since Perkin spoke fluent English; and, even if he confessed in French, Henry's command of that language was excellent.

If Perkin said "Werbecque" and the scribes wrote "Osbeck," Henry would surely have spotted the error. It seems improbable that this thorough and cautious man would not have carefully studied a document of this importance to his own title.

Why would Perkin say "Osbeck" if, in fact, he was Pierrechon Werbecque? Possibly he was *not* Pierrechon and did not know the correct name of the man whose identity he was being given, or perhaps, thinking to save his life, he had acquiesced in that identity, but hoped to insert something else in his confession that would convey to future readers that it was not authentic.

Possibly, as was common in the fithteenth century, Perkin's name was spelled differently on different occasions. That might explain the use of "Warbek," "Werbek" and "Werbecque." But "Osbeck"? It seems unlikely.

There remains the possibility that Perkin did not come up with the name at all, that he was simply forced to sign a document prepared by Henry's men that erroneously stated the name that they believed was his or that they wished to foist on him.

The confession refers to Perkin's mother as Catheryn de Faro, while the Tournai records showed the wife of Jehan Werbecque and the mother of Pierrechon Werbecque to be Nicaise Faroul or Faro. Evidently, Nicaise was also called Nicaisine or just Caisine, which, conceivably, could have been anglicized by Perkin to Catheryn or misunderstood by the king's scribes. But these explanations seem unsatisfying.

The confession refers to one of Perkin's "grandsires" as Deryck Osbeck. According to both Hawardie and Gairdner, the Tournai records showed Pierrechon's paternal grandfather to have been Dieric de Werbecque. The first name was thus correctly stated. Here again, the family name was not.

The confession tells us little about Perkin's childhood, except that, at some point, he was taken by his mother to Antwerp to learn Flemish and, after half a year, returned to Tournai because "of the warres that wer in fflaunders." Thereafter, he fell sick and remained ill for five months.

Later, according to the confession, Perkin traveled to Portugal with the wife of Sir Edward Brampton. He worked in Lisbon for a one-eyed knight named Peter de Cogna and then traveled to Ireland with a Breton merchant named Pregent Meno.

The confession goes on to relate that, in Ireland, Perkin was mistaken for the duke of Clarence's son, which he denied. Later, he was approached by two Englishmen who insisted at first that Perkin was King Richard's bastard son and then, later "agaynst my will made me to lerne Inglisshe, and taught me what I shuld doo and say. And after this they called me Duke of York, the second son of Kyng Edward the Ffourth."

It is impossible to believe that, in a short time, two strangers could teach a young Belgian to speak accent-free, upper-class English *against his will* and could sufficiently acquaint him with intimate knowledge of the family of Edward IV, to the point that he could fool some of the crowned heads of Europe, the king of Scotland and even his own aunt.

It is difficult to understand why Henry's advisors would have hit on such a seemingly transparent story if they were planning to impress the world with the authenticity of the confession. Perhaps they did not. Perhaps Perkin himself came up with that fanciful tale hoping it would be seen as untrue, just as he may have hoped that by using the name "Osbeck" others would perceive the falsity of what was "confessed."

Bacon, writing in the seventeenth century under James I, ignores Henry's version of the confession and provides a quite different story. According to Bacon, Perkin's father was "John Osbeck, a convert Jew." Bacon has Osbeck and his wife travel to England, where they live "for a time" and where Edward IV, apparently a friend, christens their son "Peter."

Bacon provides no explanation for ignoring Henry's version of the "confession." Obviously he was aware of it; and one could reasonably infer, from his disregarding it and providing his own version, that he considered "Henry's version" false. Unfortunately, we have no indication of the source of Bacon's version or of any evidence supporting it. Indeed, it seems even more improbable than the version given out by Henry and published by Andre.

Whoever Perkin was, there is some indication that he did make a trip to Portugal and that he was accompanied not merely by Sir Edward Brampton's wife but by Sir Edward himself. Perhaps, in his confession, he sought to protect Brampton by omitting any reference to him and by shifting the blame for his coaching to the two unnamed Englishmen.

The "Brampton connection" is one of the most intriguing

aspects of Perkin's story, involving some strange coincidences in itself. Sir Edward Brampton was a converted Portuguese Jew whose name originally was Duarte Brandao. Arriving in England in 1468, he had ultimately become a close friend and trusted associate of Edward IV. Having fought for Edward "in many battles," he was the first Jew ever knighted. He was designated a naval commander, given command of a large sea force, made governor of Guernsey and granted estates in the City of London and in Northamptonshire. In 1483 it was Brampton who saved the English fleet for Richard III. Later that year he took up arms for Richard in opposing Buckingham's rebellion.

As might be expected of a man with such strong loyalties to the Yorkist cause, Brampton lived in Flanders after Richard's defeat in 1485, and his English estates were confiscated by Henry VII. If Brampton was living outside England, why would Perkin feel the need to protect him by leaving him out of the confession? Perhaps he felt that, with the Yorkist cause lost, Brampton should make his peace with Henry VII and return to England. He later appears to have done just that. Or perhaps Perkin feared that English agents would take revenge on Brampton even on foreign soil. Or possibly Brampton was not with Perkin on the Portuguese journey after all.

There are apparent similarities between Sir Edward Brampton and Perkin's "father," Jehan Werbecque. Werbecque may also have been a converted Portuguese Jew, as indicated by Bacon. There is some confusion in the accounts as to whether Perkin was supposed to be the son of a Jew or merely the servant of one—presumably Brampton. Brampton was a skilled and experienced seaman. Apparently, Werbecque was a seaman as well as controller of the city.

Could they have been the same man? When the brilliant and cosmopolitan Brampton left England, did he somehow assume the identity of Jehan Werbecque? There is no evidence of this, and it seems most unlikely. Werbecque's birth and death and the identity of his parents were all listed in the Tournai records. Besides, Werbecque was a public official in Tournai. It would seem impossible for a new and different man to appear, claiming to be the seafaring controller the local people had known all his life.

On the other hand, Brampton could certainly have been a close friend of Werbecque's. There was substantial trade between London and Tournai; and, as two capable, seafaring men possibly sharing a common language and religious background, such a friendship would not be unlikely. Did Brampton smuggle the younger prince out of England to the home of a trusted friend and coreligionist in Tournai?

And what was the role of Margaret of Burgundy? She saw Perkin on a number of occasions. Would she fail to unmask someone impersonating her own nephew? Perhaps. She had been away from England for many years, having visited there briefly only once after the birth of the two princes. Would Margaret be unable to catch Perkin out in some minor detail of what was later claimed to be a quickly memorized story of family life? Here again, it is not impossible in light of her long absence from the family.

Bacon attributed Perkin's coaching to Margaret, rather than to the two Englishmen of the "confession." But having left England before either prince was born and having returned only once for a brief visit in 1480, it was not likely that she could have had the intimate knowledge of family matters necessary to do the job.

Those who insist that Perkin was an imposter do so primarily because of his confession. But there is other documentary evidence as well. Gairdner reports the discovery of two copies of a letter in French supposedly written by Perkin to his mother shortly after his capture. In it, he asks for a little money and tells her that "certains Engletz" made him claim to be Prince Richard of England. Like the confession, the original of the letter does not exist.

The purported copies contain a recitation of details about Perkin and his family life that his mother would already have known and that revisionists argue would be pointless in a letter sent to her by her own son. Gairdner, however, contends that Perkin put these family details in the letter "in order that his mother may be assured the letter really comes from her son." Gairdner may be right. The letter itself contains the statement that the recital of these events is included "so that you may hear and recognize clearly that I am your son and none other."

There are, however, other grounds for questioning the authenticity of the letter. Perkin addresses his mother as "Catherine Warbecque," not "Osbeck" as in the confession. And, as we have discussed, his mother's name, as shown in the Tournai archives, was "Nicaise," not Catherine.

The letter says "My sister Jehanne has died of the plague at the procession of Tournai." Perkin's letter was written on October 13, 1497. Pierrechon Werbecque did have a sister named Jehanne. But the Tournai archives showed that Jehanne was still alive in 1517 and living in the city with her husband. Surely Perkin could not have had a mistaken belief that his sister had died when, in fact, she was still alive and well. Moreover, there does not appear to have been any plague in Tournai anywhere near the time to which the letter refers.

The letter, which Gairdner says was written *before* Perkin's confession, also says "I hear my father has departed this life." But the confession refers to Perkin's father in the present tense. Perhaps Gairdner is incorrect as to the order of the two statements, and Perkin got news of his father's death and put that in his letter after, rather than before, his confession.

However, it has been argued that Perkin's father, Jehan Werbecque, did not die until the following year, 1498. This may or may not be so. According to Hawardie, the Tournai archives show only that Jehan died "before December 1498" and that Nicaise Werbecque, the widow of Jehan, *remarried* in that month. Those entries would not seem to preclude the possibility of Jehan having died in 1497 or even earlier. The entry recording his death "before December 1498" could mean he died "before December, *in* 1498," but that would seem a strange way of putting it.

In any event, the letter, like the "confession," may be either an outright fraud, written by Henry's agents, or a document Perkin was forced to write, in which he deliberately inserted error in the hope that discerning readers would see that he was being coerced.

Putting separate facts together can create an interesting hypothesis. It seems clear that there really was a Pierrechon or Pierrequin Werbecque born in Tournai to Jehan and Nicaise Werbecque. Perhaps, as a boy, Pierrechon was indeed taken to

Antwerp, where he spent six months. James Gairdner places the probable year of the boy's return to Tournai as 1483 or 1484. Evidently, the "warres" to which the confession refers occurred in 1484 and early 1485. After Pierrechon's return, he was very sick—so sick that his illness lasted five months.

In March 1484, Elizabeth Woodville left sanctuary, reportedly having been promised at an earlier time that if she left, her sons would be allowed to live with her. There is no clear record of where the ex-queen went after she left sanctuary. However, Audrey Williamson uncovered a Tyrell family legend that Elizabeth and the princes actually lived for a time at the Tyrell family home in Suffolk "by permission of the Uncle," i.e., Richard. Tyrell was, of course, a trusted aide to Richard, so the princes' secretly residing at his home would almost certainly have been with Richard's knowledge and consent. The Tyrell estate was near Ipswich on the coast, a convenient point of departure should prudence require the removal of the princes to Flanders.

The Great Chronicle of London reports that after Easter 1484 people began to whisper about the princes' disappearance. Were they now with their mother, temporarily ensconced in Sir James Tyrell's Suffolk manor?

Is it possible that the real Pierrechon Werbecque died in or about 1484 on his trip to Antwerp, a victim of "the warres" then occurring, or that he succumbed to the long and serious illness described in the confession? Could Brampton or Tyrell or both have smuggled Prince Richard out of England, sailing secretly from the coast near Tyrell's estate? Could they have inserted the prince into the Werbecque household to assume the identity of the deceased Pierrechon? Or perhaps as a visiting "cousin" or friend who assumed Pierrechon's identity only in his confession, thinking that it might save his life.

In late 1484, Richard sent Sir James Tyrell on a mysterious mission to Flanders, "for divers matters concerning greatly the King's weal." We have no record of the nature of this unspecified mission. Did it involve arrangements with Richard's sister, Margaret of Burgundy, to see that Prince Richard was kept safe in the Werbecque home in Burgundian territory?

In January 1485, Richard appointed Tyrell commander of the

castle at Guisnes, the logical entry point for Yorkist and other refugees fleeing England to the Continent. At or about the same time, Richard paid Sir James a huge sum, reported to be as large as the annual royal budget. The nature of this extraordinary transaction has never been discovered.

It has been suggested that the massive payment served some military purpose. But it is hard to imagine what that purpose might have been. If the payment was for the Calais garrison, there would have been no need for secrecy. And what other "military" need on the Continent would have required a payment of that size, shrouded in such secrecy?

Tyrell appears to have been involved in the abortive negotiations with the Breton treasurer, Pierre Landlais, to turn Henry Tudor over to the English. But the January 1485 payment to Tyrell was not likely to have been a bribe to Landlais, since Henry had already escaped from Brittany to France in September 1484.

Could the huge payment from Richard to Tyrell have been both a reward to Sir James for keeping Prince Richard hidden in his family home after Easter 1484 and for subsequently smuggling him out of England, as well as a fund for the young prince's maintenance and protection during the coming years in Tournai?

And what of the older prince? If, as Kendall suggests, he was seriously ill, he may have died while still in the Tower or at Tyrell's home between Easter and the end of the year, or in some later hiding place.

Another hypothesis as to the fate of the older prince is one we have already discussed—that "Edwardus," who was the focal point of the rebellion of 1487, was, in fact, Edward V, that he was killed in the battle of Stoke and that Henry Tudor's agents substituted the much younger "Lambert Simnell" for the slain "adolescent" in order to have a demonstrable commoner who could be used to ridicule the cause of the rebels and discourage further rebellions.

There is no hard evidence to support any of these theories, and, arguably, they are inconsistent with a letter from Perkin to Queen Isabella of Spain written on August 25, 1493, well before his capture. Perkin, writing as Richard Plantagenet, told his "most honoured Lady and Cousin," Isabella, that his older brother, Edward V, had been murdered, but that when the writer was delivered to "a certain lord" to be murdered as well, that lord took pity on him and sent him abroad, after requiring him to take an oath not to reveal his identity for a specified number of years.

The melodramatic story seems quite fanciful, but the letter appears to be genuine. There are four possibilities: (1) Perkin was an imposter who made up the entire story; (2) Perkin was, in fact, Prince Richard, but made up the story of his brother's murder for some reason we cannot fathom; (3) Perkin was Prince Richard, and an unidentified "lord" told him falsely that his brother had been murdered; or (4) Perkin was Prince Richard, and Edward V was in fact murdered, but for some reason Prince Richard was spared.

Scenario number three might not be as bizarre as it seems. If an unidentified man told young Prince Richard this tale of murder, he may have considered it the only way to induce the young prince to go abroad without protest and to maintain his silence. To a ten-year-old, the belief that his brother had been murdered and that the murderers could be searching for him as well would be a powerful incentive to go through with the masquerade and to keep his true identity secret. It would be cruel to fabricate a story of his brother's death, but perhaps this was the only way to ensure Prince Richard's silence. Perhaps Prince Edward was given a similar story about Prince Richard's death in order to induce *him* to remain silent as well.

If scenario number four is true, who was the unidentified man who warned the younger prince and sent him abroad? He is described as a "lord." But a ten-year-old may not have been accurate about rank. Could it have been Tyrell? Brampton? Someone sent by Buckingham? Buckingham himself?

P. W. Hammond and W. J. White point out that according to the Dutch Divisie Chronicle, "some say" that, after murdering one of the princes, Buckingham spared the other "and had him secretly abducted out of the country." This could be taken as corroboration for the story in Perkin's letter to Isabella. But Buckingham was ambitious and self-centered. He hated the Woodvilles, helped engineer Richard's seizure of Prince Edward, led the move to force Prince Richard out of sanctuary and believed in his own claim to the throne. It would be difficult to imagine Buckingham deciding to ignore his "orders" and to spare the younger prince.

The Divisie Chronicle was written about 1500, some seven years after Perkin's letter to Isabella. Possibly the Chronicle was simply repeating gossip that flowed from the letter and embroidering on its dramatic tale by casting Buckingham in the role of the mysterious good samaritan.

Despite his letter to Isabella, there is no indication that Perkin believed Richard III was responsible for killing Prince Edward. While he may have been told that the older prince was "miserably put to death," he does not impute the crime to Richard. If Perkin considered Richard guilty of murdering his brother, would he not have explicitly said so in his 1493 letter? He had nothing to fear from Richard, who had been dead ten years when the letter was written.

In his proclamation to the English before the raid from Scotland in 1496, Perkin said of Richard that his "desire of rule did blind him," but that in other respects he was noble. It has been argued that this accuses Richard of murdering the elder prince. But it seems far more consistent with a reference to Richard's usurping the throne by claiming the illegitimacy of the two princes than it does a charge of murdering Prince Edward.

Those who are convinced that Perkin was an imposter point to what they consider two telltale errors concerning his age. First, on January 24, 1495, in the presence of Margaret of Burgundy, he signed an official document making Maximilian, king of the Romans, his heir should he die without male issue, and swearing that he would not seek to set aside that obligation on the ground of being underage.

If, as seems correct, Prince Richard was born in August 1473, he was already twenty-one in January 1495. He was not, in fact, underage.

While the agreement with Maximilian could be construed as *some* evidence that Perkin was not Prince Richard, it is hardly conclusive or even compelling. A careful reading of the document shows that Perkin does not say he *was* underage. He promises not to *assert* that he was underage as a ground for evading his agreement. Conceivably, he even said he was *not* underage; but since he was plainly a very young man, Maximilian's counselors were taking no chance that he might turn out to be under twenty-one and thus able to avoid his commitment when he came of age.

This was a lawyer-drafted document, carefully prepared by Maximilian's representatives and obviously intended to be binding and airtight. The draftsman had Perkin swear not to claim *any* kind of defense to the enforcement of his promise to Maximilian and gave examples of the kind of defenses Perkin could not assert. Thus, the document provides that the young man will not seek to be excused from his promises "*no matter for what reason . . . on any pretext such as* being a minor in age, constraint, respect or error." This is no more a statement by Perkin that he actually *is* a "minor in age" than it is a statement that he has actually been subjected to "constraint" (i.e., duress) or that he has actually made his commitment to Maximilian in "error."

There is, however, an apparent error in Perkin's letter to Queen Isabella written in August, 1493. But it is also not convincing evidence that Perkin was an imposter. In the letter, Perkin says he was "about nine years old" when his older brother was murdered. Since the murder could not have occurred before mid-1483, and the probable date of Prince Richard's birth was August, 1473, he would have been ten or almost ten at the time of his brother's death. But that death supposedly occurred ten years before Perkin's letter. How many of us at twenty would remember with any degree of accuracy whether we were "about nine," as opposed to "almost ten," when some event happened years before in our childhood?

Moreover, people were considerably less careful about age in the fifteenth century. It is possible that, having been separated from his parents and his brother and having spent much of his youth away from the places of his early years, Prince Richard may really not have even known the year he was born, much less exactly how old he was when his brother was reportedly killed.

Despite Perkin's confession, the letter to his mother and these other documents suggesting defects in his story, and despite the conclusion of most historians that he was an impostor, we cannot definitively rule out the possibility that he was, after all, the younger prince.

Even More seemed to have some doubt as to whether the princes were really killed. He tells us that, of the various accounts of what happened to them, he has provided the version given him by "suche men & by such meanes as me thinketh it wer hard but it shoued be true"—presumably his mentor-host John Morton. But More prefaces his remarks on the subject by noting that their "death and final infortune hathe natheles so far comen in question, that some remain yet in doubt, whither they wer in [Richard's] dayes destroyde or no."

We have already discussed that More may have abandoned his "History" half complete because he discovered facts contradicting the account he had been given by Morton and others. Perhaps those facts indicated that no murder had been committed.

Perhaps there was truth in the "rumours and whisperings" reported by Bacon that "the two young sons of King Edward the fourth, or one of them, which were said to be destroyed in the Tower, were not indeed murdered, but conveyed secretly away, and were yet living."

Perhaps Perkin was, indeed, the younger prince. If so, it becomes even more plausible to believe that Lincoln, Margaret and the Woodvilles supported Simnell's rebellion with the idea of placing Prince Richard on the throne if the rebellion succeeded, but keeping him abroad and in safety until its outcome was determined. Then, after the rebellion failed, Margaret determined to try again, this time with the prince himself, since he was now old enough to rule directly in his own right. Elizabeth Woodville could no longer join in the plot. She had died shortly before in her convent at Bermondsey.

That Perkin was Prince Richard would also fit the alternative scenario that "Edwardus" of the rebellion of 1487 was Edward V, who was killed at Stoke. Having failed with the older prince, Margaret may have tried again with the younger.

We have hypothesized that if Tyrell or Brampton brought about the princes' escape, they did so in obedience to Richard's order. Could they have done this against Richard's wishes or at least without his knowledge? Possibly, but it is not likely. Such a risky venture on their part could have been designed to prevent Richard from harming the boys, or it could even have been undertaken on secret instructions from Henry Tudor designed to eliminate potential rivals by kidnapping and killing the two boys. Either scenario seems fanciful and most improbable, given both men's relationship with Richard and, in Brampton's case, his even closer relationship with Edward IV.

While the bold and daring Brampton might have intervened to save the boys if he thought they were in danger from Richard, it seems completely unlikely that Tyrell would have joined him in acting against Richard's interests or that he acted alone in that manner. And unless they were treacherous double agents all along, it is difficult to imagine Tyrell or Brampton harming the princes to aid Henry Tudor's cause.

If the younger prince was smuggled out of England and hidden on the Continent, it seems far more likely that this was done at Richard's direction. Can we believe that instead of murdering the boys, Richard would have wanted to hide one or both of them in some safe and foreign location? It is not as impossible as most traditionalists assume.

Certainly Richard realized that if the princes were known to be alive, they would constantly serve as a rallying point for conspiracy and rebellion. Perhaps, however, he was unwilling to order the murder of his brother's sons. If they could be hidden away overseas and somehow induced to remain silent as to their true identities, might he not have taken the risk of leaving them alive? Presumably, if they showed up some day, Richard would have already have consolidated his power and, in that event, he still had the *Titulus Regius* card to play.

Richard may also have recognized that the two princes were an even greater threat to the aspirations of Henry Tudor than they were to his own position. Unlike Richard, Henry could take no comfort at all from *Titulus Regius*. If the princes were illegitimate, then so was their sister, the Princess Elizabeth. And Henry's proposed marriage to the princess, a child of Edward IV, was his strongest ground for claiming the throne. If she was illegitimate, it was no ground at all.

If, on the other hand, the boys were both alive and legitimate, they were the rightful heirs, and no one would back Henry's claim, possibly not even his mother. Either way, Henry had no real chance at the throne so long as one or more of the princes lived.

But if their deaths could be arranged, that was something else. That could create a real opportunity for Henry, particularly if the murders could be blamed on Richard. With the princes dead, Henry could go after the crown of "Richard the usurper" taking the position that Edward's children were legitimate and promising to marry Edward's eldest daughter.

Richard certainly realized the enormous advantages that would flow to Henry from the princes' deaths. He may have perceived them to have been in real danger from Henry's adherents, agents and spies or from killers hired by Henry's determined mother, her powerful husband, Lord Stanley, or even the ever scheming Bishop Morton.

Given all of these factors, the best solution could have seemed to remove the boys to some safe and secret place—preferably outside the kingdom—and to find a way, if possible, to keep them from speaking out. The answer may have been to tell each one that his brother had been murdered and that the murderers would be looking for him as well.

Perhaps the princes (or the surviving prince if one had died) were not meant to remain abroad forever. Perhaps, on the death of his own son in April 1484, Richard determined to keep the surviving prince safe on the Continent, planning ultimately to disclose his existence and name him as heir or, when the prince was old enough to govern, even to reverse *Titulus Regius* and place him on the throne.

In December 1484, Richard sent Sir John Kendall to Rome as an emissary. Later, Kendall was one of Perkin's supporters. Could his 1484 mission have been to negotiate for a papal decree that, despite his father's precontract with Eleanor Butler, Prince Richard could be named heir, or, when old enough, even made king?

While the idea is a romantic one, it is difficult to imagine Richard ever being willing to take the double risk of having either prince perceived as being both alive and legitimate. If Richard ever intended to bring one of the princes back to England, it would probably have been with the continuing stigma of illegitimacy. If so, Richard would have wanted to consolidate his own power and get his hands on Henry Tudor before even revealing that one of the princes was alive and well.

If Richard had any such plan, it was ruined by Bosworth Field. But perhaps the young prince's supporters, such as Lincoln, Margaret of Burgundy, and the Woodvilles, were not ready to give up. Perhaps they hit on the notion of using an imposter like Lambert Simnell to mount a rebellion, keeping the prince safely in Burgundy pending the outcome. Or perhaps they sent the older prince himself to serve as the focal point of that rebellion. Whether that was the case or Simnell was only a stalking-horse for the younger prince, it may well be that when the rebellion of 1487 failed, Margaret waited until Prince Richard was older and ready to rule. Only then did "Perkin" come forward to claim his rights.

Was Perkin Prince Richard? There is certainly evidence tending to show that he was not, such as the confession and the letter to his mother. But that evidence is hardly unimpeachable; and, despite what seems to be a solid consensus among historians, the possibility cannot be entirely dismissed that the "pretender" was in fact the younger prince.

Of course, Prince Richard could have been alive and well even if he was not Perkin Warbeck. After trying with Simnell, the Yorkists could have put forward another known imposter in Perkin, once again keeping the actual prince safe on the Continent or in some other secret place.

Indeed, Perkin is not the only person claimed to have been the missing prince. Jack Leslau, although not a professional historian, has devoted many years to developing his theory that Dr. John Clement, president of the Royal College of Physicians, who married the adopted daughter of Sir Thomas More, was in fact the younger prince and that another distinguished Englishman, Sir Edward Guildford, was really Edward V.

Leslau bases his contention primarily on a number of clues and symbols he finds in the 1527 portrait of More's family by Hans Holbein. A copy of the painting can be seen at the Chelsea Town Hall. There is some indication that it may even be the original.

Holbein has set out the names and ages of each of the several figures. The painting shows a young male standing in a doorway somewhat above and behind the other figures. The legend over his head appears to identify him as "Johanes heresius." His age is shown as twenty-seven.

It has been assumed that this figure was John Harris, More's secretary. But, in the name "Johanes heresius," the "h" is not capitalized. The first letter of the family name of every other figure in the picture is capitalized. "Johanes heresius" is the sole exception. Leslau argues that these words are correctly translated, not as "John Harris," but as "John the rightful heir."

Supporting Leslau's thesis is the fact that Dr. John Clement, although an honored member of More's family, is not ostensibly depicted and named in the painting. Leslau infers that he is there, but that he is the figure identified as "Johanes heresius."

The figure in the doorway is a young man, considerably younger than Dr. Clement was at the time. But Leslau has an explanation. Holbein was known to use cryptic signs and symbols in his paintings to convey private or hidden meanings. This work may be no exception. A clock face in the painting is decorated with a half moon, and the door of the clock is open. Leslau theorizes that this indicates that time has been changed (the open clock door) and that someone has been depicted at half his age (the half moon).

John Clement's registration at the University of Louvain in 1489 would have made him in his fifties in 1527, when Holbein painted the More family portrait. Leslau concludes that the young man in the doorway is really the middle-aged Doctor Clement, but that he is shown at twenty-seven, which is half of his true age. This, of course, would make him fifty-four, and, since the painting was done in 1527, it would make his year of birth 1473, the very year in which prince Richard was born to Elizabeth Woodville.

Leslau finds similar clues in Holbein's portrait of Sir Henry Guildford in the royal collection at Windsor, indicating that Sir Henry's supposed half brother, Sir Edward Guildford, was in fact Edward V.

Leslau is convinced that the two princes were not killed at all, that they were hidden away and given assumed identities, finding their way into the More and Guildford families. He suggests that

More wrote his "History," depicting the princes' death, in order to throw the Tudors off Dr. Clement's trail.

But More wrote his "History" in or around 1513. Clements did not marry More's adopted daughter until 1526. He apparently was studying medicine on the Continent until 1525. Did More know the man who was Clements in the years before he left for his European studies? Had he returned to England from time to time, courting More's daughter? Was More asked or otherwise motivated to protect the man's identity in that earlier period by writing a false "History"? Possibly, but there is no evidence of this.

Besides, if the boys had been spirited away to a secret hideaway, it would most probably have been at Richard's direction or at least with his concurrence. If Richard had been responsible for their lives being spared, it would seem contrary to human nature for More to have chosen Richard for the role of the villainous murderer in his fictional drama. For obvious reasons, he could not give Henry VII that role; nor would he want to impose it on his old mentor, John Morton. But why not choose someone like Buckingham, who was no longer alive and was evidently a figure for whom More had little respect?

If Dr. Clements really was Prince Richard, a more likely scenario would be that, at first, More believed what he wrote, but that he had begun to doubt his facts and had put the "History" aside. Then, later, after Clements married More's daughter and disclosed his true royal identity to the family, More pulled out his old abandoned account and turned it over to Hardying or Grafton and possibly others, with the idea that its publication would throw any pursuer off the trail.

One difficulty with Leslau's theory is that it necessarily requires More to have told Hans Holbein the potentially deadly secret that he was harboring the Yorkist heir in his household. More was a highly intelligent, experienced and discreet man. Holbein was well connected, and ultimately became the official painter to Henry VIII. It seems unlikely that More would have taken the portraitist into his confidence about a matter that could have led to the imprisonment or death of his son-in-law, if not himself.

Another problem with Leslau's theory is the difficulty of accepting that two young men resembling the missing royal princes could suddenly appear as members of prominent London families without being recognized. On the other hand, if the princes lived incognito in Europe, returning to England only as mature men, it is not likely they would have been recognized as the two boys who had disappeared so many years earlier.

There are no early records of Dr. Clements being in England. He lived for some time in Italy and obtained his medical degree at Siena in 1525. Apparently he came to England soon thereafter, as he married More's adopted daughter Margaret the next year and was admitted as a member of the College of Physicians in 1528.

Similarly, the first reference to Sir Edward Guildford was a 1509 reference in Hall's Chronicle. His daughter, Lady Jane Guildford, is buried in the Sir Thomas More Chapel of Chelsea Church. It is recorded on her tomb that her father, Sir Edward Guildford, was the son of Sir Richard Guildford and that she bore thirteen children by John Dudley, then duke of Northumberland. Somewhat strangely, the Northumberland monument bears a 1555 inscription referring to her as "Ye Right Noble and Excellent *Princess* Lady Jane Guildford."

Could it have been known among the English nobility, or at least in her own family, that Lady Jane was, in fact, a royal princess—that her father had been Edward V? Ironically, one of Lady Jane's sons, Guildford Dudley, briefly occupied the English throne as the husband of Lady Jane Grey. Thus, a great-great-grandson of Edward IV may finally have retaken the throne for the Yorkists, albeit briefly.

Leslau is seeking to have DNA tests conducted on the remains of Dr. Clements and Sir Edward Guildford. If those tests indicate that these two prominent men from entirely different families are in fact brothers, it may not prove Leslau's thesis, but it will certainly lend it enormous support.

There is one other "pretender" we should consider. In the mid-sixteenth century, an aged stonemason in Kent told his employer an amazing story. As a young man, he said, he had been summoned by King Richard to Bosworth Field on the eve of the great battle. The king revealed a stunning surprise. The youth was his illegitimate son, and, if the coming battle was won, the king would acknowledge him.

Of course, the battle was lost, and the young man fled. After many hard times, he became a mason, plying his trade in Eastwell, Kent, until he was seventy or eighty. The man's name was Richard Plantagenet, and his death in 1560 is noted in the records of Eastwell.

Richard III readily acknowledged his two illegitimate children and treated them extremely well. His son John was knighted and given many honors. His daughter was given favorable treatment and was married to the earl of Huntingdon. Why would he have treated this third child so differently? There seems to be no ready explanation, unless this child, unlike the other two, was conceived during Richard's marriage to Anne Neville and was kept secret for that reason.

But Richard married Anne in 1472. If Richard Plantagenet was conceived after that, he could not have been more than about ten years old at the time of Bosworth Field. A boy that young would not normally be described as a "young man." But the elderly mason may have been incorrectly quoted, since his story has been repeated, and perhaps distorted, by many others over the centuries.

Is it possible that the mason, "Richard Plantagenet," was in fact the younger prince, Richard of York? After being hidden for some time, could he have considered it preferable to live in peaceful obscurity as a common mason than to announce his identity and be subjected to the tender mercies of a Tudor reign?

Prince Richard would have been twelve at the time of Bosworth Field; and that might fit the age of the "young man" as the story has been retold. He would have been eighty-seven when the mason died in 1560. There is no evidence to support this hypothesis; and why would a man seeking to hide his identity choose a give-away name like Plantagenet?

Of course, it is entirely possible that the old mason made up the entire story and simply adopted the name Plantagenet because it had a nice ring to it.

Putting aside the romantic conjecture about "Richard Plantagenet," the evidence of pretenders and imposters raises doubt as to whether Prince Richard or perhaps either prince, was really murdered by anyone. That doubt cannot be magnified into a certainty or even a probability that no crime was committed. But, again, it is a possibility that cannot be ruled out.

XVI

♚ THE CONFESSION

One of the salient elements of the mystery of Richard III is that we supposedly have a "confession"—not by Richard, of course, but by James Tyrell and John Dighton. Often, criminal trials result in a conviction on otherwise weak evidence because the accused or an accomplice has confessed. Is this such a case? Before we can draw any conclusion, we need to examine the facts surrounding the confession.

Like Richard, Henry VII seemed inclined to reward Tyrell handsomely, but to prefer that he stay abroad. Henry continued Tyrell as commander at Guisnes and appointed him captain of the Port of Calais. On February 23, 1487, Tyrell was ordered to turn over all of his Welsh lands and titles in exchange for lands of equal value in Guisnes.

Tyrell continued to lead an active and successful life as a respected knight and officer of the crown. He attended the coronation of Elizabeth of York in November 1487 and fought in the battle of Dixmunde in 1489.

Sir James remained in his position as captain of the Port of Calais until 1502. In that year, he was charged with admitting Edmund de la Pole to Guisnes. De la Pole, the earl of Suffolk, was one of the last surviving Yorkist heirs. The brother of the earl of Lincoln, who died fighting Henry at the battle of Stoke in 1487, de la Pole had a reasonable claim to the throne in his own right. His mother, Elizabeth, was a sister of Richard III and

Edward IV. He had fled England and was on his way to Flanders when he was given protection by Tyrell.

This in itself may seem inconsistent with Tyrell's having murdered the princes. Is it likely that a man who risked his career and even his life by disobeying one king to aid a Yorkist heir (de la Pole) would have murdered two other Yorkist heirs (and children at that) to please another king? Perhaps not. But the two boys were dominated by the hated Woodvilles. De la Pole was not.

Evidently Henry VII was stunned by this betrayal on the part of the previously loyal and well-rewarded knight. At first, he was reluctant to believe the report. Finally, however, Henry ordered Tyrell's arrest for aiding de la Pole. Tyrell prepared to fight rather than surrender and, in Guisnes, he had a fortress in which he could hold out indefinitely.

However, Sir James was lured on board a British ship to attend a meeting with representatives of the Crown. He had been provided with a formal promise of safe conduct given under the Privy Seal. Notwithstanding this official guarantee, Tyrell was immediately arrested and brought back to England. There, on May 6, 1502, he was privately executed on a charge of committing treason by his aid to de la Pole. So much for the word of Henry VII and the significance of the Privy Seal.

According to More and later traditionalists, Tyrell confessed before his execution that, nineteen years earlier, in 1483, he had murdered the two princes in the Tower at the behest of Richard III and with the aid of Miles Forest and John Dighton. There was no written confession or any other written record that Tyrell had in fact confessed.

Why would Tyrell make such a confession? He was already in serious trouble for allowing de la Pole's entry. If Henry knew nothing about Tyrell's participation in murdering the princes, why would Tyrell volunteer that he had committed that far more serious crime?

Tyrell's son, who was arrested with him, was not executed, and his attainder was reversed. Perhaps Tyrell believed he would be executed anyway for admitting de la Pole and hoped that his family would receive better treatment if he gave Henry the valuable political weapon of a confession linking Richard to the murders. Or, knowing that he was going to die anyway, perhaps Tyrell simply wanted to clear his conscience. Possible, but not likely.

More expressly states that Dighton confessed as well as Tyrell and that they described the manner of the princes' deaths just as More had related it. More also says the fact that they confessed to these events was "well knowen."

Yet, significantly, More tells us that his account of the murders is reported "not after every way that I have heard, but after that way yt I have so herd by suche men & by such meanes as me thinketh it wer hard but it should be true." And, after he describes "the dolorous end of those babes," More again seeks to persuade the reader that he had selected the correct version from among others, by adding that the version he has chosen comes "from them that much knew and little cause had to lie." He also concedes that some men are still "in doubt" about whether the crime really was committed at all.

"Me *thinketh*" this was what happened? What a strange and inconclusive way to put the matter if More believed that Tyrell and Dighton had actually confessed. And if the murderers had really confessed and, as More wrote, admitted all the facts of the murders just as he related them—and, as More also said, this confession was "well knowen"—why were men still "in doubt" and why were there so many other versions of what occurred? Why was More himself asking around and choosing among the differing versions of the princes' fate, rather than sticking to the version to which Tyrell and Dighton had supposedly confessed?

If there really were such confessions, Henry showed a strange reluctance to make them public. In 1504, two years after his execution, Henry finally had Tyrell attainted. But the bill of attainder charged him only with "treason on account of his connection with Edmonde de la Pole, Earl of Suffolk." There was no reference to any murder—not even a veiled and general reference to something like "shedding of Infants blood," as in Henry's bill of attainder against Richard.

How is that possible if two years earlier Tyrell had really confessed to murdering the young man Henry considered the true king of England along with his younger brother? Henry had been on the throne for nineteen years and had consolidated his power, except for the possibility that further pretenders might rise up and claim to be one of the missing princes. If, in 1485, he had wanted to keep the fate of the princes ambiguous to prevent support for any other claimant or to avoid strengthening the continental view that England was a violent and unstable place, his wisest policy by 1502 would seem to have been the opposite.

At the time of Tyrell's supposed confession, Henry had a particularly strong motive for announcing publicly that the two princes were no longer alive. His oldest son, Prince Arthur, had died just a month before Tyrell's execution. Only Prince Henry remained to carry on the Tudor line. By 1502, two troublesome pretenders had already come forward, one claiming to be the missing Prince Richard. Each had caused a rebellion. More pretenders were likely to come.

Henry hoped that Prince Arthur's widow, Katherine of Aragon, would now marry Arthur's younger brother, Prince Henry. But Katherine's parents, Ferdinand and Isabella of Spain, had been concerned about these repeated claimants to the English throne. A public announcement of Tyrell's confession would have eased their minds. Yet none was forthcoming. Even in 1504, Tyrell was charged with having committed a far less serious and certainly less significant crime, "his connection with Edmonde de la Pole."

More's account, the first referring to the confession, was not written until 1513. Perhaps More heard about a confession some time before he wrote. Even so, there would still appear to have been a gap of years between Tyrell's supposedly confessing to the crime in 1502 and Henry's deciding to speak of it—*if he ever did.* It is difficult to find any convincing explanation for Henry's remaining silent for *any* significant period after receiving a confession that Richard had murdered the princes.

Even Bacon pointed out that Henry made no mention of the confessions "in any of his declarations." Bacon added that the king "gave out" that Tyrell had confessed, presumably meaning that Henry told others informally that there had been a confession. But there is considerable doubt that Henry even did that until years later, *if ever.*

Fabyan completed his chronicle in 1504, two years after Tyrell's execution. He reports that event, and he charges Richard with murdering his nephews. But he fails to connect the two events and makes no mention of Tyrell confessing to the murder.

Bernard Andre, Henry's personal biographer and his sons' tutor, was still writing his biography of the king when Tyrell supposedly confessed. Yet, Henry failed to tell Andre about the confession. Andre does not even mention it. Nor does he accuse Tyrell of the crime or describe the boys' death as Tyrell supposedly confessed it. Instead, he states that Richard had the princes put to the sword. How is this possible if Tyrell had already confessed to committing the crime and to the exact manner in which it was committed?

Even Polydore Vergil, Henry's official historian, whose *English History* was written between 1505 and 1517 and published under Henry VIII in 1534, says nothing about a confession. In a statement entirely inconsistent with its existence, Vergil says "with what kinde of death these sely chyldren wer executyd yt is not certanely known." How could this still have been the case thirty-two years after the confessions of Tyrell and Dighton supposedly laid out all the details of the crime?

Vergil even refers to a general belief "that the sons of Edward IV were still alive, having been conveyed secretly away and obscurely concealed in some distant region." How could there be any such general belief if, as More claims, it was "well knowen" that Tyrell had confessed to their murders.

Why would Henry VII fail to tell Vergil, his official historian, and Andre, his own personal biographer, the critical fact that, years before, in 1502, Tyrell had confessed to murdering the princes on the orders of Richard III? How could he not relate to these men, whose job was to record such things for posterity, the details of the regicide to which Tyrell supposedly confessed?

If we can believe in More's sincerity, someone told him, during or before 1513, what no one told Vergil or Andre or the public—i.e., that there had been a confession back in 1502 that gave all the details of how the crime was committed and by whom. More seems to have had some doubts about this from the beginning, and they may have grown as he pursued the subject.

More and Vergil were friends. Yet More appears never to have told his friend about the supposed confession, even though Vergil was writing an official English history that would cover the events of Richard's reign. We have already seen that, in 1529, More's nephew and ultimate publisher, William Rastell, described the death of the princes and the disposal of their bodies in a way inconsistent with what Tyrell and Dighton supposedly confessed. How is that possible if More knew of their confession? Could it be that, before Rastell wrote his own chronicle and Vergil wrote his "History," even More had come to the conclusion that the entire confession story had been concocted?

Alison Weir who, of course, pronounces the reported confession absolutely authentic, claims that Henry's keeping it a secret is evidence of its authenticity. The claim defies logic and common sense.

Weir argues that Henry was a secretive man and wanted to avoid bad publicity about English instability that would upset Ferdinand and Isabella. Perhaps England's reputation could have been a factor in 1485. But wouldn't any such bad publicity in 1502 have been outweighed by the fact that Henry could now, finally, demonstrate that his two most serious rivals for the throne were no longer alive—murdered *nineteen years earlier* by the man Henry had defeated at Bosworth Field?

Indeed, the thing that could best allow any concern about English instability would have been proof that the princes were long dead. With such a disclosure, there could be no more fear of imposters rallying support by claiming to be one of the princes and creating an unstable and perhaps dangerous situation in Henry's domain.

It is difficult to avoid the conclusion that if Tyrell had really confessed in 1502 to murdering the two princes, Henry would immediately have trumpeted the confession not only in England but throughout Europe.

And, if Tyrell was willing to confess, why didn't Henry obtain a written and signed confession? What a fine document to show the public, to show Ferdinand and Isabella, to show everyone. Such a document, of obvious value to Henry, could have easily been obtained, whether Tyrell's confession was coerced or was voluntary. If it was coerced, it would have been just as easy to coerce a written confession as an oral one. And, if it was given voluntarily, why would Tyrell not agree to put it in writing, which unquestionably would have been of far greater value to Henry?

Bacon suggests that there may have been written statements that were "delivered abroad." But there is no evidence of this. And why would such critical documents be shipped out of England, rather than displayed to the council, to Parliament and to the public? How can we believe that Henry VII permitted any such written confession to be sent away, misplaced or destroyed?

It must be taken as highly probable that written, signed confessions were never obtained. That in itself strongly supports the inference that the two men did not confess at all.

There is another fact that seems even more indicative of the fact that there never was a confession. Supposedly Tyrell confessed that John Dighton and Miles Forest had physically committed the murder. More tells us Miles Forest died before More's "History" was written in 1513; and he appears to have died even before Tyrell's "confession." But More reports that John Dighton was interrogated with Tyrell and that both men "confessed the murther in the maner above writen." Bacon reported that as well.

Yet, there is no indication that Henry ever did anything to punish Dighton, who seems to have ended his days peacefully, the recipient of substantial favors from the king. More himself reports the amazing fact that, as of the time of his "History" (no earlier than 1513), Dighton was still alive and free.

More adds that the man was likely to be hanged before he died. This seems to be a semihumorous reference to the likelihood that Dighton would commit some new offense, rather than a prediction that he would finally be executed for murdering the true king of England more than ten years after he confessed to that crime.

Henry VII died in 1509 without ever taking any action against this supposedly confessed regicide. It has been argued that Henry wanted to keep Dighton alive to repeat the story of the murders throughout the land and, presumably, that this policy was continued by Henry VIII even after his father's death.

There is no record of Dighton ever repeating the story. But, even aside from that, the explanation seems hopelessly improbable. If there was one crime that English monarchs loathed and feared, that they wanted to deter, to punish swiftly and harshly, it was regicide, the murder of a king.

It is inconceivable that Henry VII could or would have allowed, much less encouraged, a man who confessed to committing such a murder to go about the country unpunished and boasting of his crime. If Tyrell and Dighton had really confessed in 1502 to murdering the young man Henry considered the rightful king, it is virtually impossible that eleven or more years later, when More wrote, Dighton would still have been walking around England a free man.

On any objective analysis of the facts, it must be considered *highly* improbable that there ever was a confession by either Tyrell or Dighton, and most probable that the entire story of the confession was concocted by someone endeavoring to add "evidentiary" support for the claim that Richard murdered his nephews.

XVII

⚜ THE BONES

As we have seen, among the fundamental elements to be considered in determining guilt or innocence in a murder case is the time of death and the alibi of the accused. Given the time of death, was it possible for him to have committed the crime? Or did he have an airtight alibi?

In the case of Richard III, time of death can be critical. If the princes were killed before the battle of Bosworth Field was fought in August 1485, Richard certainly had the opportunity to commit the crime. If their deaths preceded Bosworth Field, they may or may not have been killed at Richard's direction, but they certainly could have been. If, however, they were killed after Bosworth Field, Richard has a complete alibi: He was no longer alive.

An important indication of when death occurred in this case may be the physical evidence sometimes called "the bones." To understand the bones and their role in the drama, we need to know a little about the Tower of London where the bones were found.

The Tower, as we know it today, was started by William the Conqueror, although there had been earlier fortifications there—even Roman fortifications. It appears that a substantial masonry structure occupied the site of the White Tower as early as the second century. Construction of that building, which was the massive keep or central fortress, was started by the Conqueror and finished by his successor, William Rufus. Its walls were fifteen feet thick and constructed of brick surfaced with stone. It housed a small royal chapel and a large hall used as a council chamber.

Later kings improved and added to the Tower complex. In the thirteenth century, its walls were extended to include the Church of St. Peter ad vincula, and Henry III, not a strong king but one with good taste, whitewashed the keep, after which it was called the "White Tower."

By the reign of Edward IV, the Tower complex consisted of an outer wall, a moat and an inner wall surmounted by twelve stone towers. A number of buildings filled the space between the White Tower and the river. These included the royal apartments.

In November 1666, an ordinance was passed authorizing the demolition of certain of these buildings in order to clear a path from the gunpowder magazine in the White Tower to the Tower Wharf. It was projected that this path would reduce the time needed to supply the fleet with powder from twenty days to just four. The entire project took almost ten years.

In 1674, workmen removing a structure near the White Tower, discovered a chest containing two small skeletons. The larger skeleton was lying on its back. The smaller was lying face down on top of the larger. According to the great English architect Sir Christopher Wren, the chest was found "ten feet deep in the ground" as the workmen were taking away the foundation of a staircase.

There is some ambiguity as to where this staircase was located and where the bones were found in relation to the staircase. Was the staircase inside the White Tower itself? The wall of a now blocked portion of the spiral staircase within the White Tower bears an official plaque that so indicates. The sign is almost certainly incorrect.

The staircase under which the skeletons were found was in the process of being removed when the bones were found. The huge spiral staircase within the White Tower was hewn out of the fifteen-foot walls and was never removed. It was in place long before Richard's reign. If the two skeletons were found under *that* staircase, they were not likely to have Richard's nephews.

Almost certainly, the 1674 bones were found under the staircase that formerly led to the White Tower from an adjoining building being demolished at the time. An inaccessible doorway can still be seen about fourteen feet above the ground in the south facade of the White Tower facing the river. It seems quite likely that this is the doorway to which the demolished staircase led.

According to Sandford's "A Genealogical History of the Kings of England" (1677), the workmen who found the bones were taking down buildings "contiguous" to the White Tower, not excavating within the Tower itself. Sandford, who purports to quote an eyewitness account, says that the workmen were "digging down the stairs which led from the King's Lodgings to the chapel in the said Tower."

Wren also reported that the workmen were "taking away the stairs, which led from the royal Lodgings into the Chapel of the White-tower."

The royal lodgings were in a separate building, and these accounts indicate that the staircase the workmen were "digging down" was outside the White Tower, not the massive spiral staircase that still exists within the Tower itself, hewn from the stone wall.

Lord de Ros, a nineteenth-century lieutenant governor of the Tower, reported that, at Charles II's direction, a mulberry tree was planted at the spot where the bones were found. The tree subsequently died. But planting a tree at the spot certainly indicates a location outside, not inside, the White Tower, and that the staircase under which the bones were found led to the White Tower from an adjacent structure that was taken down.

No one seems to have asked why workmen engaged in removing a staircase would not simply have smashed it to ground level, rather than digging a pit ten feet below it. If this was to be an open area, what was the point of digging up a foundation that far below the ground? Why not just knock down the building and smooth over the ground? Perhaps Wren meant that the bones were ten feet under the *top* of the staircase, but within the staircase itself, so that they may in fact have been above ground level. But Wren didn't say that. He said "ten feet deep in the ground."

Wherever they may have found the bones, the workmen threw them on a nearby rubbish heap. An anonymous account written sometime later stated that pieces of rag and velvet were seen among the bones. There is no other report of this, and the rest of the anonymous account is inconsistent with other reports. It leaves out the rubbish heap and indicates that the bones were immediately recognized as the two princes and put in a stone coffin.

That is not at all what happened. Days or even weeks after their discovery, someone evidently realized the potential significance of the discovery, and the bones were retrieved from the rubbish heap. Apparently this was accomplished by Sir Thomas Chicheley, master of ordinance. John Knight, surgeon to Charles II, reported that it was done by sifting through the rubbish until the bones (or at least *some* bones) were found.

The location of the chest was considered to fit exactly the place described by More, i.e., "at the stayre foote, metely depe in the grounde under a great heape of stones." For example, the pseudonymous Miles Tudor, in his concise summary, "The White Rose Dies," states that "Sir Thomas [More] even describes with absolute accuracy the exact place where the bodies were eventually found some 200 years later." Mr. Tudor asks whether More had obtained his "uncannily accurate location of the Princes' skeletons" from John Morton.

Many writers, like Miles Tudor, have considered the location of the 1674 bones to be conclusive proof that More's account was accurate and that these must be the skeletons of the two princes. But most overlook a critical fact: More did not tell us where the bones *were*. He told us where they were *not*. Yes, he said they had been buried "at the stayre foote." But he also reported that, after the Princes were initially buried there, "metely depe" and "under a great heape of stones," Brackenbury's priest, acting on King Richard's orders, *removed the bodies to a more appropriate, but unspecified and unknown place.* More added that Tyrell and Dighton "confessed the murther in manner above written, *but whither the bodies were removed thei could nothing tel.*" Even Shakespeare, taking his cue from More, wrote that no one knew where the bodies were now buried.

Logically analyzed, the location of the 1674 bones, if they were really those of the princes, would prove More wrong, not right. But logical analysis has not always prevailed in the writings on this subject. In 1674, no one focused on the inconsistency between More's report and the place where the bones were found. The newly found bones were commonly considered to be the remains of the two princes and to prove the truth of More's account. Those conclusions retain wide and often unquestioning acceptance even today.

Where traditionalists have faced up to the inconsistency between More's account of the bodies being moved from the "stayre foote" in 1483 and the finding of the bones under the staircase in 1674, they have offered two explanations. Neither is very persuasive. The first explanation is that while most of More's "History" can be accepted as fact, he or his informants fabricated the story of the priest moving the bodies in order to justify Henry's failure to find and rebury them.

It is difficult to argue that a key part of More's "History" is a deliberate fabrication, while, at the same time, arguing that we should accept the balance as gospel. Weir adopts that inconsistent approach to More, although she does not accuse him personally of the fabrication. When his account fits her theory, she treats him as authoritative and unassailable. When it does not, she claims he is mistaken or has been misled by his informants, as in the case of the date of the murders and the reburial of the bodies.

Moreover, if the bodies were *not* moved in 1483, as More reports, that would be further evidence that Tyrell and Dighton did not confess in 1502, as More also reports. If the bodies had not been moved, Tyrell and Dighton would have known exactly where they were buried. It is inconceivable that the king's interrogators who obtained their confessions would not have demanded and obtained that information. It seems equally inconceivable that, on learning the whereabouts of a murdered English king and his royal brother, Henry VII would not have had them disinterred and properly buried with a royal requiem mass.

If he had the information, there seems no reasonable explanation for Henry's not doing this. Since he did not arrange for such a reburial, it is a fair inference that he did not have the information. This suggests either that Tyrell and Dighton did not confess, or that the dead princes were, in fact, moved. If they were moved from the "stayre foote" in 1483, they are not likely to have been the bones found under a staircase in 1674.

The second traditionalist response is the "two staircase" theory. This is the conjecture that perhaps Forest and Dighton buried the Princes "metely deep" under some *other* staircase and that Brackenbury's priest moved them to the staircase outside the White Tower under which they were found in 1674. The argument goes that since the second staircase adjoined the White Tower, which housed the royal chapel, it was considered consecrated ground or was as close to consecrated ground as the priest could get.

But once we assume that the bones were moved in 1483, all force is gone from the argument that their location in 1674 proves the accuracy of More's account, as well as from the argument that they must be the two princes because they were found where More said they were buried. Those arguments are based on the claimed similarity between the place where the bones were found and the place More specified. But, if the bones had been *moved* to the staircase under which they were found in 1674, that second location cannot be the "stayre foote" described by More. Their discovery under a staircase proves absolutely nothing about where the bodies were located *before they were moved.*

They could just as well have been buried in the garden or in the wall as under another staircase farther from the royal chapel. If the bones had been moved to where they were found, any similarity between that second location and the *initial* burial place spelled out by More is irrelevant. It provides no support for the veracity of More's account or for the claim that the 1674 bones are those of the two princes.

Moreover, the "two staircase" theory seems most improbable. It is difficult enough to imagine that none of the many Tower residents noticed Forest and Dighton digging a pit "metely deep" under the first staircase or glimpsed Brackenbury's priest (evidently a hardy fellow) reexcavating that pit to move the bodies. It is even more difficult to envision that lone priest choosing to dig another pit ten feet deep under a second staircase and still hoping to escape detection.

Over long periods of time, the ground surface of a city tends to rise, increasing the distance of an ancient and buried object from the modern surface. This might allow the argument that, when the priest reburied the bodies, they were less than ten feet deep. But the rising surface level is normally the result of the deposit of rubble, refuse and dust on the preexisting ground. It is unlikely that the ground level *under a staircase* would rise materially even with the passage of 190 years, and it seems likely that bones found ten feet under a staircase in 1674 were already ten feet deep in 1483.

Of course, if the bones found in 1674 had been buried *before* the staircase was even constructed, they might have been placed less than ten feet from the ground level at the time. That could well be the case, since ten feet seems very deep for a grave, especially one hand-dug by a priest. But if the bones were buried before the staircase was even constructed, they could not be the two princes. The forebuilding containing the staircase appears to have been in existence from the reign of Henry II (1154–89) until its demolition in 1674.

Finally, a second staircase would not have been the only place the priest could find consecrated ground nearby. Nor would it even have been the most likely, most convenient or most appropriate place. In 1483, the Church of St. Peter ad Vincula was within the Tower walls and less than fifty yards from the White Tower.

The church was mentioned in the early twelfth century as lying just outside the Tower walls. It became a part of the Tower buildings when the walls were extended in the thirteenth century to enclose parts of the surrounding city. Queens and nobles have been buried in the church. Ironically, so was Sir Thomas More.

A midnight burial in the church's crypt, which clearly was consecrated ground, could have been carried out with much less difficulty and far less chance of discovery. Plainly, it would be a more appropriate last resting place for two royal princes than a ten-foot hole under a staircase, and much more in keeping with Richard's supposed direction to move them from "so vile a corner" (i.e., at the foot of a staircase) and to bury them "in a better place because thei wer a kinges sonnes."

It seems highly unlikely that a priest given that royal order and desiring secrecy would choose to dig another hole ten feet deep beneath a second staircase, when he could have moved the bodies a short distance to holy ground in the darkened crypt of St. Peter's.

More described the initial burial place of the princes as at the "foote" of a staircase. This would seem to refer to a place outside the staircase itself and beyond the bottom step. Were the 1674 bones found in such a place? Or were they found *under* the staircase itself? The contemporary accounts suggest the latter, although they are hardly clear on the point. If so, the bones were *not* even in the place described by More as the *initial* burial place, before they were moved.

To review and summarize, the location of the 1674 bones leads us to some interesting conclusions:

1. If, contrary to More, the princes' bodies were *not* moved, and if Tyrell and Dighton confessed in 1502, as More reported, then the two conspirators knew where the princes were buried (i.e., they were still "at the stayre foot metely deep").

2. Accordingly, if Tyrell and Dighton confessed and the bodies had not been moved, Henry VII would have disinterred and reburied the princes with royal honors and a proper mass. To reject this proposition, we must adopt one of two highly improbable scenarios. Either (a) Tyrell and Dighton confessed without ever being asked where the princes were buried or, (b) Henry was told where their bodies were located, but decided not to give them a proper reburial.

   It seems impossible that the confessing murderers were not asked where the bodies were buried. And, if he knew their location, Henry would have considered it a religious and royal duty to give a proper burial to these "kinges sonnes." Besides, as noted above, he had the strongest of political motives to do so. By 1502, two pretenders had already fomented rebellion, one claiming to be the missing Prince Richard. By far the best way to put an end to the parade of such claimants would be to produce the princes' bodies and have a royal funeral.

   Ambiguity may have been an acceptable policy in 1485 when Henry first took the throne and felt justifiable concern about rivals with a stronger claim than his own, whose supporters would be deterred by the possibility that the princes might still be alive. By 1502, however, that concern was greatly reduced. By that time, one of Henry's main problems was that more pretenders would come along claiming to be Prince Richard. The ideal solution would have been to prove that both princes were dead.

3. If propositions (1) and (2) are correct, and they seem to be, we can conclude that either (a) Tyrell and Dighton did *not* confess, or (b), as More reported, they confessed, but did not know where the princes were buried, because, from a pit "metely deep" at the "foote" of a Tower staircase, the bodies had been moved by Brackenbury's priest to some unknown burial place more appropriate to royal princes.

4. If, as More reported, the bodies were moved from their place "metely deep" beneath the "stayre foot" to a more appropriate location, the bones found in 1674 ten feet under a Tower staircase are unlikely to have been the two princes. To reject this proposition, we must adopt the improbable scenario that in searching for the more appropriate royal burial place directed by Richard, Brackenbury's priest decided to excavate a second ten-foot hole beneath a second Tower staircase, when instead a much easier, more secret and far more appropriate burial could have been effected in clearly consecrated ground close by, within the Tower walls.

5. If the foregoing propositions are correct—and that seems highly probable—it also becomes highly probable that either (a) Tyrell and Dighton did *not* confess, or (b) the bones found in 1674 were not the two princes—or both.

If Tyrell and Dighton did not confess, More's account, supposedly based on their confession, becomes significantly less credible, and the case against Richard is considerably weakened.

If the bones found in 1674 were not the two princes, then that discovery, which has been taken by so many to confirm More and bolster, if not prove, the case against Richard, is irrelevant.

And what of the two *other* young skeletons reportedly found in 1647 laid out on a table and sealed in a previously unknown Tower room? Molinet, a fifteenth-century French historian, reported that this was how the princes were killed. Was he correct? Or was this sealed room the more appropriate burial place to which the princes' bodies were moved by Brackenbury's priest?

These earlier walled-up bones were also assumed to be the remains of the two princes. They are customarily said to have been found in 1647. But August 17, 1647, was not their date of discovery, but the date of the notation on the flyleaf of More's "History" that referred to an earlier discovery of the skeletons at the time when Lord Grey and Sir Walter Raleigh were imprisoned in the Tower.

The flyleaf notation made in 1647 said that when Grey and Raleigh were both prisoners in the Tower, the wall of the passage to the king's lodgings seemed hollow, and that when the wall was taken down, a small room was discovered, about seven or eight feet square. In the center of the room was a table. On it were the bones of two children, which Grey, Raleigh and others present believed were "ye carcasses of Edward ye 5th and his brother then Duke of York." Since Grey and Raleigh were only in the Tower together between 1603 and 1614, when Grey died, the discovery had to have been in this earlier period.

There are historians who contend that these bones found in the early seventeenth century were much more likely to have been the remains of the two princes than the skeletons found in 1674. Certainly the "little roome" described in the flyleaf notation fits more closely with More's description of a place more fitting to a king's son than a pit ten feet deep under a staircase.

One problem with this theory is that the flyleaf notation in 1647 said that the bones appeared to be those of "two children supposed of 6 or 8 yeares of age," which, of course, would have been too young to be the sons of Edward IV.

Still, neither Grey, Raleigh nor anyone else present was likely to have been competent to judge the age of a small skeleton. Moreover, if they really thought the bones were those of a six- and an eight-year-old, why would they have believed that these were the two princes? Raleigh at least would seem to have known better. Perhaps the reference to the ages of the "two children" was simply an error by whoever made the 1647 note on the flyleaf.

In 1674, no one focused on those earlier bones or the conclusions that had been drawn from their discovery, just as no one focused on the inconsistency between the place where the new bones were found and their supposed removal as described by More.

If the bones found in 1674 were, in fact, those of the missing princes, they are not only relevant to establishing the time of death, they are significant evidence that a crime was committed. If these really are the bones of Edward's two sons, then the boys were almost certainly murdered *by someone.* If the two princes had died of natural causes, it is not likely that they would have been thrown together in a wooden chest and buried anonymously at the foot of a staircase.

Ultimately, by order of Charles II, most of the 1674 bones were placed in a marble urn designed by Sir Christopher Wren and interred in Westminster Abbey. Charles II was understandably concerned about the deposition and killing of rightful kings, as his father, Charles I, had been deposed and beheaded.

The urn can be seen in the abbey today, in Henry VII's chapel. It bears the following inscription:

> Below here lie interred the remains of Edward V, King of England, and of Richard, Duke of York. Their uncle Richard, who usurped the crown, imprisoned them in the Tower of London, smothered them with pillows, and ordered them to be dishonorably and secretly buried. Their long desired and much sought after bones were identified by most certain indications when, after an interval of over a hundred and ninety years, found deeply buried under the rubbish of the stairs that led up into the chapel of the White Tower, on the 17th July 1674 A.D. Charles II, most merciful prince, having compassion on their unhappy fate, performed the funeral rights of these unfortunate princes among the tombs of their ancestors, A.D. 1678, the thirtieth year of his reign.

As the inscription indicates, the bones were not enclosed in the marble urn until 1678, four years after they were removed from the Tower rubbish heap. Where were the bones between the time of their removal from the rubbish and their encasement in marble? No one is sure. For a part of that time, at least some of the bones may have been stored for convenience in the tomb of General Monck in Westminster Abbey. Most of the time, however, they appear to have been in the possession of Sir Thomas Chichely.

Some of the bones may have been delivered to the Ashmolean Museum in Oxford and ultimately lost. Elias Ashmole, founder of the museum, referred in his diary to the finding of the bones, but does not go beyond that. Thomas Hearne in his "Collections" describes a visit to the Ashmolean in 1729. He inquired about the bones and was told that "they had somewhere or other such bones, very small, particularly the finger bones." But the bones were not produced, and apparently, by 1729, they were nowhere to be found.

In 1933, with the permission of the trust that administers Westminster Abbey, the tomb was reopened so that the bones could be examined using what were then "modern" scientific methods. The examination was conducted by Lawrence Tanner, the archivist of Westminster Abbey, and Professor William Wright, dean of the London Hospital Medical College and president of the Anatomical Society. Their report was published in 1934.

Tanner and Wright found two incomplete skeletons mixed with various animal bones and rusty nails. They reported no cloth or velvet. Many bones were missing. Even aside from whatever bones may have gone to the Ashmolean, some of the bones may have been taken, sold as relics and replaced by the bones of animals before the remainder were interred in Westminster Abbey. Either that, or else animal bones were in the chest when it was discovered or were in the rubbish heap and became mixed with the two skeletons that had been in the chest.

Since reliable procedures for establishing a chain of custody for the bones were not followed, we cannot even be absolutely sure that the bones interred in 1678 were the same bones found in the Tower in 1674, although it is probable that they were.

Professor Wright concluded that these were the skeletons of two children of slender build, the older twelve to thirteen years old and the younger nine to eleven. Wright based his conclusions not so much on the size of the bones, as on their development: "[T]he elder child was still in the puberty period, since the elements forming the sockets of the shoulders and hip joints showed no sign of union." Moreover, the second cervical vertebra (the "axis") of the older child lacked "the apical part of its odontoid process." That is, the tip of the vertebra was not yet ossified and rounded as it would be in the child's later development. Wright considered this latter fact conclusive evidence that the older child "had not yet attained the age of thirteen."

Considerable light is shed on Wright's objectivity by his conclusion that "I can say with complete confidence that their death occurred during the reign of their usurping uncle, Richard III." This from a scientist who had not demonstrated that these were the princes or that they were even from the fifteenth century, much less from Richard's reign.

According to Wright, the older child had a serious infection or disease of the lower jaw, which he suggests is consistent with the condition of Edward V. Although Edward was attended by Dr. Argentine, there is no evidence that he had such an affliction. Indeed, More purports to quote a speech by Elizabeth Woodville in which she describes the *younger* prince as "sore diseased with sicknes."

Wright also noted a "blood stain" on the skull of the older child. He considered this indicative of death by suffocation, as described by More.

A concurrent dental examination was conducted by Dr. George Northcroft, a former president of the British Dental Association. Based on the children's dentition, Northcroft agreed with Wright's conclusion as to their ages at the time of death. This was difficult because only the right half of the lower jaw of the younger child was present, and the jaw of the older child contained no teeth. Northcroft, however, believed that the state of development of the missing teeth could be determined from the empty sockets. He opined that, based on that development, the older child was between twelve and thirteen.

Edward V, the older prince, was born November 2, 1470, while his mother, Elizabeth Woodville, was in her first sanctuary in Westminster Abbey. This would have made him almost thirteen in 1483, when More says he was killed, but almost fifteen at the time of Bosworth Field.

There is disagreement as to when the younger prince was born. His place of birth was known to be Shrewsbury, and August 17, 1472, is sometimes given as his birth date. But that date cannot be correct, since his older sister Margaret was born on April 10, 1472. Given the fact that there is no report of Prince Richard being born prematurely and that premature babies almost never survived in the fifteenth century, any date for the prince's birth before January 1473 seems virtually impossible.

A sixteenth-century Shrewsbury chronicle, presumably based on local tradition, records Prince Richard's birth as having occurred during the period from September 1472 to September 1473. The queen was in Shrewsbury in August 1473.

Tanner refers to a document in French acknowledging a gift and referring to the recent birth of Edward IV's second son. The document is dated September 3, 1473. Tanner considers this proof that Prince Richard was born in August of that year. That seems a reasonable conclusion. If it is correct, the younger Prince would have been ten when More has him killed and twelve at the time of Bosworth Field.

Wright pointed out "the presence of wormian bones of unusual size and of almost identical shape" in both skulls and what he and Dr. Northcroft considered evidence of "tooth surpression" in both children "occurring in the same regional plane." They concluded from this that the two children were probably related.

In 1984, Dr. Jean Ross, then of Charing Cross Hospital Medical School, came to a similar conclusion as to the consanguinity of the two skeletons. In addition, an examination of the bones of Anne Mowbray, a relative of the two princes and the child "wife" of Prince Richard, showed that she possessed some similar dental anomalies.

These reports have been considered by many writers as proof that the skeletons were those of the two princes, that they had

been killed in 1483, not 1485, and, therefore, that they had probably been killed with the knowledge, if not at the direction, of
Richard.

There are serious problems with drawing these conclusions
from the bones, even if we assume, as seems probable, that the
bones examined in 1933 were the same bones found in the Tower
in 1674. The scientific processes available in 1933 did not permit
even an approximate dating of the skeletons. The Tower had been
in use for many centuries before 1483. P. W. Hammond and W. J.
White, in their excellent analysis of the subject, note that in 1977
the skeleton of a boy between thirteen and sixteen was discovered
buried in the Tower grounds and was scientifically dated to the
late Iron Age. Dozens of other skeletons have been found within
the Tower walls, in the crypt of St. Peter ad Vincula and in the
moat (when it was drained in 1830). The bones discovered in 1674
could have been Roman bones, and Roman female bones at that.

Unfortunately, neither Wright nor Tanner nor Norcross made
any attempt to determine the sex of the skeletons they examined.
They simply *assumed* that the bones were male, an assumption for
which there was no basis other than the erroneous assertion that
the bones had been found where More said they were buried and
therefore must be the two princes.

There were, at the time, methods of determining the probability that a skeleton was male or female. Today, there are additional and more reliable methods. Hammond and White find
support in tooth measurement statistics for the position that at
least one of the skeletons may have been female. Theya Mollesen
of the British Museum has pointed to physical features she considers indicative of the probability that both skeletons were male.
Hammond and White find her reasoning unpersuasive.

In the absence of a further examination, the best we can do as
to the gender of the bones is to assess probability; and there is no
agreement among experts even as to which gender is the more
probable.

Some traditionalists have argued that velvet was unknown in
England until the fifteenth century, so that if there was a bit of
velvet in with the bones, as the anonymous comment indicated,
these were bones from that century or later. Others have replied

that the report of velvet in with the bones is not reliable and that, in any event, velvet was known in England long before the fifteenth century.

Moreover, given the very lax chain of custody of the bones in 1674, the velvet could have been in the rubbish heap or inadvertently included later—if there was velvet at all. No velvet was found in 1933 by Wright and Tanner.

Medical writings after the time of Wright and Tanner have brought out that a bloodstained skull does *not* indicate death by smothering, if indeed the stain was even human blood. Wright conceded his inability to prove that it was.

And, while common skeletal and dental characteristics could be evidence of a family tie, the characteristics common to these two skeletons are not so unusual as to create a high probability of such a relationship.

For example, according to Hammond and White, large wormian bones, a feature Wright and Tanner considered evidence that the two skeletons were related, have been found in approximately fifty percent of skeletons from the Middle Ages. Moreover, the skull of Anne Mowbray, who was related to the two princes, did *not* contain the kind of wormian bones treated by Wright and Tanner as indicative of consanguinity.

Common missing teeth, another factor given weight by Wright and Tanner, is also an unreliable factor, in that a substantial number of missing teeth was a common feature of skeletons from the Middle Ages and, in any event, could often have been the result of teeth being knocked out or lost to infection, rather than the consequence of a congenital tendency.

Several different problems inhere in trying to determine how old the two children were at the time of their deaths. The size of the bones is not a useful indicator in determining their age. Humans in the fifteenth century were normally smaller than they are today. One need only look at the doorways of ancient European homes or the size of medieval suits of armor to realize that, in general, people were significantly shorter. There are no reliable figures for the average size of children in the fifteenth century, but it would be a fair inference that it was considerably smaller than the average in the 1930s.

Hammond and White point out that although Anne Mowbray was almost nine when she died, the size of her bones compared to modern averages would make her appear to have been only six, and that applying the same modern averages to the bone length of the two skeletons examined by Wright and Tanner would make the two deceased children appear to have been only eight and ten, respectively, at the time of their death.

If the same ratio between actual age and apparent skeletal age that was found in the case of Anne Mowbray is applied to the two Wright and Tanner skeletons, the child whose bone length compared to modern averages appeared to make him (or her) eight would actually have been twelve and the child whose bone length appeared to make him (or her) ten would have been fifteen. Of course, we cannot take bone length averages and apply them to individual skeletons. Anne Mowbray may have been uncommonly short and, since we know that Edward IV was six-foot-three, one might expect his sons to have been uncommonly tall.

More significant to the 1933 examination, however, was the factor of bone development. As pointed out, Wright concluded that structural development consistent with a child of thirteen or more was not present in the skeleton of the older child, and, therefore, that the child was not yet thirteen at death. Hammond and White suggest that, using modern statistics, the structural development in question would be present at twelve, rather than at thirteen, so that the same argument would lead to the conclusion that the older skeleton was not yet even twelve and so could not have been Edward V.

Similarly, Paul Murray Kendall cites scientific opinion to the effect that the skeleton of the older child may have been too *young* to be the older prince, a conclusion that might not give sufficient weight to the effects of a fifteenth-century diet and possible bone disease.

Modern studies suggest, as do Hammond and White, that reaching any firm conclusions about calendar age from development of the bones is simply not justified. In a 1963 lecture, Dr. Richard Lyne-Pirkis, an English anatomical expert, described a careful and comprehensive study by Dr. Wingate Todd and his successors at Case Western Reserve University. In this study, the skeletal development of a diversified group of about a thousand children was regularly measured from birth until the children were twenty.

The conclusion of this controlled study was that there was no reliable way to determine calendar age from skeletal development and that the degree of skeletal development varied by as much as two years from the children's calendar age, even in children with a normal modern diet. In the case of children with diets less enriched than those of those of the average modern child—something reasonable to assume in the case of fifteenth-century children—skeletal development would be as much as another year slower. The Case Western study showed that the same was true of dental development. The rate of that development could not be reliably used to determine calendar age. The variations were too great.

Dr. Lyne-Pirkis added that that the jaw disease evident in the older skeleton was probably osteomyelitis, a disease that can slow bone growth appreciably—perhaps by as much as three years.

Based on Dr. Lyne-Pirkis's views and the Case Western study, the calendar age of the two skeletons cannot be determined conclusively from their skeletal or dental development, since a child whose age might be thought to be twelve based on skeletal or dental development could very easily be fourteen. Moreover, the same conditions in a fifteenth-century child lacking the vitamins and minerals available in a modern diet and suffering from osteomyelitis, could well make that child fifteen or sixteen.

As Dr. Lyne-Pirkis put it, the bones "belong to children of different ages, and we assume that their age lies roughly between, shall we say, the age of probably about seven or eight and fifteen or sixteen. And that's really as far as anybody could go. . . ."

Accordingly, if these were the bones of the princes, they could have died in 1485 or later, rather than in 1483. If so, the bones do not necessarily eliminate Richard's alibi, even if they are the bones of the two princes. And there is no reliable proof that they are.

Of course, the *average* age of children with specific skeletal or dental development can be computed. But, as in the case of bone size, averages are misleading when used to predict the characteristics of any one person in the sampled population. For example, if ten fish are caught in a stream on a particular day and five fish weigh one pound and the other five weigh three pounds, the *average* fish will weigh two pounds, even though not a single two-pound fish was caught. We cannot conclude that any member of a sampled group had any particular characteristic because the *average* member did.

Thus, even though the "average" child achieves a certain skeletal development at thirteen, most of the sampled children may achieve that development at either twelve or fourteen, creating an "average" of thirteen that actually fits very few of the sampled children.

What can be more helpful than the average is the extent and frequency of variation from the average. For example, even though children achieve a particular degree of skeletal development at ages varying from ten to eighteen, if sixty percent of children achieve that skeletal development between thirteen and fourteen, we can state that it is *more probable than not* that a child whose skeleton has not yet reached that stage of development was not yet thirteen at death.

Hammond and White show that, while the 1674 bones may be *consistent* with the ages of the two princes in 1483, they are also consistent with entirely different ages. In addition, it is arguable that the "age gap" (i.e., the difference in age between the two skeletons) is too small for them to have been the remains of Edward V and his brother.

Of course, Hammond and White are dealing with averages, and it is entirely possible that, as Shakespeare says (*Richard III*, act II, scene iv), the younger prince was big for his age and had nearly overtaken his older brother in size. If so, the difference between the two would be considerably less than the difference between the average ten-year-old and the average thirteen-year-old.

At least part of the mystery could now be solved. Given today's technology, the bones in Westminster Abbey can be dated to within a very few years. Certainly we can establish whether they are from the latter half of the fifteenth century as opposed to the time of the Norman Conquest or the Roman occupation.

Moreover, modern DNA technology will soon allow us to determine something even more significant. We have the remains of Edward IV. While current DNA analysis seems focused on tracing the female line, it will not be long before it can provide a conclusive answer as to whether or not these skeletons were Edward's sons.

Unfortunately, such experiments require the permission of the Trust charged with administering the abbey, and that permission may well be refused. In recent years, the Ricardian Society applied for permission to disinter the skeletons in order to carbon date them. Permission was denied, even though it had been more than fifty years since the last experiments were performed.

Someday, of course, permission will be granted. Someday, technology will be sufficient not only to tell us if these were really the two princes, but also probably to determine with precision whether death occurred in 1483 or 1485. When that occurs, we may at least have narrowed our list of possible killers.

Based on the data now available, what can we rationally conclude about the bones examined in 1933 by Tanner and Wright?

First, they are probably the same bones (minus some) that were found ten feet deep under a Tower staircase in 1674.

Second, they may or may not be the two princes and may or may not even be male. Only further testing will tell us.

Third, Tanner and Wright are incorrect in the certainty with which they conclude that the older child was not yet thirteen. That age may be probable; but it may also be that the older child was less than twelve, in which case it could not be Prince Edward, or more than fourteen, in which case, even if it were Prince Edward, he could have died in 1485 or later.

If, on the other hand, these are the remains of the two princes, and if the older child was not yet thirteen, they died in 1483, not 1485. If so, Richard's alibi would be gone. His guilt would still not be established, since others could have committed the crime in that year. Still, the probability of his guilt would certainly be increased.

XVIII

THE PROCLIVITY TO KILL

Another factor in assessing Richard's guilt of murdering his nephews is whether he had a proclivity to commit such crimes—i.e., the "character" issue.

Alison Weir draws some harsh conclusions about Richard's character, and particularly what she calls his "ruthlessness." For example, Weir points out that Richard's father and brother were killed when he was only eight, that he "suffered the agony of exile" and that he "saw his brother, the King, betrayed by Clarence and Warwick." Then she adds, in a striking nonsequitur, "*it is therefore fair to say that, by the age of eighteen he had* become hardened to violence and had *developed a ruthless streak in his character.*" (Emphasis added.)

There is absolutely nothing preceding the words "it is therefore fair to say" that could logically justify Weir's conclusion that Richard had "developed a ruthless streak." He may indeed have developed such a "streak," but the facts cited by Weir fail to support that conclusion.

Later, when Weir gives an example of what she calls Richard's ruthlessness, she errs. She asserts that, after the battle of Tewkesbury, Richard ordered several Lancastrians dragged from sanctuary in Tewkesbury Abbey, after which they were executed. However, as both Charles Ross and Paul Murray Kendall make clear in their biographical works, it was Edward IV, not Richard, who did this. Richard did preside over the subsequent trial of the Lancastrians for high treason; but that is hardly the same as dragging them from sanctuary. Even Edward's conduct has been defended on the ground that Tewkesbury Abbey was not a duly established sanctuary. But if it was, it was not Richard who violated it.

Putting Weir aside for the moment, we must analyze the evidence of Richard's character as it relates to the likelihood of his killing his nephews. Richard's consistently kind treatment of Clarence's son, Warwick, his sister's son, Lincoln, and other potential rivals provides some exculpatory evidence.

Warwick appears to have been well treated by Richard throughout his reign, even though he was nearly as formidable a threat as the two princes. But for his father's attainder, Warwick's claim to the throne was better than Richard's. As discussed above, reversing an attainder was a common thing. Richard's own attainder by the Parliament of Henry VI had been reversed. The same could easily have been done for Warwick had he gathered powerful supporters and overthrown Richard.

If Richard was the kind of man who would kill to avoid the threat of a rival claimant, why did he allow Warwick to remain alive and in England, where he could attract disaffected nobles to his cause at any time?

As we have seen, Warwick may have been feebleminded, or at least not very bright. Perhaps that mitigated Richard's fear of him as a rival, as distinguished from his fear of the two princes, who were intelligent and potentially able. Richard made Warwick his heir when his own son died. That might seem odd if Warwick were seriously impaired. On the other hand, if Richard were really the scheming monster portrayed by Shakespeare, what better way to insure his own safety than to designate a moron as his successor?

Perhaps Richard did have concern about Warwick, but, having killed the princes, found himself unable to undertake still another murder. Perhaps he was more fond of Clarence's son than he had ever been of Elizabeth Woodville's two boys. At least, with his father dead, Warwick had no family to rally behind his claim, while the princes' Woodville connections might have made them seem more dangerous.

None of these explanations is completely satisfying. While hardly conclusive, Richard's treatment of Warwick seems out of character for a man who killed his two nephews.

Similarly, Richard was consistently kind to his sister's son, the earl of Lincoln. An able young man, Lincoln was also a potential claimant to the throne, although his claim was weaker than Richard's. The kind of mentality that would have killed young Edward V and his brother, even after they were declared illegitimate, would seemingly not have hesitated to kill both Warwick and Lincoln.

On the other hand, Richard has been charged with committing other murders and having thus exhibited a proclivity to kill when it suited his interests. The first such charge is that Richard killed Edward, the Lancastrian Prince of Wales, after the battle of Tewkesbury. Richard was eighteen at the time. The prince was seventeen. They both fought in the battle.

No contemporary account attributes the prince's death to Richard. Instead, they report that the prince was "slain in the field" or while "fleeing" at the end of the battle. There is no mention of Richard being present. De Commynes reported simply that "the prince of Wales was killed on the battlefield." The Annals of Tewkesbury Abbey state that "when King Edward IV arrived with his army, he slew Prince Edward in the field." The "Historie of the Arrivale of Edward IV" says that "Edward, called Prince, was taken, fleeing towards the town and slain in the field." The Croyland chronicler reports that the Prince was killed "either on the battlefield or afterwards at the avenging hands of certain persons."

Warkworth's chronicle has the prince killed after begging for his life to "his brother-in-law the Duke of Clarence." This version may be fanciful, but Kendall adopts it, writing that, fleeing toward Tewkesbury, the prince was overtaken by troops commanded by Clarence and, after pleading with Clarence for his life, was immediately killed.

Years later, in the reign of Henry VII, Fabyan wrote in the Great Chronicle that, after the battle, the prince was taken to Edward IV's tent, where he was questioned by the victorious Edward and gave an answer Edward found offensive. Edward then "smote hym on the face with the bak of his gauntelet" and he was slain by "the Kynges servantys." Fabyan provided the same account in the chronicle that bore his name, stating that, after being struck with Edward's gauntlet, the prince "was by the Kynge's servantes incontynently slain." No one would have referred to Richard, the king's brother, a royal duke and, later, the king himself, as one of the king's "servants."

Vergil, the Tudor historian, altered this tale, providing the ambiguous report that Edward thrust the prince from him "with his hand, whum furthwith, those tha wer present were George duke of Clarence, Richerd duke of Glocester and William lord Hastinges, crewlly murderyd." This altered version of an altered version was essentially repeated by Hall and Holinshed. These were, of course, neither contemporary accounts nor unbiased ones. Even if we can accept the assertion that the prince was killed in Edward's tent, rather than in battle or fleeing the field, there seems no factual basis for substituting this quartet of noble murderers for "the Kynges servantes."

Considering all of these reports, there is no convincing evidence that Richard killed the Prince of Wales, and, on the state of the record today, he must be absolved of that charge.

The next charge is that Richard murdered Henry VI, when the old, dethroned King was imprisoned in the Tower after the battle of Tewkesbury. Edward IV had an obvious motive for killing Henry VI. Since the Prince of Wales was now dead, Henry's own death would put an end to any effective Lancastrian claim and significantly strengthen Edward's hold on the throne. Richard was intensely loyal to his brother. In a sense, Edward's motive was, vicariously, Richard's motive as well.

Other than de Commynes, no contemporary account accuses Richard of complicity in this crime. Most modern historians acquit him of it.

In 1499, during Henry VII's reign, an assembly of English churchmen petitioned the pope that Henry VI's remains be moved to Westminster Abbey. The petition blames the old king's "pitiable death" on Edward IV. It does not implicate Richard.

De Commynes, who also wrote in the reign of Henry VII, said that Richard either killed the old king or was present while others did. The latter charge may be true. The former is most unlikely. Most of the Tudor historians piled on. Vergil and More say that Richard personally murdered the old king. More even claims that Richard did this "without commandment or knowledge of the King [i.e., Edward]." This seems not only unlikely, but impossible.

If Henry was murdered, as appears probable, Edward, and most likely the council as well, ordered his death. What is extremely unlikely, however, is that Edward directed his brother to do the killing personally. On the other hand, Richard was the constable of the Tower, and it is probable that, in his official capacity, he would have been designated to convey the order to the appropriate Tower official, and perhaps even to be present as a witness when the deed was done.

The official account at the time was that Henry died of natural causes. His body was displayed to the public, so there could be no doubt that he was, in fact, dead. Of course, the public had no chance for a close examination of the corpse, and there were many ways in which Henry could have been killed without it being discernible from a casual and distant observation of his body. When Henry's skull was examined in 1910, it was reported to have been "much broken" and the hair "apparently matted with blood."

Weir quotes someone she assures us is a "reliable contemporary chronicler" who says that, the day *after* the old king's death, the crowd could see him bleeding on the pavement and that, even later that second day, the corpse "bled new and fresh." Fresh bleeding the day *after* his death? Not likely. But Weir tells us to accept this chronicler as "reliable."

Henry VI was thought to have been killed on May 21, 1471, a date on which Edward IV and Richard were present at the Tower. Their presence is not in itself a suspicious fact, since the Tower was frequently a site for important meetings. Both brothers apparently left London on May 23. It is not impossible that the deposed king was still alive at that time, but it is probable that he was not.

Henry's death cannot be taken as showing Richard's proclivity to kill when murder fitted into his plans. If Henry was murdered, Richard was probably aware of the act and condoned it. It is not unlikely that he conveyed the order to the Tower at the direction of Edward and the council and remained on as an official witness to the old king's death. It is highly unlikely, however, that he struck the fatal blow; and it is almost certain that he did not kill Henry without express authority from the king and council.

The next "victim" is Clarence, theatrically drowned in the "Malmsey butt." Shakespeare, of course, blames Richard, but all the evidence is to the contrary. Mancini reported that Richard was distraught at Clarence's execution and returned to his northern estates. As we have discussed, More suggested that Richard's anguish may have been a sham. But Mancini and others thought his grief was genuine. As Mancini put it, Richard "was so overcome with grief for his brother, that he could not dissimulate so well, but that he was overheard to say that he would one day avenge his brother's death."

With the exception of Shakespeare, no one writing at the time, or even in the Tudor period, lays this crime at Richard's door. Shakespeare, of course, was looking for drama and seeking to create a dramatic supervillain, rather than to report the facts.

Richard did have a possible motive for killing Clarence. Like the two princes, Clarence was ahead of Richard in the line of succession. But at the time Clarence was executed, Edward IV was still a young man, with two male heirs. There was no reason to believe that Richard's succession was likely even if Clarence was removed from the scene. Still, Richard might have anticipated that Clarence's death would bring him Clarence's share of his late wife's estate, since they were married to sisters.

The better case is that the Woodvilles pressed both the king and Parliament for Clarence's execution. We have already reviewed their motives. Clarence had been insultingly hostile to the Woodville family, and there was the prospect that Dorset and Rivers would be enriched by his death—which, in fact, occurred.

Perhaps, as we have said, the Woodvilles were determined to see Clarence executed not only because he was referring to Edward as a bastard, but also because he had discovered and was beginning to speak of the Eleanor Butler precontract. The

Woodvilles knew that the unstable Clarence could neither be controlled nor trusted. The charge of Edward's illegitimacy was not so dangerous, but if the secret of the precontract got out, the queen would be humiliated and Woodville power could be seriously eroded.

In any event, there is no evidence whatsoever of Richard's participation in this crime—if indeed it can be considered a crime, since Clarence had a public trial and his execution appears to have been demanded by Parliament.

Moreover, given the fact that Clarence's death had been ordered by the king and sanctioned by Parliament, there would have been numerous executioners available and no need for Richard, a prince of the blood and the brother of the accused, to carry out the order himself or secretly to hire the killers, as he does in Shakespeare's play.

It has been argued that, if Richard did not kill Clarence, he schemed to have him condemned and executed. Even that would be sheer speculation. There is no such evidence. And certainly, based on the available evidence and common sense, he must be exonerated of doing the actual killing or even hiring the killers.

Perhaps the least believable of the crimes charged to Richard is poisoning his wife in order to marry his niece, Elizabeth. Queen Anne died in March 1485 after a lingering illness much like that which took the life of her sister, Isabel. The cause of death in both cases probably was tuberculosis.

The preceding Christmas, young Elizabeth stirred gossip by appearing in the same gown as that worn by the queen. It is difficult to read much into this event other than that people were as prurient then as now. It hardly shows that Richard was publicly displaying Elizabeth as Anne's replacement.

The Croyland chronicler reported gossip to the effect that Richard was considering a marriage to Elizabeth "after the death of the Queen," which tells us at least that the queen was known to be extremely ill. But, whatever plans he may have entertained in realistic anticipation of Anne's dying, it seems unlikely that Richard actually desired her death. They had been virtually life-long companions.

Alison Weir, always certain that she knows Richard's state of mind five hundred years ago, asserts that his "motive for marrying [Anne] was not so much love as the desire to acquire her lands." She cites no evidence that supports this assertion.

But, even if Richard's initial motive was to acquire or control Anne's property, he appears to have grown genuinely fond of her during their years together. They had gone through Anne's kidnapping by Clarence and her rescue by Richard, the birth and death of their child, as well as many other triumphs and crises. They appeared to enjoy each other's company and were often together, much more so than most royal couples.

Sir George Buck wrote that he had seen, among papers in the cabinet of the earl of Arundel, a letter from Princess Elizabeth to the duke of Norfolk seeking the duke's assistance in bringing about her marriage to Richard and saying that the king "was her joy and maker in this world and that she was in his heart and thought." According to Buck, the princess "hinted her surprise at the duration of the Queen's illness and her apprehension that she would never die." Buck did not copy the letter. He merely paraphrased it—or at least his memory of it.

Alison Hanham argues that Buck invented the reference to marriage, that it was not in the original letter and that Elizabeth's impatience for the queen to die could have referred to the possibility of Elizabeth's acquiring an interest in dower lands on her death. But nothing in Buck's romantic paraphrase of the letter would be shocking or inconsistent with the known facts. The youthful Elizabeth may well have had the feelings described by Buck. Richard was still young at the time. He was, according to all reliable reports, an attractive, intelligent man and a celebrated warrior. He had been loyal to, and seemingly beloved by, Elizabeth's father. Most of all, he was the king.

Certainly it would have been characteristic of Elizabeth Woodville to push for a marriage between her daughter and the king and even to urge her daughter to write such a letter.

Did Richard reciprocate Elizabeth's feelings supposedly expressed in the letter? She was an attractive young girl. But unlike his brother Edward, Richard was no libertine. He had two (and possibly three) illegitimate children; but, for a young and vigorous member of the royal family in the fifteenth century, this was not at all unusual. Moreover, the two known children whom he acknowledged appear to have been fathered before his marriage to Anne. If Richard had any romantic feelings about Elizabeth, it is unlikely that he would have expressed them to her or anyone else before Anne's death.

If romance did not move Richard to consider a marriage to Elizabeth, were there reasons of state to do so? In early 1485, Richard's only son had died. The queen was seriously ill and had no realistic chances of producing an heir. Richard must have considered the political desirability of remarrying upon Anne's death. Elizabeth could have been one of the choices he considered.

In December 1484, Henry Tudor had announced his own intention to marry Elizabeth, thus "combining the houses of York and Lancaster." A marriage between Richard and Elizabeth after Queen Anne's death may have been suggested, if only to frustrate Henry's plan. But Richard could have achieved the same result by marrying Elizabeth to some other noble, rather than marrying her himself. It is odd that he did not adopt that course. It seems impossible that the idea failed to occur to him or his advisors.

There were reasons why Richard's marrying Elizabeth was not sound policy. *Titulus Regius* had made her illegitimate along with her brothers. Was the king of England going to marry a bastard? Reversing her illegitimacy would compel the reversal of *Titulus Regius,* casting doubt on Richard's own claim. Indeed, it would then be arguable that Elizabeth's claim was better than his. Nor would marrying Elizabeth bring the military and political advantage of a marriage to the daughter of a strong foreign power.

If Richard truly intended a marriage with Elizabeth, why did he take the unusual and possibly humiliating step of publicly denying it shortly after Anne's death? The conventional wisdom is that he was convinced by his close advisors Catesby and Ratcliffe that, even if a marriage between uncle and niece would be valid under canon law (given the pope's permission), the match would be extremely unpopular with the common people, especially in the North, where Queen Anne was beloved. With a Tudor invasion anticipated, the king was in no position to antagonize a large segment of the public, especially the northerners on whom he had so often relied.

As we have discussed, Kendall believes that Catesby and Ratcliffe had another, personal agenda, that they were vehemently against placing another Woodville queen on the throne, fearing Woodville revenge for their part in the execution of Rivers and Grey. Whatever its motivation, we cannot conclude from Richard's denial that he did not, in fact, entertain the match.

Nevertheless, whatever he may have felt or thought or considered with regard to remarriage, there is not a shred of evidence that Richard poisoned his wife.

Finally, Richard is accused of murdering Hastings, Rivers, Grey and Vaughn. Richard apparently believed that Hastings was involved in a plot against his life, along with the queen and her Woodville relations. Only three days earlier, on June 10, he had written to the city of York referring explicitly to the Woodville threat and asking for armed assistance. At some point, he seems to have become convinced that Hastings was a part of the conspiracy.

Hastings' wife had family connections with the Lancastrians that may have increased Richard's readiness to believe the worst. Richard had agents in France, just as the French had spies in London. An English agent or any one of a number of political sources could have informed Richard that Hastings had joined forces with Morton and the Woodvilles and that, as a group, they were now supporting Henry Tudor. Evidently Buckingham, who may have had his own spies (and his own agenda), was vehement in his warnings to Richard that Hastings was conspiring with Morton, Stanley and others. Finally, Richard had the report of Catesby, Hastings' trusted aide, that his old friend and benefactor had joined the conspirators.

Whether the information from these sources was true or not, it seems probable that Richard accepted and believed it. It is far more likely that Richard thought he was executing a trusted friend who had betrayed him and even planned to kill him than that he was carrying out an act of cold-blooded terrorism against a loyal and innocent associate in order to intimidate others.

There is controversy as to whether Hastings was executed on the spot, as More and Shakespeare indicate, or a week later, on June 20, which would have allowed for a trial. It has been argued that the latter is the case, since the summary execution of a council member, immediately upon his arrest before his fellow council members, would have seemed unthinkable.

Maybe so; but Richard was decisive and impetuous, and he prized loyalty above all else. Betrayal by a friend could well have caused him to demand immediate punishment. Also, as we have discussed, Hastings had his own formidable men at arms, and it may have seemed dangerous to allow him to remain alive, awaiting trial. While Richard was still only protector, he was about to become king, and it is highly probable that if he gave orders to execute Hastings, even without a trial, those orders, even if normally unthinkable, would have been obeyed.

A contemporary letter dated Saturday, June 21, refers to Hastings as having been executed on "Friday last." It is unlikely that this could mean anything but Friday, June 13, the day of Hastings's arrest. If the execution had been on Friday, the 20th, one writing on the 21st would almost certainly have said "yesterday" rather than "Friday last." At least two other documents show the 13th as the day of Hastings's execution. All these references could of course be inaccurate, but it seems unlikely.

Even if Hastings was executed on the same day he was arrested, it is not impossible that some sort of summary trial could have been conducted, with Hastings's confession being extracted and offered. But this is improbable.

Technical justification can be offered for Hastings' death, even if there was no trial at all. Hastings was accused of treason. Edward IV had made Richard constable of England for life, and with that office came the power to determine and punish treason without judicial proceedings. Moreover, it was not generally considered murder in 1483 for a royal duke to arrest and summarily execute someone who, posing as a friend, had betrayed him and plotted his death.

But those technical defenses do not answer the charge that Hastings' death shows Richard's proclivity to kill, and to do so swiftly and decisively when he considered such action essential to his own interests.

The moral issue here is not an easy one. It seems likely that Richard believed his old comrade had grossly betrayed him. Ordering an immediate execution in those emotional circumstances, while perhaps harsh and even draconian, seems a very different kind of act from the cold-blooded killing of two innocent boys who were his brother's sons and who had not betrayed him in any way.

Richard did not execute John Morton, although he was considered a key member of the same conspiracy. Did this show Richard's reluctance to kill? Probably not. It was one thing to execute a nobleman without a trial. It was quite another to treat a bishop in that fashion. Indeed, even if Morton had been tried, canon law would have forbidden Richard to execute him without permission of the pope. Moreover, Richard probably expected no loyalty from Morton and did not feel the rage toward the cynical bishop that he felt at Hastings' disloyalty or at Buckingham's later betrayal.

Richard also took no action against Lord Stanley, even though Stanley was also believed to have been involved in Hastings' plot and even though Stanley's wife was one of the chief conspirators. Lady Stanley was attainted and put in her husband's charge—not a very significant punishment considering the seriousness of her crime.

As we have said, this may not have been so much the result of a merciful nature as a matter of practical politics, given the strength of the Stanley family and its men at arms. Had Lord and Lady Stanley been executed or even banished from the realm, the result of Bosworth Field—and thus the entire course of English history—might have been changed.

Probably the most significant evidence of a readiness to kill on Richard's part is the execution of Rivers, Grey and Vaughn. It appears that they did have a trial before the duke of Northumberland, after which they were convicted of treason, condemned to death and executed. There is evidence that Richard had ordered their deaths even before the trial, and he had requested that they be charged with treason as early as May 10.

Rivers, an intelligent and scholarly man, appears not to have considered Richard wholly unreasonable in the matter, since, as we have discussed, he appointed Richard supervisor of his will only two days before his execution.

As in so many situations, Richard showed generosity to Rivers' widow, a trait difficult to reconcile with terrorism being his motive. When men like Hastings, Rivers and Buckingham were executed for treason, it would have been within Richard's power to seize their estates for himself. Although in need of money, Richard did not follow that practice.

Given the attitudes and actions of the fifteenth century, Richard's execution of Rivers, Grey and Vaughn, after at least paying lip service to the forms of a trial, cannot realistically be called murder.

If, as appears likely, they did not join in any conspiracy while held in separate northern castles, they were quite probably a part of the Woodvilles' earlier plot to disregard the will of Edward IV, to seize the fleet and the treasure, to deceive Richard and possibly even to kill him.

Moreover, Richard probably held the entire Woodville clan responsible for the death of Clarence, an act that seems to have angered and embittered him. While these earlier acts may not have provided a sound legal basis for the executions of Rivers, Grey and Vaughn in June 1483, they at least provide an emotional context that distinguishes their deaths from the killing of two innocent children who had done Richard no wrong at all.

The execution of Buckingham can hardly be called a murder. The mercurial duke openly led a rebellion against the reigning king. He was supported by the king's enemies, and he conspired to bring about Henry Tudor's invasion of England. Very clearly, he was guilty of treason; and, in accordance with the law, his conduct warranted execution. Even here, however, Richard was generous to Buckingham's widow, awarding her a pension and paying the duke's outstanding debts.

In summary, Richard's conduct with respect to these other deaths, even where legally or morally unjustified, does not provide significant evidence that he killed his two young nephews in the Tower.

XIX

♛ THE BEHAVIOR OF CONTEMPORARIES

In a modern court of law, the opinions of third parties as to the defendant's guilt or innocence would be, as lawyers sometimes say, "irrelevant, incompetent and immaterial." We must convict criminal defendants by factual evidence adduced in a courtroom, not by the opinions of their fellow citizens.

But evaluating a person's guilt of a crime committed in the fifteenth century is quite a different proposition. Weight is often given to what contemporaries or near contemporaries thought, usually as reflected in what they wrote. Indeed, much of the case against Richard is based on the opinions of those who wrote in Tudor times.

But the actual behavior of contemporaries may be a better indicator of the truth than any written or spoken assertions, especially the assertions of those who were highly motivated to express biased views. If we examine the *conduct* of Richard's contemporaries and carefully consider the possible explanations for that conduct, we may be able to draw reasonable inferences as to what they really believed about his guilt or innocence. Then, if we weigh their opportunity to know the truth, we may be aided by their opinion in forming our own.

Buckingham, Stanley and Northumberland, for example, turned against Richard, the first leading a rebellion to depose him, the other two betraying him in his confrontation with

Henry Tudor. Was this evidence that, having observed Richard, they considered him guilty of murdering the two princes? Some historians have considered it so. But, as we have already discussed, there were cogent and probable reasons for the behavior of each of them other than a belief that Richard murdered his nephews. If the conduct of the three men can even be considered evidence of Richard's guilt, it would seem of low probative value.

And what of the behavior of the Woodvilles? The former queen, Elizabeth Woodville, released her younger son from sanctuary after Richard had arrested Rivers, Grey and Vaughn and had actually executed Hastings. If Elizabeth considered Richard likely to murder the boy, wouldn't she at least have called the council's bluff, making them either back down or take her son from sanctuary by force? At this time, there were no rumors that the older prince had been killed, so we can only consider the former queen's conduct evidence of what she thought about Richard's proclivity to kill, not on the issue of whether, later, she thought he did kill.

Elizabeth Woodville left sanctuary with her five daughters in March 1484. By that time, it had already been rumored that Richard had murdered her sons. This had even been publicly proclaimed in France. These reports and rumors must have been known to the ex-queen.

If Edward IV's sons were dead, Elizabeth certainly knew that his daughters were almost as dangerous to Richard. If their illegitimacy were reversed, their claim to the throne, like that of their brothers, would be better than Richard's; and public opinion could coalesce around them. Would Elizabeth Woodville turn her daughters over to Richard if she thought he had killed her sons?

After leaving sanctuary, the former queen appeared to be on the friendliest of terms with Richard. As Gairdner put it, Elizabeth was persuaded "zealously to befriend [Richard]." This would also suggest that she did not believe he had recently murdered her two young sons. And her belief would be based on a reasonable opportunity to assess the facts. At the very least, she must have asked where the boys were and how they were. She must have asked to see them. What answer did Richard give—"I killed them madame, but let's dance"?

Of course, fifteenth-century attitudes were not the same as today's. Death and dynastic struggles were part of life, and it is possible that Elizabeth simply recognized the realities of the situation and behaved in a manner that served her own best interests. If Richard had killed her sons, expressions of rage would not bring them back and would only jeopardize her own safety and that of her daughters. Richard had given a public oath to respect the princesses' safety and to treat them well. Despite their ancestry, they were females and not as likely as the two princes had been to attract the support of discontented nobles. Perhaps the king would keep his word. What was the alternative—to spend the rest of their lives in sanctuary? To risk death? Why not just go along?

On the other hand, Elizabeth wrote to Dorset, her oldest son, urging him to return to England and to make his peace with Richard. Unless this was a sham, done solely to impress the king, it is further evidence that Elizabeth did not see Richard as a danger to her children. It was probably not a sham, since Dorset actually tried to leave the Continent in 1485 but was apprehended and forced to remain. Richard's proclamations against Henry Tudor in December 1484 and June 1485 condemned those supporting Henry, but the list no longer included Dorset as one of the conspirators. Evidently, even after Richard was widely rumored to have killed the two princes, the Woodvilles had seemingly made their peace with him.

Finally, we have the apparent support of Elizabeth Woodville for the cause of Lincoln and Lambert Simnell in 1487 and the fact that Henry Tudor evidently believed that Dorset also supported that cause, since he arrested the marquess at the time. If, as appears to be the case, the Woodvilles backed Lincoln and Simnell, that would be a significant indication of their belief, at that time, that one or both princes were still alive and that one of them, rather than Simnell, would take the throne if Lincoln's rebellion succeeded. It is difficult, if not impossible, to imagine any other reason why the Woodvilles would support a rebellion intended to depose Henry VII and his Woodville queen, the former Princess Elizabeth of York.

And what can we infer from the behavior of that Woodville

princess before she became Henry Tudor's queen? Seemingly, in late 1484 and early 1485, her relationship with Richard was good—or maybe better than good. In the letter summarized by Sir George Buck, the princess supposedly expressed the wish that Queen Anne's illness would soon take her life so that Elizabeth might marry Richard, whom she described as "her onely joy and maker in this World."

This was well after the rumors circulated that Richard had murdered the princes. It is understandable that Elizabeth might overlook many things in order to marry the reigning king. But is it possible that she would have had such romantic yearnings for the man who had recently killed her two younger brothers?

Given the morality of the period and the fact that Edward IV's children had been raised apart from each other and may not have been that close, it is possible—but not likely. Of course, Elizabeth may not have written what Buck said or may not have really meant what she said in the letter, simply intending those sentiments to be passed on to the king in order to gain his good-will for her family.

There is also the possibility that Elizabeth did not *know* Richard had murdered her brothers. But it is likely that, by late 1484, she and her mother had reasonably good information about the two boys. And, even if she only knew they were missing and perhaps dead, she must have entertained the possibility that Richard had killed them—unless she knew that someone else had done so.

Considering everything, the behavior of the dowager queen, Elizabeth Woodville, her adult son Dorset, and her oldest daughter strongly suggests (even if it does not prove) that they believed in Richard's innocence; and, at the times they engaged in that behavior, they would seem to have been in a good position to assess his guilt.

The same can be said for Sir Robert Brackenbury. He certainly would have known if Richard had arranged for the princes' murders in the Tower. Brackenbury had a reputation for honesty and integrity. Yet, he remained loyal to Richard, fighting and dying for him at Bosworth Field. Would he have done so if he knew that Richard had murdered his young nephews? It seems unlikely.

Weighing the actual behavior of these contemporaries, the probable reasons for that behavior and the likelihood that they knew whether or not Richard committed the crime, their conduct tends to support the inference of innocence rather than guilt. It is, of course, not conclusive; but it seems more persuasive than the biased assertions of contemporaries such as John Rous or even the accounts of Thomas More, who was five years old when the events he described took place.

XX

"FALSUS IN UNUS . . . "

"*Falsus in unus, falsus in omnibus*" is an ancient and commonly applied principle of law. If a witness is found to have testified falsely about one matter, it may be inferred that his testimony as to other matters is false as well.

This does not mean that a person who lies about one thing is *necessarily* lying about everything. It is simply a permissible inference. Put in a different way, if we know a witness has fabricated a part of his testimony, we may, as a matter of common sense, assign less weight to the balance of what he has to say.

This age-old principle has some application to the question of Richard's innocence or guilt. If Tudor adherents and sycophants deliberately created and perpetuated false reports concerning Richard, we are justified in considering the balance of their assertions less likely to be true.

We have already seen that one or more of them appear to have fabricated the story that Tyrell and Dighton confessed to killing the princes at Richard's direction. And there are other apparent fabrications. For example, if Tudor sympathizers falsely portrayed Richard as a deformed hunchback, perhaps they also created a false report that he murdered his nephews.

To the cynical propagandist there would have been good reason to invent the legend of Richard's deformity. The average sixteenth-century Englishman still held the ancient view that a deformed body signified an evil mind and a corrupt soul. After all, the Bible itself, in Leviticus 21:20, specifies that having a hunchback precludes a man's entering Heaven. This, of course, does not prove that Richard's deformity was invented. It simply provides a motive for inventing it.

It is virtually certain, however, that Richard bore little if any resemblance to Shakespeare's grotesque monster with his hunched back and withered arm, scuttling about on uneven legs. Richard's prowess in battle with lance, sword and battle-ax is acknowledged by even the most staunch supporter of the Tudor cause. His fighting abilities were noted at Barnet and Tewkesbury and in the final charge at Bosworth Field when he killed Sir William Brandon, unhorsed the giant warrior Sir John Cheney and, when surrounded by overwhelming numbers of the Stanleys' troops, fought on to the end, striking out in all directions, seeking to kill as many of the enemy as he could before he died.

Obviously, his sword arm could not have been withered. Nor could his other arm. To fight from horseback, as Richard often did, wielding a heavy lance, sword or battle-ax in one hand while controlling a charging war-horse with the other, would have been impossible for a man with a withered arm.

Not one drawing or painting of Richard, whether made in his own reign or under the Tudors, showed a withered arm. The closest thing is a painting sold in Belgium in 1921. This shows Richard's left arm ending in a stump—which, of course, is not the same thing at all and is undoubtedly fanciful.

Those who have withered arms normally have tiny, ill-formed hands. It would be rare to see a normal adult hand growing from a withered arm. Yet, every picture of Richard that shows his hands portrays both as normal in size.

More, who had no direct personal knowledge, reported that Richard's left shoulder was higher than his right. Rous reported just the opposite. Given the constant practice at swordplay in which Richard would have engaged as a youth, it is not unlikely that one shoulder, probably his right, would have developed more musculature than the other and would appear to be higher. But that is a far cry from being a hunchback.

If Richard were as deformed as Shakespeare describes him, he would have required specially made armor with a vast bulge to contain his hump, and probably an unusual piece for his withered arm. A king would have had two, three or even more sets of armor. It would be most unlikely that such bizarre artifacts, so useful for Tudor propagandists, would have been destroyed. Yet they do not exist and no one has even written about them.

With the exception of the grossly unreliable Rous, not a single writer who could have actually seen Richard says that his appearance was irregular in any way. The Great Chronicle makes no mention of any deformity. Whoever wrote or supplied the information for the Croyland Chronicle had certainly seen Richard on many occasions. Yet the chronicle, written in Henry Tudor's reign, when there was certainly no motive to flatter Richard, contains no hint that Richard was deformed in any way. Nor does Mancini, even though he had undoubtedly seen Richard and would almost certainly have pointed out to his interested patron any physical deformity he observed.

De Commynes, who had actually seen Richard, was inclined to give detailed physical descriptions of important figures. Reflecting the French point of view, he was highly critical of Richard. Certainly, if Richard had a humped back and withered arm, de Commynes would have noted it. Yet, his "Memoirs" contain no suggestion of any such deformity.

More relates that, during Dr. Shaa's address to the London crowd on June 22, 1483, Richard actually appeared and that Shaa pointed to him and told the crowd "This is his father's own figure, this his own countenance, the very print of his visage, the sure undoubted image, the plain express likeness of the noble duke, whose remembrance can never die while he liveth." Since many in the crowd had seen Richard's father, this claim would have drawn hoots of derision had Richard been the deformed monster of Shakespeare's play. If Richard had been that visibly deformed, it is extremely unlikely that Shaa, an experienced public orator, would have even considered making that argument to the crowd.

Alison Weir makes the point that a resident of York called Richard a "crook back." The same man added that Richard was a "hypocrite" who had been "buried in a ditch like a dog." But those remarks were supposedly made six years after Richard's death, in a drunken argument over whether Northumberland had betrayed Richard at Bosworth Field. We have no indication that the man who used the term "crook back" meant it literally as a reference to Richard's physical appearance, rather than to the humpback boar on Richard's personal badge, since Richard was often called "the boar" (or even "the hog"), a characterization that might fit with dying "like a dog." Even if the remark was made and was intended to be taken as a literal description of Richard, in the absence of any indication that the speaker had ever seen Richard, it cannot be given much weight as showing that the king was actually deformed.

Weir says that Rous described Richard as having a "humped back." This is not accurate. Even in his most virulent anti-Ricardian period, Rous says only that Richard "was small of stature, having a short face and unequal shoulders, the right higher and the left lower." That is not the same as having a "humped back," and it is hardly a description of Shakespeare's grotesquely deformed villain.

In fact, the original English version of the Rous Roll, still in the British Museum, contains two line drawings of Richard made by Rous himself. One shows a slim young man holding a heavy sword in one hand and a symbolic castle in the other. There is no hint of any deformity. The other drawing shows the same man with a sword in one hand and an Oxford cross in the other. Again, there is no deformity.

Even more significantly, the Latin version of the Rous Roll, *redone by Rous in Tudor times to eliminate anything favorable about Richard,* creates a new drawing of Richard that still shows no deformity. If Richard really had a hunched back and withered arm, Rous, who clearly was trying to eliminate anything positive about the late, defeated king, would surely have drawn in Richard's grotesque physical characteristics, rather than leaving a falsely flattering portrayal when there was no longer any need to flatter and every reason to deform.

The British Museum houses another manuscript containing a near contemporary drawing of Richard—again showing no deformity. This is "The Pageant of Richard Beauchamp—Earl of

Warwick." This illustrated history of the maternal grandfather of Anne and Isabel Neville, the wives of Richard and Clarence, shows the Beauchamp family tree with sketches of each family member. It was originally attributed to Rous, who was the official historiographer of the Beauchamp family. Later scholars, however, demonstrated that it was not Rous's work. It is believed that the sketches were by a Flemish artist retained by the countess of Warwick. The sketches are believed to have been made in about 1493, eight years after the death of Richard III, a time when there was no conceivable motive to flatter him or improve his appearance. Yet Richard is portrayed with no deformity whatsoever.

Nicolas von Popplau, a Silesian knight on a diplomatic mission for the Emperor Fredrick III, kept a travel diary recording his visit to England during Richard's reign. Von Popplau was widely known for his great learning, his prodigious strength and his skill at jousting. He wielded a lance so long and heavy that he was reportedly the only man strong enough to use it.

The Silesian knight met Richard at Pontefract in May 1484. He describes the English king as three fingers taller and somewhat thinner than von Popplau himself, with "subtil Arme and Schnekel," i.e., "slender arms and legs." There is no mention of any deformity.

Richard told von Popplau "I wish that my kingdom lay upon the confines of Turkey; with my own people alone and without the help of other princes I should like to drive away not only the Turks, but all my foes."

Von Popplau's diary appears to be free of bias or intent to please any particular faction and, since he includes a physical description of Richard, it seems inconceivable that he would have omitted the fact that the king of England was a hunchbacked, withered-armed monster, hobbling about on ill-matched legs. This seems particularly true in light of Richard's warlike statement about driving out the Turks. For such an expression of machismo to come from someone with a twisted body and deformed limbs would almost certainly have evoked comment in the Silesian's diary.

The aged countess of Desmond is reported to have said many

years after Richard's death that she was present at a court occasion during the reign of Edward IV and to have described Richard as "the handsomest man in the room except his brother Edward, and was very well made."

John Stow, who wrote in the sixteenth century, interviewed old men who had actually seen Richard. Not one reported any deformity. Their consensus was that Richard was well made but "of low stature."

There are a number of existing oil portraits of Richard. Ultraviolet examination of at least one such painting shows that it was intentionally doctored in later years to add an enlarged shoulder in keeping with the "Tudor myth."

The facial expression has been altered in other Tudor paintings, creating a look of tension, perhaps even pain. Possibly these changes were designed to make Richard look sinister. If so, they have not achieved their aim.

Alison Weir, of course, puts a different spin on this doctoring of Richard's portrait in Tudor times. According to Weir, "portraits of Richard, held to have been painted with the aim of flattering him, were altered in Tudor times to reflect what people believed he really looked like." If Weir were correct, any portrait of Richard done after his death in 1485 should show his deformities, since there was no longer any reason to flatter him.

The drawings of Richard in the Beauchamp Pageant and in the altered version of the Rous Roll are, of course, in this category. Each was done after Richard's death. Yet, neither shows any deformity. And, as we have said, even though Rous doctored his Roll to eliminate anything favorable about Richard, there still is no humped back or withered arm.

There are also three oil paintings to consider, each of which has been copied a number of times. The first is in the Society of Antiquaries in London. It has been tree-ring dated to the period 1516–22.

Tree-ring dating tells us the age of the wooden panel on which the portrait was painted. It does not tell us the interval between the cutting of the tree and the painting of the portrait. A portrait tree ring dated to 1516 could have been painted in 1530. It could not have been painted *before* 1516.

This first painting indicates no deformity either visible to the naked eye or revealed by X-ray analysis. There is no hump and no withered arm. Richard is looking to his right and is either playing with, putting on or pulling off a small ring that is partially on the fourth finger of his left hand. From the position of his left forefinger it appears more likely that he is putting the ring on.

It has been argued that the partially removed ring is a symbol of Richard's realization that he was not entitled to the throne, which would make sense in the case of a Tudor-era portrait. But the society's portrait of Edward IV, which analysis shows was painted on a panel cut from the same tree, shows Edward looking to his left and wearing no ring.

It may be that the two portraits were meant to be connected and hung as a diptych, with Richard putting on the coronation ring while Edward, his brother and predecessor, looks on with approval. Of course, the society's paintings of the two brothers may be Tudor era copies of earlier portraits done before Bosworth Field, rather than under Henry VII.

Nevertheless, if that was the case, the Tudor copyist, who treated the two images as separate portraits rather than duplicating what would have been a pro-Ricardian scene, did not add any hump or withered arms in the portrait of Richard, even though it would have been politically correct to have done so.

Thus, whether the portrait was originally done under Henry VII and is meant to show Richard's awareness of being a usurper, or it was a Tudor copy of an earlier work, it is evidence of the absence of any deformity.

The second portrait, which may be the earliest surviving original, is in the royal collection at Windsor. It is tree-ring dated to the period 1518–23. An X-ray taken in 1973 revealed that Richard's right shoulder was altered by subsequent painting to make it appear significantly higher than his left and that the eyes were narrowed, presumably to create an evil countenance. The alteration of the right shoulder is actually discernable to the naked eye, and Richard's necklace is painted by a different artist than the original one.

This painting, in its altered form, appears to have been the prototype used in a number of later copies. If the original painting was made in 1518–23 (which was more than thirty years after Richard's death), it is difficult to understand why the deformity was not shown when the painting was originally done—unless, of course, Richard had no deformity and even the original artist, although working in the reign of Henry VII, saw no reason to add one.

In this painting, Richard wears a black velvet gown with a lining of brown fur and slashed sleeves in the fashion of the 1470s. His black cap was of the type often worn in the 1480s. These elements do not mean that the painting was done in that period. A sixteenth-century artist would have had knowledge of the costuming of the earlier period.

Here again, Richard has a ring half on and half off his finger. In this instance, there may be a different significance. In a portrait of Edward IV from the same series in the royal collection, Edward is making a similar gesture. Edward's portrait was part of a husband and wife pair with his queen, Elizabeth Woodville. The couple would have been hung facing each other, and the gesture with the ring would have symbolized marriage. It may be that, similarly, a portrait of Richard's queen, Anne Neville, accompanied the original of his portrait, with the ring serving the same gestural purpose. But this is sheer speculation.

The third key painting is the "broken sword" portrait. It is also at the Society of Antiquaries in London. The painting shows Richard holding a broken sword, symbolizing his moral and military failure. Clearly it was painted after Bosworth Field, and it has been tree-ring dated to the period 1533–43. Yet, at least in its present form, it shows neither a hump nor a withered arm. X-rays taken in the 1950s have been described as showing that the original painting portrayed Richard with a "prodigious hump" on his left shoulder and his left arm springing "unnaturally from that shoulder." If so, these deformities were subsequently painted out.

Because the work was definitely created in Tudor times, the inclusion of these deformities would not be difficult to explain. That is, of course, the monstrous Richard the Tudors sought to portray. It is conceivable that a later owner, reluctant to live with the image of a grotesque monster, or more sympathetic to Richard, had the deformities painted out.

The librarian of the Society of Antiquaries was kind enough

to allow me to examine the actual X-ray. I am hardly an expert at reading X-rays of aged paintings. For that purpose, one would need an expert in the restoration of such works, or perhaps a good radiologist.

This X-ray, like so many others, is cloudy and ambiguous. It appeared to me that the original left shoulder shown in the X-ray was somewhat higher than that in the present painting, and the curve of the shoulder seems somewhat different. I would not, however, have characterized the X-ray as showing a "prodigious hump." The area of the X-ray showing the left arm as originally painted is quite difficult to make out. The arm may originally have been painted in a different and awkward position. But, here again, I would not have characterized the X-ray as showing a left arm that appears to spring "unnaturally from that shoulder." Nor does it appear to have been depicted as "withered."

On the other hand, a version of the broken sword portrait from the same workshop was sold in Brussels in 1921. This painting is said to have had a "stump" for an arm and to have had a large hump as well. This may indicate that the Society of Antiquaries' painting once had the same features, notwithstanding my own inability to perceive them in the X-ray.

Interestingly, the portrait in the royal collection has definitely been altered to change the shoulder line, making the *right* shoulder higher than the left. The later copies of that portrait do the same. But if the broken sword painting, as originally done, had a "hump," it was *on the left.* This inability on the part of Tudor artists to agree on which side had the hump (like the similar disagreement between More and Rous as to which shoulder was higher) is rather striking, since there were people alive at the time who had seen Richard.

Portraits of Richard done in his own reign and showing a deformity would, of course, be significant evidence that he was deformed. There are none. Portraits of Richard in that period without any deformity (and there are several) are some evidence that he had none. They are, however, susceptible to Weir's argument that the artists were all flattering the king by leaving out his hump and withered arm. Portraits of Richard done in Tudor times showing deformities would be but slight evidence of their actual existence.

But portraits *without deformities done in Tudor times* are difficult if not impossible to square with Weir's argument. These include the portrait in the royal collection, as originally painted, the portrait with the ring at the Society of Antiquaries, the drawing of Richard in the Beauchamp Pageant, Rous's drawing in the Latin version of his Roll, as altered after Richard's death and the broken sword portrait, at least as it now appears.

Considering the portraits of Richard, as a whole, they tend to support the inference that he had neither a humped back nor a withered arm, and that this was an invention in Tudor times designed to denigrate him visually, just as Rous and others did with the written word and Shakespeare did on stage.

Rous reports that Richard was two years in the womb, emerging at birth with fully developed teeth and long hair. More, who repeated the story that Richard was "crook-backed" and had a withered arm, provides a somewhat less bizarre tale of Richard's birth, and does so as a rumor rather than as fact. Obviously the Rous version is untrue. Hair? Perhaps. Teeth? Rare, but not impossible. But two years in the womb? Never.

Yet Weir treats Rous as a reliable source. She adds that as an infant, Richard was a "weakling." What is the "evidence" on which Weir bases this assertion? A writer during Richard's infancy used the words "Richard liveth yet." But these words came from a rhyming list of the order in which Cecily Neville's children were born. The rhymester noted those children who had died while others, like Richard, still lived. The quoted sentence, wrenched out of context by Weir, seems wholly unrelated to weakness.

A further sign of the tendency in Tudor times to blacken Richard's reputation by altering the facts is the substitution of Elizabeth Lucy for Lady Eleanor Butler as the woman with whom Edward IV supposedly had a precontract. As we have discussed, this substitution can be seen in More's "History."

Elizabeth Lucy, one of the king's mistresses, was a courtesan of low station. There is no evidence whatsoever of any marriage or precontract between her and Edward IV. Nor could there have been, since she appears to have been already married at the time to "one Lucy," a commoner. Any claim of a precontract between the King and Elizabeth Lucy would have been readily dismissed as patently false. Describing Elizabeth Lucy as the other party to the precontract would strongly support the argument that the story was an absurd fabrication created by Richard to cover up his usurpation of the crown.

Eleanor Butler was another matter entirely. Lady Eleanor was the highborn daughter of John Talbot, the first earl of Shrewsbury, usually called the "Great Talbot" since he was a famous hero of the war against the French. She was also the grandaughter of the Earl of Warwick and the aunt of Anne Mowbray, who was married to Prince Richard. A match between Lady Eleanor and Edward would have been infinitely more suitable and acceptable than his marriage to Elizabeth Woodville. Their precontract was confirmed by Stillington's eyewitness testimony. It could not be taken lightly and presented a serious impediment to the legitimacy of the two princes and substantial support for the claim of Richard III.

Apparently for this reason, Lady Eleanor was replaced in Tudor times by the easily dismissed Elizabeth Lucy. More, elaborating on this fabrication, even tells us that the duchess of York had raised the claim of Elizabeth Lucy's precontract years before as a means of preventing her son, Edward IV, from marrying Elizabeth Woodville, and that Edward only married his queen after Elizabeth Lucy admitted in an official inquiry that the claim was false.

This "admission," which would presumably have occurred in 1464, before Edward's marriage to Elizabeth Woodville, was, of course, calculated to make a claim in 1483 of a precontract between Edward and Elizabeth Lucy seem even more preposterous. But it is all untrue, all a sham. Edward married Elizabeth Woodville secretly and kept the marriage secret for months— even from his mother. Elizabeth Lucy never claimed to have contracted marriage with the king, and there was no official inquiry into her having had such a contract.

Is it possible that More was unaware of these facts? It would be nice to believe that the sainted Sir Thomas did not *knowingly* substitute the wrong woman or *intentionally* fabricate this tale about the rejection of a claim by Edward's mother, and that he was misled by his informers—most likely John Morton, whose anti-Ricardian schemes we encounter at every turn.

More did make a number of errors in his "History" that seem

to reflect carelessness, rather than intentional deception. For example, he reported that Edward IV was fifty-three, rather than forty, when he died and that Warwick had been negotiating for Edward's marriage to the Spanish Infanta, rather than Bona of Savoy, at the time of the king's marriage to Elizabeth Woodville. But More's use of the name Elizabeth Lucy rather than Eleanor Butler could hardly have been inadvertent. He refers to Mrs. Lucy no less than six different times as the woman claimed by Richard to have had the precontract with Edward. Nor could his tale about the duchess of York's premarital claim and the official inquiry have been written by accident.

Clearly, those who were around in 1483 knew full well that the claimed precontract was with Eleanor Butler. After all, even aside from its being publicly described by Shaa and Buckingham and presented to the council, Lady Eleanor and her precontract with Edward had been openly discussed before the entire assembly of the three estates in 1483 and the Parliament of January 1484. It was included in the Rolle adopted by that 1483 assembly and in the parliamentary act of January 1484.

The Rolle enacted by the three assembled estates and presented to Richard on June 25, 1483, and its confirmation by a lawful Parliament in January, 1484, as *Titulus Regius,* both specify that "[A]t the time of . . . the same pretensed Mariage, and bifore and longe tyme after, the seid King Edward was and stode maryed and trouth plight to oone *Dame Elianor Butteler, Daughter of the old Earl of Shrewsbury,* with whom the same King Edward had made a precontracte of Matrimonie, longe tyme bifore he made the said pretensed Mariage with the said Elizabeth Grey. . . ."

Similarly, the Croyland chronicler describes the claim as that Edward "had been precontracted to a certain Lady Eleanor Boteler before he married Queen Elizabeth."

One may decide that Stillington's disclosure about a precontract was a total fabrication. But clearly, the precontract that was *claimed* and acted on by Parliament was with Lady Eleanor Butler, not Elizabeth Lucy.

And those who were around in 1464, when Edward married Elizabeth Woodville, knew that Edward's mother, like Warwick and everyone else, had been unaware of his secret marriage until months *after* it occurred, that she never asserted a precontract with Elizabeth Lucy as a means of *preventing* the marriage and that there never was any official inquiry into a precontract with Mrs. Lucy.

Between 1485 and 1513, someone deliberately substituted the married courtesan for the highborn widow as the other party to Edward's precontract, and created this fable about the duchess and the official inquiry. Probably whoever did these things believed that all copies of *Titulus Regius* had been destroyed and was unaware that the monks of Croyland had retained an account of the real party to the precontract.

But for the account preserved at Croyland and one isolated copy of *Titulus Regius* that escaped Henry Tudor's ban, the world would forever have dismissed Richard's title to the throne as founded on what would have seemed a preposterous and obviously fabricated tale that King Edward had betrothed himself to a common courtesan named Elizabeth Lucy, who was already married at the time, a claim already considered and officially rejected years before. That is the depth of the crime against truth committed by someone, whether it was More himself, Morton or some other proponent of the Tudor cause from whom More got his "facts."

Most probably, the fabrication was done by More's informants rather than by Sir Thomas himself. But, at least at the time he first wrote, More can be charged with extreme negligence in failing to check his facts. Possibly he did ultimately check them, realized that they were grossly incorrect and, for that reason, abandoned the "History" entirely.

If More or his informants were corrupt or even negligent enough to have given the world false information about such matters as Richard's supposed deformity, the identity of the other party to Edward IV's precontract, the "official inquiry" assertedly brought about by Edward's mother to prevent his marriage to Elizabeth Woodville, Sir James Tyrell's status and knighthood in August 1483 and the supposed "confessions" of Tyrell and Dighton, is there a permissible inference that their account of the princes "murder" is equally false?

Applying the *falsus in unus* principle, such an inference can certainly be drawn. Does it prove Richard's innocence? By no means. Does it constitute exculpatory evidence? Indeed it does.

XXI

♛ OTHER SUSPECTS

In most murder trials, the defendant's lawyer tries to convince the jury that someone else committed the crime, or at least could have done so.

Richard's defenders have done the same. Clements Markham, for example, argued that the true murderer was Henry VII. Henry is, of course, a prime suspect. Any defense lawyer worth his salt would try to pin the murder on the king who succeeded Richard and took over the Tower after Bosworth Field.

If the princes were still alive when Henry entered the Tower in 1485, he had a stronger motive to kill them than Richard had in 1483. Despite his extremely weak claim to the throne, Henry was determined to rule. Clearly, live sons of Edward IV would have been a serious obstacle to that goal toward which he had striven for so long and for which he had just risked his life.

Unlike Richard, Henry could not rely on *Titulus Regius* and the boys' illegitimacy. Henry's adherents expected him to bolster his very weak claim by carrying out his oath to marry their sister, the Princess Elizabeth. But *Titulus Regius* made her illegitimate along with her brothers. That, of course, is why Henry so vigorously suppressed it.

Lessening Henry's motive, however, is the fact that, even if he killed the princes, there were other rivals with better claims to the crown than his own. One was young Warwick, Clarence's son. Unlike Richard, Henry imprisoned Warwick and later had him killed, although he waited until 1499 to do so.

Why would Henry kill the princes, only to leave Warwick alive as a threat for the next fourteen years? One answer is that the two princes were a far greater danger. After all, Edward V, if he was still alive in 1485, was the rightful king—unless he was illegitimate. And if he was illegitimate, so was Henry's wife. Besides, Warwick, safely ensconced in the Tower, posed only a limited threat; and even that threat was minimized if the young man was known to be weak-minded, as was rumored.

Another potential rival was Lincoln, the son of Edward IV's sister. Lincoln was killed at the battle of Stoke in 1487. His younger brother, Edmund de la Pole, was ultimately persuaded by Henry to return to England. Later, when Edmund's life seemed in jeopardy, he managed to escape to the Continent, where he was aided by Tyrell.

Perhaps Henry's delay in executing some rivals showed a reluctance to kill that may be considered evidence that he did not kill the two princes. But, again, he may have considered the princes a direct and immediate threat, while the others were less dangerous and could be dealt with later.

Does the Princess Elizabeth's willingness to marry Henry in January 1486 support the inference that he did not kill her brothers? It is unlikely, though not impossible, that he could have hidden the crime from his wife.

On the other hand, it is not impossible that the princess would have married Henry, even if he had killed her brothers and she knew it. Fifteenth-century attitudes were different from those prevalent today; and, in any event, even if she considered Henry guilty, her choices were limited and extreme. She could either become queen of England, or else face banishment or even death by speaking out about the murder of her brothers.

If the princes were alive and in the Tower when Henry took power in 1485, he certainly had the opportunity to kill them. His silence about their fate and the absence of a hue and cry over their whereabouts, might indicate that he did find them alive.

Henry may have had an even better opportunity to kill them in the summer of 1486. At that time, the new queen and her mother, Elizabeth Woodville, appear to have been at Winchester awaiting the September birth of Prince Arthur. If the princes had been alive but imprisoned until then, Henry could have seized on that opportunity to have them killed. Certainly there were men who would have committed the crime at Henry's direction. If we can believe what More tells us about him, even Tyrell might have done so. With Richard dead, the Tyrell described by More might have been looking for a way to ingratiate himself with the new ruler.

Could this have been the reason for Henry's double pardon of Tyrell in 1486, first on June 15 and then, one month later, on July 17? Could it have been the reason for Henry's order in February 1487, in substance exchanging Tyrell's lands in Wales for new holdings in Guisnes, where he was apparently expected to remain?

If Henry had the princes murdered that summer, the queen and her mother would almost surely have learned of the murder when they returned to London with Prince Arthur at the end of 1486 or the beginning of 1487. Was the queen dowager's rage at the murders the true reason for Henry's suddenly sending her to a convent in February 1487? Was he forced to choose between killing his mother-in-law or sending her to a nunnery?

These are all interesting speculations. But there are alternative explanations for each of these events, and there is no more hard evidence against Henry than there is against Richard.

There are other suspects as well. The neurotic, unpredictable duke of Buckingham was executed in October 1483 after his failed rebellion. Some writers have suggested or even contended that Buckingham, rather than Richard or Henry, killed the two princes. De Commynes, for example, says that Richard "had his two nephews murdered." But he also says that it was the duke of Buckingham "who had put the two children to death," and that "a few days later King Richard himself had Buckingham put to death."

It has been contended that these entries are inconsistent. But what de Commynes appears to be saying is that Buckingham committed the murders at Richard's behest, after which Richard killed the duke.

The author of the anonymous "Historical Notes" says that the Princes "wer put to deyth in the Towur of London be the vise of

the duke of Buckingham." This may mean at the duke's direction
or, in the alternative, upon the advice he gave to someone else—
possibly Richard. Humphrey Lloyd, said to have written in the
late sixteenth century, reported that Richard murdered the
princes after "first taking counsel with the Duke of
Buckingham." The source for the "Historical Notes" may simply
be the rumors reported by others, and there is no reason to
believe that Lloyd's charge was reliable.

On the other hand, Buckingham cannot be discounted as a
suspect. It is probable that Buckingham stayed behind in London
when Richard left on his royal progress in July 1483 and that he
joined the royal party at Gloucester. Although first peer of the
realm, he is not among those listed as having been present in
Oxford, an earlier stop on the king's progress. At Gloucester,
Buckingham and Richard had a brief meeting, after which the
duke left for his own estate at Brecknock.

If, as More reports, the princes were killed in this early period
of Richard's reign, Buckingham had the opportunity to kill them
before leaving London. Or did he? Could Buckingham have
gained sufficient access to the princes to carry out the murders?
Probably. He was now lord high constable of England and the
most important man in the kingdom next to the king himself. He
had authority there superior to that of Brackenbury or anyone
else, other than Richard.

It was Buckingham who suggested that the princes be housed
in the Tower in the first place. If he sought access to the princes
in Richard's absence, he need not have said he was there to murder them, and it is difficult to imagine Brackenbury or anyone
else denying him such access.

Once Buckingham and his men were in a room with the two
boys, it would have been a simple matter to kill them. If it was
night, the bodies might have been smuggled out without detection. And, even if they were seen, would anyone try to arrest or
impede the all-powerful duke?

Kendall says that it was undoubtedly Buckingham who told
the Woodvilles and Lady Stanley of the princes' murders just
before the rebellion of 1483. He asks how Buckingham would
have known of the crime, since he left Richard at Gloucester and

Richard supposedly gave the deadly order to Tyrell days later in Warwick.

If we were to accept More's account, however, the original order directing Brackenbury to kill the princes was sent via John Grene from Gloucester. More says it was given only after Buckingham left Gloucester for his estates at Brecknock. Still, it is conceivable that Richard told the duke of his plan before his departure. If so, it would have been reasonable for the duke to assume that, after he left, the king's plan had been carried out.

Did Buckingham have a motive to kill the sons of Edward IV? Absolutely. As second peer of the realm, he had a claim to the throne himself, albeit inferior to that of Richard and the two princes. As we have seen, the duke was descended from Thomas of Woodstock, the youngest surviving son of Edward III.

More writes that, at Brecknock, before the duke's rebellion, Morton suggested to Buckingham that he had the proper attributes "for the rule of a realm." The "realm," of course, was England. Evidently Buckingham shared this view even before it was expressed by Morton. More describes the duke as coveting Richard's crown. Sir George Buck refers to his "[a]mbition and aime to be soveraigne."

Perhaps Buckingham planned to kill the boys and blame the crime on Richard, hoping to foment a rebellion over the issue and to overthrow Richard and assume the throne himself. Or perhaps, he was in league with Henry Tudor from the beginning and intended either to put Henry on the throne or to aid a rebellion by Henry and then arrange Henry's "death in battle," leaving Buckingham a clear field if Richard were defeated. Either way, the elimination of the two princes would have been an essential step, whether it was Henry's idea or Buckingham's.

Buckingham was the sort of man who would need less of a motive than others. What, after all, was the motive for his rebellion against Richard in October 1483? To put himself on the throne? Possibly. To put Henry Tudor there? That was the announced purpose; but was it the truth? Given Buckingham's character and attitudes and the fact that his claim was superior to Henry's, it seems unlikely. Henry could hardly be more generous to Buckingham than Richard had been. Richard had rewarded the duke handsomely just before Buckingham betrayed him.

It would seem more in character for Buckingham to have planned to have Henry killed in the rebellion, so that he could take the throne himself. He would, of course, have pretended that he was supporting Henry's claim in order to secure the support of the Lancastrians, the Woodvilles and Lady Stanley. But had the rebellion against Richard been successful, it seems likely that Buckingham would have tried to betray Henry as well, in order to seize the crown he undoubtedly thought should be his all along.

It has been argued that since Buckingham was married to Elizabeth Woodville's sister, the two princes were his nephews, and therefore it was unlikely that he would kill them. Buckingham had spent much of his early life in the home of Elizabeth Woodville, which might create the inference of an additional tie to the Woodvilles and the princes.

This argument is of very doubtful merit. Every indication is that Buckingham deplored the Woodvilles and was incensed at their having forced him, through the king's intercession, to marry the queen's sister, a woman he considered far beneath his social station.

At some point in the rebellion of 1483, Morton escaped and fled to the Continent. Did he fear that the impetuous duke had done something Morton considered too extreme, too dangerous? Was it the murder of the princes? More likely Morton simply lost faith in the rebellion's success.

If More was correct and the princes were killed before Buckingham's rebellion, an intriguing scenario becomes possible. Buckingham, resentful and envious of Richard, perhaps angered by Richard's giving Parliament final say over the award of the Bohun inheritance, decides that he, not Richard, should wear the crown. After all, the same Plantagenet blood flows in his veins as in Richard's, and he considers himself the more gifted man.

But even if the duke can somehow organize or join in a successful rebellion against Richard, the two princes stand in his way to the throne. It is one thing for the three estates to put aside the boys' claim for Richard, the only surviving brother of Edward IV, the designated protector of the realm and a highly regarded military leader. It is quite another to cast them out in favor of Harry Buckingham, who has no such credentials.

Buckingham is perceptive enough to realize that if he rather than Richard is the rival claimant, there will probably be a powerful movement to reverse the declaration of illegitimacy and put Prince Edward on the throne. But if the princes are dead, and if Richard can be blamed for their death—at least by public gossip—two birds could be killed with one stone, and the duke might have a good chance at the crown.

With that in mind, Buckingham waits until Richard leaves on his royal progress. Then, as lord high constable of England, he enters the Tower with one or two trusted henchmen. He gains access to the princes on some innocent pretext. Once there, his aides quickly kill the two boys. They dispose of the bodies under the staircase, in the Thames or in some other unknown place. This done, Buckingham joins the conspiracy between Lady Stanley and the Woodvilles and begins to spread the rumor that Richard killed his nephews, an activity in which his co-conspirators enthusiastically join.

Richard, hearing the dangerous rumor, considers himself powerless to speak out. He has no proof against Buckingham. The boys were in Richard's control and he would seem the obvious beneficiary of their deaths. Who would believe that he had not ordered them killed?

Then, Morton convinces Buckingham that the confederacy to overthrow Richard can only be kept together and succeed if the candidate is Henry Tudor, who will then marry Princess Elizabeth, uniting the houses of York and Lancaster. Otherwise, they will not have the support of Lady Stanley, the Lancastrians or the Woodvilles. Without that support, they will almost certainly fail. Reluctant at first, Buckingham finally pretends to go along, assuming that it will be a simple matter to arrange for Henry's death in battle if Richard fails to accomplish that for him.

Buckingham's character is not inconsistent with his committing the crime. He appears to have been single-minded and brutally pragmatic in advancing any cause to which he was committed, especially his own. We know, of course, that he betrayed Richard's trust in conspiring with the Woodvilles and Lancastrians and leading the rebellion of 1483.

And there are other indications. It was Buckingham who

provided most of the "warnings" to Richard that Hastings was plotting against him. Were those warnings false? Or at least grossly exaggerated? Did Buckingham coax the self-serving Catesby into making a false or overstated reports of Hastings' "treason"? Did Buckingham scheme to eliminate Hastings as a rival and as a man who might stand in the way of the duke's own cause? Again, two birds with one stone. Hastings is taken off the board, and Richard gets the blame.

We know that Buckingham was at the heart of the decision to arrest Rivers, Grey and Vaughn. Was he also the instigator of the decision to execute them? Probably. He was Richard's closest advisor at the time, and he despised the Woodvilles. More importantly, they too could stand in the way of his plans; and here, once again, was an obstacle that could be eliminated in a way that painted Richard as a ruthless killer.

Did Buckingham play his own game from start to finish? Did he deliberately use Richard to eliminate those men, such as Hastings and Rivers, most likely to block his own rise to power, while at the same time injuring Richard's reputation and popularity by positioning him as the cruel king who directed those seemingly arbitrary killings?

Did he kill the two princes in the ultimate phase of his diabolical plot? Having wiped out Hastings, Rivers, Grey and Vaughn and having damaged Richard's reputation in the process, did he plan to: (1) eliminate the two boys, who blocked his path to the throne; (2) blame their murders on Richard, further eroding his public support; (3) join the now enraged Woodvilles, Lady Stanley and Henry Tudor in overthrowing Richard; and (4) find a way to eliminate Henry and take the throne himself?

An alternative scenario hypothesizes a more loyal but unstable Buckingham who remains behind in London and kills the princes to serve what he believes to be Richard's interest. Proudly, he joins Richard at Gloucester and tells him the news, expecting to be rewarded or at least praised. Instead, the king, stunned at the unexpected murder of his nephews, expresses outrage, not gratitude.

But, again, Richard can take no action against Buckingham, because the public will never believe that Richard was not implicated in the murders. The duke, surprised, angry and humiliated at Richard's reaction and fearing the king's ultimate retribution, leaves the progress and rushes back to Brecknock.

Persuaded there by the wily Morton, Buckingham joins the conspiracy of the Woodvilles, Lady Stanley and Henry Tudor and begins spreading the story that Richard has murdered his nephews. Morton, having learned the truth from Buckingham, decides that the risks of being tied to the mercurial duke are now too great, and he flees to the Continent to await the outcome. If Henry and Buckingham win, he will return and emphasize his significant role in their plot and his long support for the Tudor cause. If Richard wins, he will remain safely ensconced in Brittany.

According to Audrey Williamson, Buckingham wrote to Henry Tudor on September 24, 1483, referring to the liberation of the two princes as an aim of Henry's invasion. This was well after the duke left London to join Richard and his progress. Does this reference to still living princes eliminate Buckingham as a suspect? Not really. The duke may have been deliberately misleading Henry and concealing his own guilt by pretending to believe the princes were still alive.

Seeking, as always, to demonstrate Richard's guilt, Alison Weir necessarily argues for Buckingham's innocence. She asserts that the duke could not have entered the Tower without the permission of Brackenbury, the king or the council. Weir cites no authority for her statement; and, as we have said, given Buckingham's exalted status and his position as lord high constable, it seems most unlikely that, if he said he was there on some business other than murdering the princes, Brackenbury or anyone else would have refused him permission to enter and to have an audience with the two boys.

Weir also contends that Buckingham started his revolution because he knew that Richard had killed the princes. Her "support" for this is her assertion that since Richard had just awarded Buckingham the Bohun inheritance, there could have been no other motive for his revolution than Richard's murder of his nephews.

That, of course, is another demonstrable non sequitur. Other possible motives are the duke's apparent envy of Richard and resentment at his coronation, the fact that Richard made the Bohun grant conditional on parliamentary approval, which Buckingham may have considered a ruse by Richard to deny him his rights, and, above all, Buckingham's own desire to be king, which he may not have abandoned when he agreed to back Henry Tudor.

If Buckingham did kill the princes, a number of questions would be answered. Much of Richard's suspicious conduct would be understandable. Even though innocent, he would have found it difficult to produce the bodies of the princes or to announce their murders, since no one would believe he was not a party to the crime.

Similarly, the conduct of Elizabeth Woodville in coming to trust Richard, releasing her daughters to him and urging Dorset to return and make his peace with the king, would be explained by her having learned that Buckingham, rather than Richard, had killed her sons.

If Henry knew or believed that Buckingham was the murderer and that others might know it, he might have decided to remain silent on the subject when he took the throne in 1485. He might have felt that there was too much risk in openly blaming Richard and that ambiguity was his best policy. This would explain why there was no hue and cry over the princes being missing and why Henry may have hit on the ambiguous phrase in Richard's bill of attainder charging him with "shedding Infants blood," hoping the public would blame Richard and yet not explicitly accusing him.

If, while writing his "History," More came to believe that Buckingham, rather than Richard, had committed the crime, one sensible course of action would have been to put the work aside. Better to go on to other things than to undertake a major revision of what he had already written—a revision that would hardly be pleasing to Henry VIII. Could this be why he abandoned the "History" just after the part about Buckingham's meeting with Morton at Brecknock?

If DNA and other advanced scientific methods show that the skeletons found in 1674 were, in fact, the two princes, and that their deaths occurred in 1483, rather than in 1485, Buckingham's guilt would be as consistent with that finding as Richard's.

Despite all this, the case against Buckingham is based essentially on speculation. He had the motive, the opportunity and the character; and the behavior of others was consistent with his being the murderer. But, here again, there is no substantial evidence that he actually committed the crime.

Are there other potential suspects? Yes, but the case against them is weak. John Morton, for example, would have been motivated to have the princes killed because their claims to the throne were infinitely better than Henry Tudor's and because he might induce the public to blame Richard for the crime. It might have been difficult for Morton to have accomplished the murder during Richard's reign. But if the princes remained alive after Bosworth Field, he could have done it. If Morton was responsible for the crime, he would certainly have hired someone else to commit the physical act, and it is unlikely that he would have acted without Henry's approval, if not at his direction.

While Morton may be an unappealing figure and one possessing both motive and, at least during Henry's reign, opportunity to kill, there is no evidence whatsoever of his guilt.

Could the murderer have been the perfidious Lord Stanley? In 1483, after Buckingham's rebellion, Richard made Stanley constable of England for life. Evidently Richard believed that although Lady Stanley had supported the rebellion and the claims of her son, Henry Tudor, her husband had remained loyal. As constable, Stanley, like Buckingham before him, had complete access to the Tower.

Stanley had a potential motive as well. Although Henry had sailed back to Brittany when Buckingham's rebellion failed, he was expected to attempt another invasion as soon as he could obtain the necessary support both in England and on the Continent. If such an invasion succeeded and Richard was killed, Stanley's stepson would be king. His future and that of his family would be insured. The princes were clearly an obstacle in Henry's path to the throne. Their death would make real the Tudor dream and considerably enhance the position of the Stanleys.

On the other hand, unlike his brother, Lord Stanley was a cautious, prudent man. It is very difficult to reconcile the record of his conduct over the years with the commission of a risky double murder in the heavily populated Tower.

Finally, John Howard, the loyal duke of Norfolk, who died fighting for Richard at Bosworth Field, has also been considered a suspect. Howard appears to have been appointed constable of the Tower for a short time prior to Brackenbury's appointment in July 1484. His household records for May 21, shortly after Edward V moved to the Tower, reflect his ordering two sacks of lime and charging them as Tower expenses. But the purchased lime could have had a perfectly innocent use, and there is no indication that it had anything to do with the princes.

Howard's supposed motive was that the younger prince held the title duke of Norfolk and therefore blocked Howard's attaining that title, which had belonged to his family. But only Prince Edward was in the Tower at the time Howard was constable. His younger brother was still in sanctuary at Westminster. And why would Howard kill both boys when only one held the Norfolk title?

Once it became clear that Richard would become king, Howard had no need to kill either prince to obtain that title. Richard seems to have been more than willing to take it from the younger prince, who had been declared illegitimate, and to bestow it upon the loyal Howard, whose claim to the title was better, who deserved a reward for his services and who, as duke of Norfolk, could act as earl marshall at Richard's coronation.

Notwithstanding his purchase of some lime, there is no evidence at all of Howard's guilt. He was a man of action, but nothing in his background or life suggests that he would kill two children to achieve a goal that appeared attainable without committing such a heinous crime.

In addition to the identified suspects, we have the unnamed "certaine personnes" who committed the unspecified but apparently serious crime referred to in Richard's letter of July 29, 1483, to his chancellor. Richard's obvious reluctance to name the individuals or specify their crime would be consistent with his having learned that "well-meaning" supporters had taken it unto themselves to murder his nephews, thinking that was what he wanted. But the letter, while strange, could have so many other explanations that we cannot accord much weight to this possibility.

If we are to give serious consideration to a suspect other than Richard, it almost certainly must be Henry VII or Buckingham, both of whom had the motive, the opportunity and probably the requisite will. There is no hard evidence that either committed the crime. But is there such evidence against Richard?

XXII

♛ SUMMING UP

Having analyzed the facts, or what after centuries we perceive to be the facts, what can we conclude as to Richard's guilt or innocence? If we apply the standards of a court of law in a criminal case, our conclusion is relatively easy. Richard would be acquitted of the crime by virtually any jury that heard the case. The possibility that no murders were committed, or that if they were, Henry or Buckingham committed them, together with the paucity of admissible evidence against Richard, would almost surely raise a "reasonable doubt" in the jury's mind; and that, of course, would call for an acquittal. No jury could be faulted for reaching such a verdict.

But this is not a criminal trial. Finding a "reasonable doubt" is not sufficient. We must ask ourselves whether Richard's guilt is or is not probable and consider the degree of its probability.

First, we must deal with the issue of whether a crime was really committed. There is a significant possibility that the princes were not murdered by anyone, but were smuggled out of the country and hidden away in some protected place, perhaps under new identities.

It makes no sense that Lincoln and Margaret of Burgundy would mount a rebellion in 1487 to put Lambert Simnell, an obvious imposter, on the throne. Clearly, they intended the crown for someone else.

The fact that, as seems likely, the Woodvilles supported Simnell's rebellion strongly suggests that the "someone else"

Margaret and Lincoln had in mind was not weak-minded Warwick or Lincoln himself, but one of the two missing princes, and that the true aim of the rebellion was to put a Woodville prince on the throne. Why else would Elizabeth Woodville and her family support a rebellion aimed at displacing her daughter's husband and preventing her daughter's children from succeeding to the throne?

The former queen may have been dissatisfied with her position under Henry VII and his delay in holding her daughter's coronation. But he was her son-in-law, and her grandchildren would someday rule the kingdom. It seems impossible that she would have expected her own position or that of her daughters to be improved if Lincoln or Warwick became king. But it would certainly be better if one of her dutiful and loving sons was alive and could take the throne.

If that could be brought off, Woodville power and her own position would be even greater than during the reign of Edward IV. The fact that one of the princes was alive and would rule if the rebellion was successful seems the only cogent explanation for why the ex-queen and her family would support the rebel cause. And it seems highly probable that this is what Henry VII believed they were doing and that, in fact, he was correct in that belief.

When the rebellion of 1487 failed, Margaret may have tried again, this time with Perkin Warbeck. Despite the skepticism of some historians, the possibility that Perkin really was Prince Richard cannot be ruled out.

And, even if Perkin, like Lambert, was an imposter, albeit a far more skilled one, that fact would not eliminate the possibility that Margaret had selected Perkin as another stalking-horse for Prince Richard, who remained alive and well in Burgundy and who would have come forward to claim the throne had Perkin's rebellion succeeded.

Is there *proof* that the princes were not murdered? Of course not. It simply remains a reasonable possibility.

Assuming, however, that the princes were killed, what is the affirmative evidence of Richard's guilt?

We cannot accept the revisionist claim that there is *no* such evidence. That overstates the case. Richard's motive itself is evidence. So is the fact that the boys were in his custody when last seen and that he failed to explain their disappearance. But there is very little beyond that.

The bones found in 1674, taken with the testimony of Wright and Tanner, may be considered "evidence" that the crime was committed and that Richard has no alibi. But the contrary views of later experts create serious doubt as to whether these really were the two princes and whether they were necessarily killed in 1483. And, even if the bodies were not moved and the 1674 skeletons were, in fact, the two princes, and, in addition, they were killed in 1483, the killer was not necessarily Richard. It could, for example, have been Buckingham, who had the motive, the opportunity and the character to commit the crime.

Even if it could be considered evidence against Richard, the claim that Tyrell and Dighton confessed cannot be given significant weight. The failure to obtain a signed written confession when it would have been easy and valuable to have done so, along with Henry's continued silence on the subject and his allowing Dighton to continue free for years after supposedly confessing that he murdered the true king of England, all indicate that the supposed "confessions" never occurred.

Then, of course, there is Henry's failure to disinter the princes and give them a proper requiem mass. This also indicates that there was no confession, unless the bodies had been moved, so that Tyrell and Dighton were unaware of their location. And, if the bodies had been moved from under the Tower staircase, in 1483, the bones found under just such a staircase in 1674 were not likely to be the two princes.

In a court of law, we could not, of course, even consider the hearsay and the opinions offered by More, Vergil and other writers. But, again, we are not in a court of law. We can consider such matters even though they would never be admissible in evidence. The *contemporary* opinion of those who were in a good position to know the truth does not give us any strong and reliable indication of Richard's guilt. The conduct of Elizabeth Woodville and her daughter seems far more consistent with their belief in Richard's innocence than in his guilt. The same could be said for

Brackenbury. It is arguable that Buckingham and the Stanleys considered Richard a murderer. If so, Sir William Stanley was certainly less sure later, when he expressed the belief that Perkin Warbeck might be Prince Richard, an assertion that cost Sir William his life.

Contemporary writers express varying opinions or none. Mancini, who is quick to accuse Richard of usurping the throne, did not know whether or not the princes had been killed by anyone. He simply tells us of a concern expressed in the London streets, hardly a strong indication that the princes had actually been murdered or that Richard had murdered them.

Professor Ross says that Mancini made it clear that the public believed the princes were dead before June 1483 but "admits he does not know how they died." But Mancini said more than that. Writing in December 1483, Mancini said he did not know *if* they died, not just *how* they died. Even from that later vantage point, after interviewing such witnesses as Dr. Argentine, Mancini continued to have doubts as to whether the princes had, in fact, been "done away with," and certainly he was not prepared to accuse Richard of the crime—if indeed a crime had been committed.

De Commynes says that Buckingham actually murdered the princes, but he also expresses the opinion that this was done at Richard's behest.

The Croyland Chronicle was written in 1486, under Henry VII, when it was politically advantageous to attack Richard. It was written by a southerner, a man plainly resentful of Richard, open in his accusation that Richard usurped the throne and ready to condemn him whenever he could. The author was either an insider or at least got his information from an insider. Yet even that account, written three years after the supposed crime by someone who should have had access to the true facts, does *not* assert that Richard murdered the princes or even that they were murdered. The chronicler tells us only that, in the summer of 1483, "*a rumour arose*" to that effect. He does not comment on the truth or falsity of that rumor. This is hardly convincing evidence of Richard's guilt. Indeed, if we are considering the opinion of contemporaries, the fact that the chronicler does *not* accuse Richard of the crime would seem evidence tending to show his innocence.

Subsequent accounts tend to be hopelessly biased, demonstrably unreliable or both. This includes More, with his stories of Richard displaying a withered arm and of Tyrell and Dighton confessing, and his substitution of the married courtesan, Elizabeth Lucy, for the highborn widow, Eleanor Butler, as the party to the precontract. We know that More was far off the mark about other matters, such as Edward's age, Tyrell's status in August 1483 and when and why Tyrell was knighted. And for some reason, More chose not even to finish or publish his "History."

If we are accepting such writings as evidence, More's may qualify; but it is hardly conclusive or even convincing. Yet, it was the basis for so many subsequent accounts, including those by Hall, Holinshed and, most importantly, Shakespeare; and it was heavily relied on by Gairdner, an otherwise careful historian.

Rous, of course is worse. His hypocritical assertions appear to be deliberate fabrications, rather than innocent or careless errors based on false information supplied by others.

There is, of course, the argument that Richard had a proclivity to kill, based on the claim that he murdered others. There is no basis for concluding that he murdered the Prince of Wales or his own wife. None. Buckingham's death can hardly be called a murder. Hastings' execution is questionable: Maybe he was *not* conspiring against Richard with Morton and the Woodvilles. If he was, or if Richard believed he was, his death *may* have lacked the customary formalities—remember, as Constable of England, Richard had the power to try and punish treason—but it would not be much of an indication that Richard would be ready to murder his young nephews.

Rivers, Grey and Vaughn come closest to indicating Richard's willingness to kill when necessary to remove opponents or obstacles, without regard to legal cause. But here again, they undoubtedly participated in Woodville plotting before their arrest and perhaps even had a hand in bringing about Clarence's execution. If their own executions lacked a sound legal basis, at least they were carried out against a background of what probably seemed to Richard moral justification. Moreover, they were adults and unrelated to Richard.

Do their executions create a likelihood that Richard killed his brother's two young sons? No. On the other hand, they cannot be ignored and must be considered as providing a legitimate argument for the traditionalists.

Cutting the other way are elements of Richard's character that may seem inconsistent with his murdering his nephews. Loyalty was a dominant theme in Richard's life—perhaps the most dominant. And, of all his loyalties, his loyalty to his brother, Edward IV, was the most striking. Given that staunch loyalty, would he have murdered Edward's sons, especially after they had been declared illegitimate? The revisionists can rationally argue that this demonstrable character trait offsets whatever inference can be drawn from the executions of Rivers, Grey and Vaughn.

But is it possible that Richard was simply pragmatic about the situation? Edward, after all, was dead. Nothing Richard did now could hurt him or help him. Richard sanctioned a harsh attack on Edward's reign in the Rolle prepared in June 1483 and allowed that attack to be repeated in the parliamentary act of January 1484. Does this indicate that the fierce loyalty Richard demonstrated during his brother's life ended with his brother's death?

Moreover, Richard hardly knew the two princes. Probably he had only met them two or three times in his life. He may have thought of them more as Woodvilles than as the sons of his late brother.

Traditionalists add some other factors in support of their position. There is Weir's contention, for example, that Buckingham must have known the truth and that the duke had no reason to rebel in 1483 unless he believed that Richard murdered the princes. But the duke did have other reasons, including not only his apparent anger over Richard's handling of the Bohun inheritance, but also his envy of Richard's position and perhaps, most importantly, his own designs on the throne.

Weir also argues that Richard's donating funds to found a chantry in York Minster at which one hundred priests would pray for his soul shows his consciousness of guilt. But founding chantries at which priests prayed for one's soul was a common practice of medieval royalty. The will of Henry VII bequeathed funds to cover *ten thousand* masses at twice the normal rate. Richard had established other chantries even before he became king. While the one at York was significantly larger, it was probably intended as his tomb and monument.

Even Rous praised Richard for founding this impressive chantry, expressly noting the number of priests who were to pray there. Vergil also considered it a good deed, although perhaps motivated by the desire to win public support. Gairdner (after More the dean of traditionalists), in listing Richard's laudable accomplishments, cites the hundred-priest chantry as a prime example of the king's "munificence." It requires quite a stretch to join Weir in inferring that Richard murdered his nephews from the fact that he endowed the chantry at York Minster.

Similarly, Weir incorrectly states that a prayer to Saint Julian in Richard's Book of Hours had been chosen as his personal prayer. Saint Julian murdered his parents before changing his ways, and Weir contends that Richard's selection of this particular prayer as his own is further evidence that he murdered his nephews. A.J. Pollard points out, however, that a page of the book is missing, and that the prayer to Saint Julian was a totally separate prayer from the personal prayer selected by Richard and was placed in the book many years before Richard's birth. The personal prayer actually chosen by Richard and copied into his book of hours was to Saint Michael, the soldier.

Considering all the evidence of every kind—admissible or not—the soundest conclusion we can come to at this point in history is that we do not know the answer, that the mystery remains unsolved.

Certainly there are facts that provide rational support for the traditionalist argument that Richard is guilty. But there are logical answers to those points and other indications that Richard was not the murderer. Just as good a case can be made against Buckingham, for example. Nor can Henry be ruled out as a suspect. Nor can we assume that the princes were even killed.

If the princes were murdered, Richard must still be considered a prime suspect. As much as the revisionists may admire Richard for his loyalty and courage as well as his competent rule and concern for the people, we must recognize that he really *might* have killed his nephews. "Might," of course, allows the possibility of "might not"; and, at the very least, the revisionists are fully justified in expressing strong doubts as to Richard's guilt.

Having said we would consider the degree of probability that Richard murdered his nephews, can we actually quantify that degree? We can try. But our methods will necessarily be crude and our results inexact.

There are two propositions that are essential to Richard's guilt. Both must be true if he was guilty. One proposition is that the princes were actually murdered. The second is that if they were murdered, Richard was responsible. The probability of both propositions being true must be weighed in assessing the probability of Richard's guilt.

If there is a fifty to seventy percent chance that the princes were murdered rather than hidden away somewhere, and, if they were murdered, there is likewise a fifty to seventy percent chance that Richard rather than Henry VII, Buckingham or someone else committed the crime, then, mathematically, the probability that *Richard* murdered his nephews is in the range of twenty-five to forty-nine percent.

If these are the correct parameters, it is more probable than not that Richard was innocent. Are they correct? No one can say with any degree of certainty. Considering everything, they appear to be a reasonable assessment.

But assigning numbers to the probability of Richard's guilt is a matter on which reasonable minds can differ. When DNA tests are finally run, and we know if the bones discovered in 1674 are really the remains of the two princes, an assessment of probability should be easier and the odds discussed here may radically change.

Unfortunately, an objective analysis of the facts known today does not allow for certainty or even near certainty as to Richard's innocence or guilt. We can only look to the future. And, DNA tests or not, we may never know the answer.

XXIII

♛ WHAT IF?

One of the fascinating aspects of history is the speculation as to what would have happened if a particular battle had been won rather than lost, if an individual leader had not been assassinated or if some other critical event had not occurred.

If the Persians had beaten the Greeks at Marathon, would we be speaking Persian today?

What if Caesar had not crossed the Rubicon or Cleopatra and Anthony had won at Actium? Or Napoleon had been victorious at Waterloo?

And so we might ask, What if Richard had allowed Edward V to rule?

Let us speculate. Richard resists the suggestions of Buckingham. He does not arrest Rivers in Northampton in April 1483. Instead, finding that young King Edward has already left Stony Stratford for London, Richard rides into the capital with Rivers, ready to serve as a loyal uncle and protector.

The Woodvilles, with the boy king in their control, press forward with their plans for an immediate coronation. Once Edward is crowned, they declare the protectorate at an end based on historical precedent. Richard is allowed to remain as a council member in a government dominated by the Woodvilles. He and Hastings become more and more isolated and find themselves standing alone and ineffective against Woodville power.

But Richard remains a serious threat to the Woodville interests—and, as we know from the example of Humphrey of Gloucester, ex-protectors can be short-lived.

One night, returning to Crosby Hall after a late council meeting, Richard is set upon by dozens of armed men. Instead of meeting his end at Bosworth Field, he is struck down in the streets of London fighting ferociously against similarly overwhelming odds.

An enraged Hastings conspires with Buckingham and Lady Stanley to mount an invasion by Henry Tudor. Secretly, Buckingham plans to seize the throne himself. If the invasion succeeds, he will arrange to have Henry killed in the fighting. But, with a nonthreatening boy king on the English throne, neither the French nor the Bretons are inclined to back the invasion, and few English nobles are ready to rebel against the rightful king in the face of entrenched Woodville power. Hastings and Buckingham are found out and executed.

In 1485, instead of warning Henry Tudor of the English-Breton plot that threatens his safety, John Morton, now the servant of the Woodvilles, becomes the architect of that plot. The Bretons turn Henry over to the English, who quickly try and execute him for treason.

In 1490, Edward V dies, a victim of the osteomyelitis that is claimed to have been slowly killing him even in 1483. Prince Richard, now seventeen, takes the throne as Richard III. The new king is tall and vigorous like his father, Edward IV. Like his father, he is also attracted to pretty women.

Since Richard's childhood marriage to Anne Mowbray was ended by her early death, Rivers and his other advisors urge an advantageous royal marriage. Only in that way can there be a male heir. But the handsome young king, preferring the single life, makes one excuse after another to postpone the inevitable.

Finally, he relents. The Spanish had previously spoken of a diplomatic alliance with England. Those discussions are revived. Ultimately, in 1500, they lead to the marriage of twenty-seven-year-old Richard III and Katherine of Aragon, then only fifteen.

There is, of course, no Henry VIII, and no English reformation, since the driving force for that change was Henry's desperate need to divorce Katherine in order to marry Anne Boleyn.

England, now closely allied with Spain, continues as a Catholic country.

At thirty, Richard III reasserts the ancient English claim to the French throne. With Spanish aid, he successfully invades the Continent to enforce those claims.

Through well-planned intermarriage, his heirs, who are also the heirs of Ferdinand and Isabella, go on to rule a united empire that includes England, France and Spain. Religious wars are fought in the seventeenth century. But, facing the massed power of the Euro-Empire, the Protestant forces are defeated. Roman Catholicism remains the established religion throughout Western Europe.

The Euro-Empire develops valuable American colonies, which become a refuge for Protestant dissenters. They attempt a revolution; but, opposed by the combined might of England, France and Spain, it fails.

Without Louis XVI and Marie Antoinette, without the example of a successful American revolution, and with a more enlightened imperial government based on the English parliamentary model, there is no French Revolution, no Napoleon, no Waterloo.

In the latter part of the nineteenth century, the Junkers fail to pull Prussia away from the empire. Perhaps there is a Bismarck, but he falls far short of maneuvering the rest of Europe into permitting a Prussian war with France.

By the twentieth century, America and Germany have joined England and France as the most powerful dominions of the Euro empire. Each is governed by its own parliament and an imperial governor. The economy of the empire as a whole is considerably aided by the use of a single currency, a central banking system and an empire-wide free trade policy.

In 1905, an isolated Russia is menaced by the expansionist and militarily powerful Japan. The Empire acts in what it considers the interests of global stability. It concludes a mutual defense and trade treaty with the tsar, and, at the same time, convinces him significantly to increase the power of the Duma, making Russia a far more limited monarchy. The imperial army and navy crush the Japanese forces. Under the peace treaty, the Japanese home islands are demilitarized for twenty-five years.

A surprise concord stuns the world by uniting the religions of the Eastern Orthodoxy with the Church of Rome, vastly increasing the power and influence of the pope.

Of course, there is no Queen Victoria or Kaiser Wilhelm. While a German nationalist party is allowed to participate in elections for the Parliament of the German Dominion, it enjoys no success at the polls, given the buoyant imperial economy and efficient parliamentary government.

There is no World War I, no Nicholas and Alexandra. Despite the political, economic and religious reforms imposed by the empire, Marxists seek to foment a revolution in Russia. It lacks popular support and is easily put down by loyalist forces.

Without the impact of a devastating military defeat or the threat of communism, and with a successful economy, the National Socialists remain a lunatic fringe in Germany, unable to gain any power.

Japan reemerges as a major economic and military power. Facing the might of the entire world, however, and with no ally, the Japanese leaders reject a radical plan to attack Pearl Harbor. They decide to gain power and influence through industrial development rather than through military adventure.

There is no World War II. No one develops an atomic or hydrogen bomb. So far, none is needed.

Of course, it might not have happened like that at all. But whether the changes were these or others, our lives would in all probability have been profoundly changed if, on that one April morning, Richard had awakened peacefully, breakfasted with his friend, Lord Rivers, and ridden with him to Stony Stratford to extend loyal greetings to his nephew, the king.

SELECTED BIBLIOGRAPHY

BOOKS

The History of the Reign of King Henry the Seventh
Francis Bacon
The Folio Society, London, 1971

The History of the Life and Reigne of Richard the Third
George Buck
EP Publishing Limited, Yorkshire, 1973

Memoirs: The Reign of Louis XI, 1461–83
Philippe de Commynes (translated by Michael Jones)
Penguin Books, Middlesex, 1972

Richard III: A Reader in History
Keith Dockray
Alan Sutton Publishing Limited, Gloucester, 1988

The New Chronicles of England and France, in Two Parts
Robert Fabyan (Henry Ellis, editor)
F.C. & J. Rivington, London, 1811

History of the Life and Reign of Richard the Third
James Gairdner, LL.D.
Greenwood Press, New York, 1969

Richard III: A Medieval Kingship
John Gillingham, Editor
Collins & Brown Limited, London, 1993

Richard III: Loyalty, Lordship and Law
P.W. Hammond, Editor
Alan Sutton Publishing Limited, London, 1986

Richard III and His Early Historians 1483-1535
Alison Hanham
Clarendon Press, Oxford, 1975

Richard III and His Rivals
Michael Hicks
The Hambledon Press, London, 1991

British Library Harleian Manuscript 433, Volumes One-Four
Rosemary Horrox and P.W. Hammond, Editors
Alan Sutton Publishing Limited, Gloucester, 1980

The Princes in the Tower
Elizabeth Jenkins
Coward, McCann & Geoghegan, New York, 1978

Richard the Third
Paul Murray Kendall
W.W. Norton & Company, New York, 1955

Richard of England
D.M. Kleyn
The Kensal Press, Oxford, 1990

The Betrayal of Richard III
V.B. Lamb
Alan Sutton Publishing Limited, Gloucester, 1959

The Usurpation of Richard III
Dominic Mancini (translated by C.A.J. Armstrong)
Alan Sutton Publishing Limited, Gloucester, 1969

Richard III: His Life and Character
Sir Clements R. Markham
E.P. Dutton and Company, New York, 1906

The History of King Richard III
Thomas More (edited by Richard S. Sylvester)
Yale University Press, New Haven 1963

English Historical Documents, Volume IV 1327–1485
A.R. Myers, editor
Oxford University Press, New York, 1969

Richard III and the Princes in the Tower
A.J. Pollard
Alan Sutton Publishing Limited, Gloucester, 1991

Good King Richard?
Jeremy Potter
Constable and Company, Ltd., London, 1983

The Crowland Chronicle Continuations
Nicholas Pronay and Joh Cox, editors
Alan Sutton Publishing Limited, London, 1986

Edward IV
Charles Ross
University of California Press, Berkeley, 1974

Richard III
Charles Ross
University of California Press, Berkeley, 1981

The Rous Roll
John Rous (introduction by Charles Ross)
Alan Sutton Publishing Limited, Gloucester, 1980

Richard III
William Shakespeare

The Crown and The Tower: The Legend of Richard III
William H. Snyder, Researcher and Editor
Alan Sutton Publishing Limited, Gloucester, 1981

The Great Chronicle of London
A.H. Thomas and I.D. Thornley, editors
George W. Jones, London, 1938

Richard III
Pamela Tudor-Craig
National Portrait Gallery, London, 1973

The History of England during the Middle Ages
Sharon Turner
Longman, Rees, Orme, Brown and Green, London, 1830

Polydore Vergil's English History
(full title: *Three Books of Polydore Vergil's English History,
    Comprising the Reigns of Henry VI, Edward IV, and Richard
    III*)
Sir Henry Ellis, K.H., Editor
AMS Press, London, 1968

The Anglica Historia A.D. 1485–1537 of Polydore Vergil
Denys Hay, editor
Butler & Tanner Ltd., London 1950

Historic Doubts on the Life & Reign of Richard the Third
Horace Walpole (introduction, notes by P.W. Hammond)
Alan Sutton Publishing, Gloucester, 1987

*A Chronicle of the First Thirteen Years of the Reign of King Edward
    the Fourth*
John Warkworth, D.C. (edited by James Orchard Halliwell,
    1839)
AMS Press, Inc., New York, 1968

The Princes in the Tower
Alison Weir
Pimlico, London, 1992

The Mystery of the Princes
Audrey Williamson
Alan Sutton Publishing Limited, Gloucester, 1981

ARTICLES

Shiela Bignall, "Who Was Nicholas von Popplau?", *Ricardian Register*, Vol. XXII No. 3 (Fall, 1997), pp. 30-34

Michael Bongiorno, "Did Louis XI Have Edward IV Assassinated?", *Ricardian Register*, Vol XXII No. 3 (Fall, 1997), pp. 23-24

James Edward Gilbert, "Richard III: A King amidst the Turmoil of Fifteenth-Century History," *Ricardian Register*, Vol. XXII, No. 2, Summer, 1997, pp. 4-20

Richard Firth Green, "Historical Notes of a London citizen, 1483-1488," *English Historical Review*, Vol. 96, pp. 585-590

J.W. Hales and F.J. Furnivall, editors, "Ballad of Bosworth Field" from Bishop Percy's Folio Manuscript "Ballads and Romances," Vol. 3, pp. 233-259, London 1868

P.W. Hammond and W.J. White, "The Sons of Edward IV: A Re-examination of the Evidence on their Deaths and on the Bones in Westminster Abbey," from *Richard III: Loyalty, Lordship and Law*, pp. 91-103

Alison Hanham, "Sir George Buck and Princess Elizabeth's Letter: A Problem in Detection," *The Ricardian*, Vol. VII, No. 97, June 1987, pp. 398-400

Michael K. Jones, "Richard III as a Soldier," from *Richard III: A Medieval Kingship*, p. 103

Jack Leslau, "Did the Sons of Edward IV Outlive Henry VIII?", *The Ricardian*, Vol. IV, No. 62, September 1978, pp. 2-14

Mortimer Levine, "Richard III—Usurper or Lawful King?", *Speculum*, Vol. XXXIV (July 1959), pp. 391-401

Dr. Richard Lyne-Pirkis, speech "Regarding the Bones Found in the Tower," text courtesy of Richard III Society

Mary O'Regan, "The Pre-Contract and Its Effects on the Succession in 1803," *The Ricardian*, Vol. IV, No. 54 (1976), pp. 2-7

Colin Richmond, "1485 and All That, or What Was Going on at the Battle of Bosworth?", from *Richard III: Loyalty, Lordship and Law*, pp. 172-206

Colin Richmond, "1483: The Year of Decision (or Taking the Throne)", from *Richard III: A Medieval Kingship*, pp. 39-56

Gordon Smith, "Lambert Simnell and the King from Dublin," *The Ricardian*, Vol. X, No. 135, December 1996, pp. 498-536

Lawrence E. Tanner & William Wright, "Recent Investigations Regarding the Fate of the Princes in the Tower," *Archeologia*, Vol. 34 (1934)

INDEX